ACCLAIM FOR TED DEKKER'S NOVELS

"Ted Dekker has been here for years, but he's finally arrived. [T]his is what true storytelling *is*."

—*The Bookshelf Reviews* advance praise for *Skin*

"[C]ompelling, thought-provoking fiction that is wildly out-of-the-box, speculative, [and] boundary-breaking."

—TitleTrakk.com advance review of *Skin*

"*Saint* is filled with intense, edge-of-your-seat action that will keep you turning pages until you are finished. There's something compelling about [Dekker's] writing style that sets it apart from anyone else I've ever read and *Saint* certainly doesn't veer from that path.

—epinions.com

"*Saint* reads like *The Bourne Identity* (Robert Ludlum), meets *The Matrix*, meets *Mr. Murder* (Dean Koontz)."

—5 out of 5 stars from *The Bookshelf Reviews*

"Fans of Dekker and supernatural suspense will relish this creative thriller."

—*Library Journal* review of *Saint*

"A master of suspense reminiscent of Dean Koontz and John Grisham, Ted Dekker keeps readers on their toes trying to solve the mystery of Saint's identity."

—Romance Junkies

"Toss away all your expectations, because *Showdown* is one of the most original, most thoughtful, and most gripping reads I've been through in ages . . . Breaking all established story patterns or plot formulas, you'll find yourself repeatedly feeling that there's no way of predicting what will happen next . . . The pacing is dead-on, the flow is tight, and the epic story is downright sneaky in how it unfolds. Dekker excels at crafting stories that are hard to put down, and *Showdown* is the hardest yet."

—infuzemag.com

"Dekker is a master of suspense and even makes room for romance."

—*Library Journal*

"[*Showdown*] strips the veneer of civilization to the darkness of the soul, revealing the motivations and intents of the heart. This is a difficult book to read and definitely not for the squeamish. It brings home the horror of sin and the depth of sacrifice in a way another book would not—could not."

—Author's Choice Reviews

"One of the highlights of the year in religious fiction has been Ted Dekker's striking color-coded spiritual trilogy. Exciting, well written, and resonant with meaning, *Black, Red,* and now *White* have won over both critics and genre readers . . . An epic journey completed with grace."

—Editors, BARNES AND NOBLE

"Calling [*Showdown*] unique is an understatement. Ted Dekker has successfully laced a contemporary thriller with searing spiritual principles."

—In the Library Reviews

"Put simply: it's a brilliant, dangerous idea. And we need more dangerous ideas . . . Dekker's trilogy is a mythical epic, with a vast, predetermined plot and a scope of staggering proportions . . . *Black* is one of those books that will make you thankful that you know how to read. If you love a good story, and don't mind suspending a little healthy disbelief, *Black* will keep you utterly enthralled from beginning to . . . well, cliffhanger. Red can't get here fast enough."

—FuseMagazine.net

"If you're looking for a book that will keep you up at night and yet offers hope at some point, then *House* is a must read for you. My words will never suffice how spectacular this book is, so go out and get this book for yourself. But don't forget to lock the windows and doors and whatever you do . . . stay out of the basement."

—1340mag.com

"Ted Dekker is clearly one of the most gripping storytellers alive today. He creates plots that keep your heart pounding and palms sweating even after you've finished his books."

—Jeremy Reynalds, Syndicated Columnist

"[*Thunder of Heaven* is] a real page-turner . . . scenes read like the best of David Morrell . . . his description is upsettingly precise."

—Booklist

SKIN

www.teddekker.com

OTHER NOVELS BY TED DEKKER

Saint

Showdown

Obsessed

Black

Red

White

Three

Blink

The Martyr's Song

When Heaven Weeps

Thunder of Heaven

Heaven's Wager

House (coauthored with Frank Peretti)

Blessed Child (coauthored with Bill Bright)
A Man Called Blessed (coauthored with Bill Bright)

TED DEKkER

Thomas Nelson
Since 1798

thomasnelson.com

Published in Nashville, Tennessee by Thomas Nelson, Inc. in association with Creative Trust, Inc., Literary Division, 5141 Virginia Way, Suite 320, Brentwood, TN 37027.

Thomas Nelson, Inc. titles may be purchased in bulk for educational, business, fund-raising, or sales promotional use. For information, please e-mail SpecialMarkets@ThomasNelson.com.

Publisher's Note: This novel is a work of fiction. Names, characters, places, and incidents are either products of the author's imagination or used fictitiously. All characters are fictional, and any similarity to people living or dead is purely coincidental.

Library of Congress Cataloging-in-Publication Data

Dekker, Ted, 1962–
  Skin / Ted Dekker.
    p. cm.
  ISBN-13: 978-1-59554-277-9 (hard cover)
  ISBN-10: 1-59554-277-9 (hard cover)
  ISBN-10: 1-59554-291-4 (IE)
  ISBN-13: 978-1-59554-291-5 (IE)
  1. Serial murderers—Fiction. 2. Nevada—Fiction. I. Title.
PS3554.E43S57 2007
813'.6—dc22   2006032513

Printed in the United States of America
07 08 09 10 RRD 6 5 4 3 2 1

1

When the rain isn't so much falling—be it in bucket loads or like cats and dogs—but rather slamming into the car like an avalanche of stone, you know it's time to pull over.

When you can't see much more than the slaphappy wipers splashing through rivers on the windshield, when you're suddenly not sure if you're on the road any longer, and your radio emits nothing but static, and you haven't seen another car since the sky turned black, and your fingers are tense on the wheel in an attempt to steady the old Accord in the face of terrifying wind gusts, you know it's so totally time to pull over.

Wendy leaned over the steering wheel, searching for the yellow lines that separated the two-lane highway. No real shoulder that she could see. What was to keep another car from rear-ending her if she pulled over here?

She'd seen the black clouds pillaring on the horizon as she headed across the Nevada desert. Heard the tornado warnings on the radio before it had inexplicably fried. The fact that this wasn't tornado territory had the announcers in a bit of a frenzy.

Wendy had ignored the warnings and pressed on into evening. She'd given herself two days for the long haul between San Diego and western Utah. The call from her mother asking her to come had frozen Wendy for a good ten seconds, phone in hand. Had to be Thursday, this week, her mother had insisted. It was now Tuesday night. Wendy wondered if she'd see the rest of the Brotherhood cult or just her mother. The thought of either was enough to keep her awake at night.

The tribe, as its leader Bronson called it, was a somewhat nomadic group of twenty or so members, going where God led them. God had evidently led them to the remote Utah-Nevada border now.

Wendy had been born into the cult and had managed to escape eight years earlier, on her eighteenth birthday, the day she was to wed Torrey Bronson as his third wife. Twice she'd hired private investigators to locate the tribe and report on her mother's condition. Twice the report had come back favorable. But the investigators had never actually talked to her mother—speaking to anyone from the outside world was strictly prohibited. Even making eye contact was good for a day in isolation. Physical contact, heaven forbid, was grounds for severe punishment.

Inside the cult there was plenty of touching and hugging and kissing, but no physical contact with strangers ever, period. That was the Brotherhood way.

Wendy had fallen in an Oklahoma ditch when she was seven years old and broken her leg. A farmer had heard her cries and taken her to the others who were searching. Before setting the bone, "Father" Bronson had beaten her severely for allowing unclean hands to touch her. The lashing hurt more than the broken leg. It was the last time

Wendy had touched or been touched by anyone outside the tribe before escaping.

And when Father Bronson had taken it upon himself to break her two thumbs and two forefingers as punishment for kissing Tony, another thirteen-year-old in the tribe at the time, he'd made it excruciatingly clear that he'd claimed her for himself alone.

She'd fled the cult, but not the wounding of such a perverse childhood. Few knew the extent of the damage; she hid it well behind soft eyes and a light smile. But to this day even the thought of physical contact with men unnerved her.

No issue in Wendy's tumultuous life consumed her as much as this failing. Touch was her personal demon. A beast that prevented her from expressing the deep caring she'd felt in any relationship with a man, isolating her from love, romantic or otherwise.

Now, driving through nature's fury, she felt oddly isolated again. It was suddenly clear that her decision to continue into the dark clouds had been a mistake.

As if hearing and understanding that it had played unfairly with her, the storm suddenly eased. She could see the road again.

See, now that wasn't so bad . . . Time to retreat to the nearest overcrowded motel to wait out the storm with the rest of the traveling public.

She could even see the signs now, and the green one she passed said that the turnoff to Summerville was in five miles. Exit 354. A hundred yards farther, a blue sign indicated that there were no services at this exit.

Freak storm. Flash floods. Truth be told, it was all a bit exciting. As long as the storm didn't delay her, she kind of liked the idea of—

Her headlights hit a vehicle in the road ahead. Like a wraith, the cockeyed beast glared at her through the rainy night, unmoving, dead on the road. A pickup truck.

She slammed her foot on the brake.

The Accord's rear wheels lost traction on the wet pavement and slid around to her left. She gripped the steering wheel, knuckles white. Her headlights flashed past the scrub oak lining the road.

For an instant Wendy thought the car might roll. But the wet asphalt kept the Accord's wheels from catching and throwing her over.

Unfortunately, the slick surface also prevented the tires from stopping her car before it crashed into the pickup.

Wendy jerked forward, allowing her forearms to absorb most of the impact.

Steam hissed from under her hood. Rain splattered. But Wendy was unhurt, apart from maybe a bruise or two. She sat still, collecting herself.

Oddly enough, the airbags hadn't deployed. Maybe it was the angle. She'd hit the other vehicle's front bumper in a full slide, so that her left front fender had taken the brunt of the impact before becoming wedged under the grill.

She picked up her cell phone and snapped it open. *No Service.*

No service for more than half an hour now.

She tried the door. It squealed some, then opened easily before striking the smallish pickup, which she now saw was green. She climbed out, hardly noticing the rain. The pickup was missing its right front wheel and sat on the inner guts of the brake contraption—which explained the tire she now saw in the road. Her eyes returned to the pickup's door. The side window was shattered. The front windshield seemed intact, except for two round holes punched through on the driver's side.

Bullet holes.

Of course she couldn't be sure they were bullet holes, but it was the first thought to cross her mind, and since it had done so, she could hardly consider that mere debris had punched those two perfect circles through the glass.

Someone had shot at the driver.

Wendy jerked her head around for signs of another car or a shooter. Nothing she could see, but that didn't mean they weren't out there. For a moment she stood glued to the pavement, mind divided between the drenching she was receiving from the rain, and those two bullet holes.

She remembered the pistol in the console compartment between her Accord's front seats. Louise had talked her into buying it long ago, when they'd first met at the shelter. Wendy had never received the training she'd intended to, nor had she ever fired the gun. But there it lay, and if ever there was a time for it . . .

She flung the Accord's door wide and ducked inside. Finding and dislodging the black pistol case from between the seats proved a slippery, knuckle-burning task with wet fingers. Yet she managed to wrench it out. She disengaged the sliding mechanism that opened the case, snatched out the cold steel weapon, and fumbled it, trying to remember what the safety looked like.

Meanwhile, her butt, which was still sticking out in the rain, was taking a bath. The gun slipped from her hands and thudded on the floor mat. She swore and reached for it, found the trigger, and would have blown a hole in the car if the safety had been off.

Thank God for safeties.

Now she found the safety and disengaged it. However unfamiliar she was with guns, Wendy was no idiot. Neither was she anything similar to gutless.

Whoever was in the truck might still be alive, possibly even injured, and out here in this storm. And Wendy was the only one who could help. Sniper lurking or not, she would never abandon anyone in need.

Wendy turned the key in the Accord's ignition. The car purred to life. It was still steaming through the hood, but at least it ran.

She took a calming breath, then slipped back out of the car and hurried around to the truck's passenger door, staying low.

With a last look around the deserted highway, keeping the gun in both hands down low the way she'd often seen such weapons wielded on the big screen, she poked her head up and looked through the passenger window.

Empty.

She stood up for a better look. The driver's window was smeared with something. Blood. But no body. Someone had been shot. The truck had apparently sideswiped another car and lost its front wheel before coming to a rest.

Wendy scanned the shoulder and ditches for any sign of a fallen body. Nothing.

Still no sign of a shooter, no sign of any danger.

"Hello?"

No response to her call.

Louder this time. "Hello? Anybody out there?"

No, nothing but the rain drumming on the vehicles.

She started to shove the gun into the back of her Lucky jeans, which were now drenched right through to her skin, but a quick image of the gun blowing a hole in her butt stopped her short.

It was then, hand still on the pistol at the small of her back, that she heard the cry.

She jerked the gun to her left and listened. There it was again, farther down the road, hidden in the growing dark. An indistinguishable cry for help or of pain.

Or the killer, howling at the moon in victory.

The cry did not come again. Wendy crouched low and ran down

the roadside toward the sound, gun extended. She wanted to yell but was torn, knowing that in the very unlikely case the sound *had* been made by whoever had shot at the truck, she would be exposing herself to danger.

That she was now running away from the safety of her car through the dark rain, toward an unidentified stranger, struck her as absurd. On the other hand, she would gladly spend the rest of her life pulling little girls with broken legs out of the ditches into which they had fallen, regardless of the consequences.

She'd run less than fifty yards when a van loomed through the rain. She pulled up, panting.

The van had apparently swerved off the road and down the shallow embankment on the left, where it now rested in complete darkness. It wasn't the kind of minivan in which moms hauled their children to soccer matches. It was the larger, square kind—the kind killers threw their kidnapped victims into before roaring off to the deep woods.

A streak of fear passed through her. Refusing to be gutless was one thing. Acting foolishly out of some misguided sense of justice was another. This was now feeling like the latter.

2

ow many?" Colt asked.

"Three," the dispatcher said.

"You're saying three tornadoes have actually been spotted, or the weather service is warning of the possibility that—"

"Spotted, not speculated." Becky was as nervous as a mouse, and her quick eyes betrayed her. Otherwise, she was handling her duties as dispatcher quite well, all things considered.

Summerville's police station was situated at the center of the small town at Main and Rolling Hill, an absurd name for a street in a town that was as flat as a tortilla. The dispatch doubled as a reception area out front. Double doors led to a large open room containing seven desks, only half of which were used for more than counter space and the filing cabinets each housed.

The chief's office bordered the common area on the right, next to a conference room that doubled for the occasional interrogation. Behind it all sat an overbuilt jail—five cells.

Summerville wasn't a town that saw too much trouble, certainly not of the magnitude that now threatened with three tornadoes bearing down from the east. In the full year since Colt had packed his life into the back of a midnight blue Dodge Ram and headed north to his new appointment as one of four deputies in Summerville, the department had responded to forty-seven domestic violence calls, seven accidental deaths, one murder, and more than six hundred miscellaneous violations and accidents, including everything from drunk driving to stranded cats. All in all, a fraction of what the residents of Las Vegas endured in a fraction of the time.

Colt knew, because he'd practically fled Vegas for the relative calm of a small town post. Unfortunately, a full year of this relative calm hadn't changed him. A traumatic childhood had reduced him to a clumsy, insecure mess around women, and only slightly better around men. Being a cop in the City of Sin somehow hadn't helped him hone those skills. He was exceptional with a gun, but that really wasn't what the job in a small town required.

Now that small town was in the direct path of not one but three tornadoes.

"I didn't know we had tornadoes in Nevada," Colt said absently, looking past the blinds at the rain. It had eased off considerably.

"We don't. Freak storm, they're saying. Global warming or something."

"Where's Chief Lithgow?"

"With the maintenance crew."

"Doing?"

"Shutting down the main roads till this blows over."

Colt lifted his baseball cap off his forehead and walked toward the door. It was his day off, and he'd come in to see if they needed any help. Sounded like they had the situation under control.

"I'll be on the radio if you need me." He reached for the door. "Tell the chief—"

"Officer down, officer down!" Eli Seymore's voice squawked on the radio like a chicken eyeing a freshly ground ax. "We got us trouble. There's someone out here with a gun, and he's shot the chief. Request backup." And then as if an afterthought, "Right now!"

Becky's face turned white. "You sure?"

"Yes, I'm sure! He's right here. Man, oh man. Man, oh man! Send an ambulance." The officer sounded like he was nearly in tears.

"Where is he?" Colt asked.

"Where are you?" Becky repeated.

"One block west of the main . . . Oh my . . . Crap, crap, crap. There he is! He's—" Sounds of gunfire popped on the radio speaker. Eli swore. Judging by the sounds immediately following, he dropped the radio and scrambled for safety.

"Call the dispatcher in Walton and advise them of our situation," Colt said, referring to the larger town fifty miles southeast. He yanked the door open. "I'm on my way."

A hundred possible scenarios careened through his mind as he ran for his cruiser. The most obvious he dismissed immediately. This wasn't Vegas. Minimal drug crime—nothing organized, anyhow. Most likely cause for any shooting was a domestic dispute. Passions and guns didn't mix any better in the village than they did in the big city.

East end of town. Maybe that brute Mike Seymour had finally made good on his threat to tear the town apart if his old lady, as he liked to call Laura, didn't stop eyeing every man who walked by.

No. Not even Seymour would shoot the chief.

Colt slid into the cruiser, fired the engine, and flipped the radio on with the subtle movement of a man who'd been doing nothing else for six years. The speakers filled with Eli's panicked voice. He'd reacquired his radio.

"He's coming right at us—" *Pop, pop, pop.*

"Colt's on his way," Becky said, her dispatcher voice now knotted with fear.

No response this time. Eli was taking fire.

Colt peeled out of the parking lot, sirens already screaming. You could never underestimate the power of that distant wail coming your way. It was thought that sirens alone were responsible for stopping over thirty thousand crimes in the United States every year.

"I'm on my way, Eli. What's your exact location?"

No response.

"Eli?"

Static.

Colt swore. He keyed the mic again. "Where are Steve and Luke, Becky?"

"Steve's on his way back from the Stratford Ranch. Cattle loose again. Luke's on his way to Eli."

"Luke, you there?"

"Here. What do you have in mind?"

"Where you at?"

"Coming down Cimarron."

"Okay, head up Third to the end of town and double back on First. I think they're on First near the west end."

"Copy. Come in quiet, then?"

"Quiet."

He, on the other hand, would go in siren blaring and guns blazing if need be. It had been over a year since he'd encountered a gunman. The metallic taste at the back of his mouth, compliments of adrenaline, was as sweet as it was bitter.

The chief's been shot, Colt.

Okay then, check that. The taste was purely bitter.

He flew up Main Street to Seventh and took a right turn at 65. In Vegas he'd be dodging heavy traffic, but this was Summerville. The streets were already deserted due to news of the storm. A little gunfire would empty them completely. Word traveled faster through the phone wires than over the news networks in small towns.

Driving with his left hand, Colt reached for his gun belt and pulled out his service revolver. The judgment of Sergeant Brice Mackenzie from the training academy echoed through his mind.

"You might not be the most handsome stud to join the force, but you sure can shoot."

Fitting that his name was Colt, they all said. During his most insecure years, he'd flaunted his gun handling. But now, at age twenty-seven, he'd accepted himself for what he was. Not a gunman, heavens no. He was simply a strong, caring, sensitive man who happened to be more comfortable around a gun than around a woman.

And he was fine with who he was. At least on occasion. Especially occasions like this.

He holstered the pistol and keyed the radio. "Approaching First now."

"Copy."

He had no idea what he'd find once he turned onto First Street, but it might be a fusillade of bullets, so he would go in kamikaze, not cautious. Foil the shooter's aim. Unnerve any but the most seasoned gunman.

The wind had eased, and the rain had tapered off to a drizzle. Both good and bad depending on who was doing the shooting. Ditto the deepening darkness.

Colt braced himself and spun the wheel into the corner. The cruiser slid wide on the wet pavement, squealing as rubber bit past water and into the asphalt. The streetlights revealed Eli's predicament in yellow hues.

Two cruisers were parked at angles one block up—Eli's and Chief Lithgow's. No sign of fire from either. Colt assumed both were down.

The shooter walked under one of the lights, directly toward him, undeterred by the siren, the lights, and the show of force that had announced the cavalry's approach for some time now.

Jeans and a black T-shirt. Baseball cap turned backward. Hard to make out any details of his face from this distance.

Colt increased speed, bearing down on the man.

The windows on a dozen houses and shops behind the man were shattered. The shooter had made no attempt to conceal his intentions whatsoever.

The gunman suddenly appeared to be walking in slow motion as Colt's conditioned mind was separating details, a skill required for survival in high stress environments involving guns. Or was it something else? This man seemed to command the space around him with complete confidence.

Without breaking stride, the gunman fanned his weapon and took two shots at the cruiser. The first put a hole precisely where Colt's head would have been had he not ducked the moment the shooter lifted his arm.

The second drilled a hole in the passenger's headrest. Impressive shooting in such poor light. With a moving target. Scary impressive. The only person Colt had met with such skill was Mark Clifton, a detective from Walton—Nevada's best gun handler, unchallenged. Still, this man seemed too fast.

Change of plans.

Colt cranked the wheel to his left and braked. The cruiser's back end swung right and slid to a halt broadside to the shooter. Colt was out of his door, on the pavement, gun in hand, when the next slug popped the passenger window.

He rolled onto his belly, brought the gun to bear on the shooter from under his cruiser, and fired off two shots. But the man was moving already, like a shadow on speed. Two feet to his right so that he was hidden by one of the cruiser's wheels.

No target, no shot—didn't take the best gun handler in the force to know that much. Nor the fact that this killer knew exactly what he was doing.

Colt heard a car skid to a stop farther up the street. That would be Luke—a solid kid with rookie-level experience. They had the shooter boxed in.

For a few long seconds nothing happened. Water ran down the street, splashing along the gutters, soaking Colt's jeans and T-shirt. No shooter.

And then Colt knew why there was no shooter. He'd vanished into the smashed glass of the Sears catalog store ten paces behind where Colt had last seen him. An educated guess, of course, but one worthy enough to bring Colt first to his knees, then to his feet.

"They're both down!" Luke screamed from the cruisers.

Keeping a wary eye on the broken windows along the far sidewalk, Colt ran toward the first cruiser.

Eli lay in the gutter, faceup, unmoving. Eyes wide to the falling rain. A bullet had punched a small hole in his forehead.

"He's dead," Luke said, thirty yards away. His voice was breathy and shaking. "The chief—"

"I think the shooter went into one of the buildings across the street," Colt cut in. "Keep an eye out."

He dropped to one knee beside Eli, keeping the cruiser between himself and the shooter's possible location. The immensity of their predicament hit him as he lifted Eli's radio to call in the officer's death. Adrenaline yielded to a moment of horror.

A shudder passed through his body.

He turned the radio off and clipped it on his belt. "Eli's dead. Call it in, Luke. Cover my back."

Colt took one breath of resolution and ran for the broken window through which he suspected the shooter had disappeared. Behind him, Luke called in the incident, demanding more backup, even though they both knew there was no more backup this side of Walton.

Worse, Colt knew the killer was gone. No one who possessed the skill of this man could possibly be ignorant enough to hole up in the Sears building and wait to duke it out. He was undoubtedly out the back and in the wind.

"Stay here," he shouted back.

"Where you going?"

Calling out his intentions for the killer to hear would have been stupid, so he didn't.

It took him less than a minute to reach the back alley and work his way behind the Sears store. The rear door had been kicked open from the inside.

No sign of the killer.

A gust of wind pushed the door open. The alley was dark, and Colt could just read the words painted on the gray door in red paint.

Hello Colt
It's payback time
Red

Colt felt a chill crash down his back. Payback time? Who? For what?

His days as a cop in Vegas flashed through his mind. Just over a year ago, the night he'd faced off with a man in the alley behind the whorehouse where his mother lived. He'd been coming to check on her after hearing that one of the girls had been beaten by a customer.

He might not have even seen the hooded man leaning against the corner if the sound of a scraping wood crate hadn't alerted him. He'd drawn his weapon and crouched; saw the form, arms crossed.

At first, neither spoke. The man faced him from the darkness behind his hood, slinking without the slightest concern. Colt stood slowly, unnerved without knowing why.

"Can I help you?" he asked, glancing at the back door on his left.

"Can you?" The man's voice sounded a bit like that crate he'd shoved.

"What are you doing here?"

"She's as ugly as you are, Colt," the stranger said.

This man *knew* him?

"Maybe you should do something about that," the man said.

"Who are you?"

"You forget already?"

Colt's mind raced for recollection, but none came. "Step out with your hands where I can see them."

The man leaned against the brick wall without moving.

"Step out!"

"I'm going to kill her for you, Colt. And then I'm going to come back for the rest of you. It's payback time."

Then he was gone. Colt watched him leave, but his movement was so quick that Colt didn't have time to process the threat, much less shoot him dead, which he had done a thousand times in his dreams following that night.

His mother had slit her own wrists two days later. They found her body in a hotel room three blocks from the house. The image of her dead body lying in a pool of red would never leave Colt.

He'd told his superiors about the threat, insisting that his mother's death was related, but there was no evidence that it was anything other than suicide. They'd found Fentanyl, a strong sedative, in her system, but they'd also found it in her own room. A strange drug, admittedly, but no evidence of foul play. And they all knew about her depression.

No amount of talking could convince the homicide department to pursue her death further. Colt had left Las Vegas three months later and come here.

He stared at the drying paint.

Hello Colt
It's payback time
Red

He headed for the street in a fast walk, turned the radio back on, and spoke in a soft but clear voice. "Becky, you there?"

Her voice came back, frazzled and quick. "Walton's sending some backup, but there's a storm between us, Colt. They don't know when they can get here."

"Okay." He steadied his own breathing. "I need you to stay focused. Can you do that?"

"Yes."

"Okay. It gets worse. I need you to call Horrence Tate, Mary Wiseman, Old Man Gerald—anyone you can think of who's been around for a while. Tell them to call everyone they know in town to lock their doors and stay inside. Don't answer the door for anyone. Tell them to spread the word. You got that?"

"Yes. Tell them it's the storm, you mean."

"No. Tell it straight. We have a killer on the loose, and I don't think he's done. Tell them not to panic, but we need them to stay locked down."

"Okay."

But she wasn't okay, Colt thought. None of them were okay.

And he in particular was nowhere near okay.

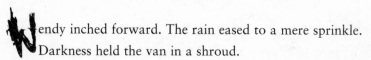

Wendy inched forward. The rain eased to a mere sprinkle. Darkness held the van in a shroud.

She approached from the right side of the vehicle. The rain, although light, would cover any sound she made. Realizing this, she ran the rest of the way, eager to get out of the open. It was the first time she'd ever run to someone's aid behind a loaded gun; but then, she'd never crashed into a bullet-riddled, bloody truck, either.

One of the side doors was open. And on the ground beside that door lay a form. A body.

Now that she was close, she could see that the van must have sideswiped the truck, because it had sustained significant damage. She could only guess the shooter had been in a third vehicle, or on foot. Confident that she wasn't coming upon a killer's van, she lowered the gun and hurried forward.

Both tires on this side of the van were shredded, bringing the vehicle low to the ground. The body belonged to a young woman dressed in jeans and a button-down shirt. She lay on her back, facing the sky, accepting the rain in her face as though totally unaware of it.

Wendy dropped to one knee and set the gun on the ground. The woman looked dead, face gray and washed clean by hard rain.

She reached for the woman's forehead, touched it gently. Hot. She had just taken the woman's exposed wrist to feel for a pulse when her eyes snapped open.

Wendy cried out in surprise and jumped back.

"Nicole?"

The door on the van's far side slammed. "Nicole!" A dark-haired man who appeared to be close to the same age as the woman raced around the van. He held a white medical kit in his hands. "What . . . Who are you?"

"I heard you. From up the road."

"You were in the truck?"

The woman, Nicole, moaned softly. Without waiting for a reply, the man hurried to her side. "She needs help."

Nicole curled into a ball, whimpering.

The man dug for something in the kit. The contents spilled on the wet ground, and he grabbed a small pack of aspirin. "If she doesn't get to a hospital, she'll die." He looked up at Wendy. "You were the one who ran into us?"

"No. I hit the same truck you did. Is she hurt?"

"Of course she's hurt." He dropped to his knees, tore the pack of aspirin open, and pressed two of the pills into her mouth. "She's already had two. She was bitten by a snake. I don't think we have a lot of time. The rain cooled her a little, but she's burning up inside. I have two spares and was . . ." He thought better of any long-winded explanations. "Does your car still run?"

"I think so, yes." Wendy moved carefully around the man and touched Nicole's face again. "She doesn't have any broken bones?"

"No. Can we take her in your car?"

"Help me with her."

The man took Nicole's arms, Wendy her legs, and they lifted her up the embankment to the road. Still no traffic. The warnings had cleared the road of all but the most stubborn or ignorant.

"Where did she get bitten?" Wendy asked. It began to rain harder.

"On her foot. Her name's Nicole, my sister. We were camping in the hills with some friends. They're still at the camp."

An odd story, but Wendy found no reason to doubt it.

"I'm Wendy."

"Carey. Carey Swartz," the man said. "I can't tell you how thankful I am. I hope we're not too late."

Wendy didn't know Carey from Adam, but she knew by the anguish in his eyes that he cared for his sister more deeply than his simple words expressed. For that alone she liked the man immediately.

They reached her Accord, and Wendy let Carey ease Nicole into the backseat.

"Where's the guy from the truck?" Carey asked.

"Gone. I think he was shot."

"You're kidding." Carey moved around to the truck and took in the bullet holes. "That's why he swerved into our lane." Behind them, steam seeped from the Accord's hood. She'd left it running, and it occurred to her that if her car overheated, they would be stranded.

They climbed into the Accord, backed away from the pickup with a creak of metal, and continued east through the rain.

"The exit to Summerville's just down the road," Carey said, leaning back over the front seat to check on his sister. "She's burning up again. Can you go a little faster?"

Wendy accelerated, glancing over at him. He had a strong chiseled chin, curly black hair, white teeth. Blue eyes flashing with empathy. Carey and his sister shared one trait: They were both extremely attractive. Beautiful, even.

"Summerville's half an hour south, off the highway," Carey said. "We have to move."

Wendy's sense of urgency refreshed, she coaxed the car up to ninety. "I think the radiator was punctured when I hit the truck. We can go fast and risk overheating, or we can go slow and risk overheating. I have no idea how radiators work, but I would think going fast would overheat quicker, but then you have more wind coming through to cool the engine, so maybe it all balances out, right?"

"Something like that. You got cell service?"

She checked. "No."

Nicole moaned behind them.

"Please hurry," he said. The understated panic in his voice was heartbreaking. Wendy knew that she should pat his shoulder or hand or something. She wanted to make such a gesture, a moment of human contact to show her concern and support. But she simply couldn't.

Despite her tremendous empathy for victims—a natural consequence of her own victimization, Dr. Rachel Lords had explained—her inability to sustain such a touch was stronger.

Wendy had spent three months on the streets of Oklahoma City after escaping the Brotherhood. She'd been eighteen and lost, but as free as a bird for the first time in her memory. She'd made friends with a woman named Louise Sinclair at the south-side shelter and had decided immediately that the only part about heaven and hell that the cult leader—Bronson—had gotten right was the part about there being a heaven populated by angels. Louise was one such angel, sent from heaven to save Wendy.

It was Louise who'd gotten Wendy thinking more about her future than her past. Louise had introduced her to Larry Crowder, the first man Wendy had ever dated, never mind that the night had ended disastrously when Larry tried to kiss her.

Louise had helped Wendy realize how beautiful she was, how she could take joy in such simple choices as wearing her hair down on her shoulders as she did now, or buying black pumps to complement her jeans if she wanted to, thank you very much. Or collecting Brighton jewelry even if it was generally worn by the over thirty crowd—she liked silver.

If not for Louise, Wendy never would have gotten her GED and won the academic scholarship to Long Beach State at age twenty. As it turned out, the Brotherhood's homeschooling had done more than a little good. Much more.

It was Louise who'd first decided that the only way for Wendy to really tackle her future was to understand her past. She'd taken Wendy to her first appointment with Dr. Rachel Lords, and together they'd explored Wendy's mind.

In the end, Wendy had come to respect herself, from her looks to her intelligence to her education to her fashion choices. But her severe nervousness around men had never subsided.

Thankfully she had no such issue with women. Only men. But it was men she loved. Or at least had tried to love on three different occasions in the last four years. All three relationships had imploded. She couldn't hold a man's hand, much less kiss him.

Headlights appeared ahead, grew quickly, then blasted by at a speed that made Wendy jerk the steering wheel.

Again twin lights materialized from the once-more strengthening storm. A truck roared by, shaking the Accord.

"Where's everyone going?"

Carey was too preoccupied to answer the question. "The exit's just ahead. Take a right."

They headed south on a smaller two-lane road spotted with cars headed the opposite direction. Wendy banged on the radio in an attempt to revive it. No luck.

It occurred to her then that she'd left her gun on the ground beside the van. Didn't matter—even if she did have use for a gun, they didn't have time to turn back now.

"You grow up around here?" she asked.

"Summerville? No. I grew up in Walton, about an hour past Summerville."

"How big is Summerville?"

"Nothing but a watering hole. Maybe two thousand people, maybe less. I'm not sure they even have a real hospital. Probably a clinic or something. It'll be closed at night. We'll have to find someone."

Another car passed them. This one honked. The fact that there was clearly something very wrong ahead wasn't lost on Wendy, but they just as clearly had no alternative except to plow ahead.

"Maybe there's a tornado out here," Wendy said.

"This isn't tornado country."

"And it doesn't normally rain like this, either." A gust shook the car.

"We don't have a choice."

"I know. I'm just pointing out the obvious. We're heading in; they're all heading out. I'm not suggesting we turn around. You tried a snakebite kit?"

"Yeah." Carey looked back at his sister, who was now sobbing softly. Tears misted his eyes.

"Just hang in there," Wendy said to both of them. "We'll get there in time."

Carey looked out his window.

"How hot is she?"

He checked Nicole's forehead. "Burning up."

"Hotter than before?"

"Yeah."

Wendy wasn't a doctor, but hotter than before was surely too hot for any living soul.

She pressed the accelerator, watched the speedometer creep over the hundred mark, then eased slightly. It seemed almost absurd. They were screaming at insane speeds for a town everyone else seemed to be fleeing.

4

Sterling Red stood over the dead body and tried to calm the tremble in his hands. He did so successfully, as he had a thousand times before. Indeed he could, and did, walk among them all day long, and they never knew he had the shakes.

Hello, Colt. It's payback time. Red.

Not that his name really was Red—or Sterling for that matter. But he liked to think of himself as Sterling Red when he was alone. If they had any idea who he really was, they would be truly freaking.

It was indeed payback time, and before this was over, all five of them would know just how painful revenge could be.

An eye for an eye; a neck for a neck; a head for a head.

The time has come for you to be dead.

He'd killed two cops and torn up a bit of town before walking away to make the rest of his preparations. Little did they know that he'd killed twice since shooting the two cops. The beginning of the end.

For every hundred million people, there was only one like him who could enter the game, change the game, and win the game, never thinking twice about what needed to be done.

And like him, those kind were usually born and bred in the smallest corners of the world. Places like Summerville. Places like hell.

Red turned his attention to the dead woman in the chair. *Goodnight, Honey Pie. Sweet stupid dreams.*

They were all so stupid, these women. He adjusted the baseball cap that sat backward on his head and walked into the kitchen. The old fool he'd killed lay prone. This man had sacrificed his life for a very good and noble cause indeed. He'd died for Red. For this reason Red loved him.

Outside, the rain came down. Red loved the man at his feet and he loved the rain. But more than either he loved himself, even though the real him rarely measured up to the him he loved so much.

This was the true cause of his trembling. Confronted with this conundrum 24/7, his body was in a constant state of revolt. Being both good and evil in one package really could mess with your mind if you let it, and Red had let it.

He reached down with a gloved hand and grabbed the old man by his hair, then dragged him along the hall to the back door. No blood, because he'd killed the man with a chicken from the freezer. There would be plenty of blood later. Patience was the one virtue he relished, despite knowing he actually had very little patience.

Red opened the back door and swung the man to his shoulder so as not to leave marks in the mud. He walked on the rock path to the toolshed. Inside was an empty drum, and in this drum Red stuffed the old man before securing the lid tightly. When the body started to rot, its smell should stay contained until the drum was opened.

Red walked back into the house, hungry from the exercise. He often tried to imagine what actually being Lucifer would be like. To think you really could be like God.

This would lead to massive amounts of conflict, Red thought. Lucifer undoubtedly appeared as nothing but a blur from all his trembling. He had to be so conflicted with his own inconsistency that whatever physical form he tried to take would quickly shake itself to pieces.

Everyone who had tried to be both good and evil at once knew that it was far too stressful for most mortals. It was for this reason that Red tried to be as consistent as possible in all respects. But it didn't always work so well. Which was why Red served only one master. Himself.

In this way, Red was better than them all.

Every time he thought about killing someone, he became hungry. Now, having killed four people in less than half an hour, he was ravenous. He glanced at the clock on the kitchen wall, saw that he had some time, and headed for the refrigerator.

Inside he found an assortment of foods: bagged pizza, olives, milk, orange juice, leftovers, and the usual condiments. Snapping the elastic on the surgical gloves on each hand, he withdrew a yellow plastic squeeze bottle of mustard and a glass jar of mayonnaise. He walked to the living room and sat down on the couch.

When the authorities responded to the distress call he planned to make in a few minutes, they would come here and find the lady who now lay dead in her overstuffed easy chair. But they wouldn't find the old man. Not yet.

He tilted his head back and filled his mouth with mustard. The smooth, tart taste calmed him. Next he scooped out a large helping of mayonnaise and sucked it off his fingers. Two more helpings from each and he felt quite satisfied. If he'd had more time, he might have finished off both bottles.

He couldn't just kill Colt, of course. There would be absolutely no justice in that. This time it had to be different, or all he'd done up to this point would be worthless. And truth be told, he wasn't sure he could just kill Colt anyway. The man had acquired considerable skill.

Red replaced the condiments in the fridge and picked up the phone. He called the police.

A rattled receptionist answered after ten rings. "Summerville Police Department."

"Hello, Honey Pie. I've killed some people at 534 Summerset."

The line was silent.

Red hung up and walked out into the rain without bothering to close the door.

5

The storm had stopped almost completely by the time they drove into the town. Nicole had stilled in the backseat, and Carey hoped aloud that the worst might be over.

Wendy slowed the Accord to the posted twenty-five-mile-per-hour speed limit and guided the car past the first few buildings that made up the desert town.

Dark streets. Power out except at a dimly lit gas station ahead on the left.

"You see anything?" she asked.

"There's a gas station on the other end."

They approached a dark intersection. Wendy looked both ways, saw no cars approaching, passed through, and angled for the gas station on the left.

She parked next to a big window display that promised hot coffee and cold beer. A neon sign indicated that the gas station was open.

"I'll be right back."

She barged into the station. No attendant that she could see. She ran up to the counter and banged a bell. "Hello?"

A smoldering cigarette in an ashtray had burned to the filter, leaving a long snake of ash still attached. Static sounded over the radio next to the cash register. An odor she couldn't quite place, something medicinal maybe, or cleaning chemicals, although the place was filthy. As if someone had just scrubbed the place with disinfectant and left no evidence of a job well done. Odd.

Louder this time. "Hello? Anyone here?"

The bell on the door clanged, and she whirled around. Carey stood in the doorway with Nicole staggering limply under one arm. "She threw up."

The evidence was down her chin.

"We have to get her to a doctor. Hold on a sec, and I'll get something to clean her up." Wendy ran to the bathrooms, checked both the men's and the women's for whoever was smoking that cigarette, and, finding no one, grabbed some tissue.

"Something's wrong," she said, returning. "This isn't right. Not just this, but everything. Have you seen anyone since we drove in?"

"There's a storm—"

"I know there's a storm, but that doesn't make sense, does it? It's not like there's a tornado riding down Main Street."

As if in response, the window shook with a blast strong enough to break small trees.

Through the front door they saw a cop car heading their way, lights flashing.

Wendy passed Carey the tissue. "Wait here." She sprinted across the lot, vaulted a hedge that ran the station's perimeter, and tore into the street, arms waving.

The cop's siren burped once, then twice when she didn't move. She

stood in the middle and moved to cut the car off when it angled left.
There was no way the officer could hear her, but she screamed anyway.

"Stop!"

It occurred to her that she looked like a cheerleader escaped from
wherever they lock up cheerleaders who've gone off the deep end.

The car braked to a hard stop. The door flew open. The man who
stepped half out wasn't dressed in a uniform as she'd expected him
to be. He wore a red NASCAR baseball cap, along with a T-shirt and
blue jeans, both soaked through. Only the gun on his hip gave him
away as law enforcement.

He looked like the kind of man who was comfortable using the
weapon.

Wendy's hands were still in the air. She lowered them.

"I'm sorry, ma'am, but I need you to move."

"We have a very sick girl who needs immediate medical attention,"
she said, still catching her breath. "Is there a clinic or a hospital here?"

The officer looked as if he was trying to judge the sincerity of her
claim. "The storm's closed the clinic."

"What happens if someone gets hurt by that storm? You can't
just close down a clinic!"

"True. Dr. Hansen handles all calls out of his place after hours."

"Okay, can you take us to him?"

"I . . . I don't think you understand our situation here," the cop
said. *He stood an inch or two shy of six feet,* she thought, brown
hair curled out from under his cap. Rugged. Not handsome, but
strong.

"You have a storm coming; I get that," she said. "We, on the
other hand, have a young woman who may die if you don't get us to
the doctor immediately. How's that for understanding?"

The cop looked over at their car, then back. "It's not just the storm. We have a situation with a killer here. Our chief's been killed with another officer, and we just got a call about a third murder. I really have to go."

"Then maybe it's the same killer who shot at us."

"You were shot at?"

"Not me, but I hit a truck that was shot at. There were two bullet holes in the windshield—"

The radio inside barked, and the cop ducked back into his cruiser, exchanged several short sentences with another car, then reemerged.

"Okay."

He pulled his cruiser next to the front door, stepped inside the small store, took in the scene with a glance and a sniff, and then helped Carey lift Nicole. They eased her into the black and white's backseat. Wendy felt them brush by her, accepting the incidental contact without any emotional response. Her therapy had helped her with at least that much, thankfully.

She hurried around the car and sat in the cruiser's front seat. Only then did she notice that the cruiser had two holes in the windshield, now covered with two small squares of duct tape on the outside. The side window was open, and she searched for a way to close it as they swung out of the station.

"Window's broken," the officer said.

"Oh."

"What's your name?"

"Wendy."

"Colt," he said without looking at her. Shy? Or maybe something more ominous? Or maybe very sweet. Impossible to tell.

They pulled into the rain.

Colt drove north, flying over the wet roads, eager to find the doctor, deliver these three to safety, and get back to Red, who was after him for reasons beyond his understanding.

Wendy was about five foot four, Colt guessed. Thin, with medium-length brown hair, dressed in Lucky jeans with a lime tank top over a white shirt that would have accentuated her figure even if it weren't soaking wet. Black boots designed for city streets, not horse riding.

She turned and met his eyes, and he focused back on the road ahead. The street lights flickered on. Power was acting up with the storm.

"You okay back there?" he asked, glancing into the rearview mirror.

"I'm fine. I don't know about Nicole."

"How far?" Wendy asked.

"On the north edge of town, by the library."

"Aren't libraries usually in the center of town?"

"Not when the good doctor pays for them, they're not. Tell me what happened on the road."

Wendy told him quickly, earning a raised brow when she described the shots in the pickup's windshield.

"The pattern in the windshield look anything like those?" Colt nodded at the two duct-taped holes in his own windshield.

"Actually . . ." Wendy looked at him. "Actually almost exactly like that."

"How long ago did this happen?"

"I don't know, maybe an hour ago."

"Timing would work. Which means he came in from the west."

"And killed the sheriff here?" Wendy asked.

"The chief, a deputy named Eli, and a woman. Two of my men just found Helen Healy dead in her living room across town. The killer called it in himself."

"How far to this doctor's house?" Carey asked from behind.

"We're almost there."

The rain, which had tapered off, suddenly began to fall hard again.

"Weather service has three tornadoes headed our way, and there's a chance they'll merge," Colt said. "That wouldn't be pretty. Could push them into F5s."

"That's possible?" Wendy asked.

"Evidently."

"If you're trying to make us nervous," Carey said, "I don't think we need any help."

He let it go. "I want you three to stay put once we get to the doctor's house. I get you in and you stay—"

Something thudded against the trunk. Then again. *Plunk.*

"Down!" Colt swerved. "Get down!"

"Wha—"

"We're being shot at! Get down!"

Behind him, Carey scrunched down with Nicole.

"He's here?" Wendy cried. "That's the killer?"

Colt careened around a corner and blasted into the rain, which had picked up even more. A large white building loomed on their right, monolithic in the darkness except for several thin windows that beamed with light. The lighted sign at the bottom of the wide entrance steps read *Summerville's Hansen Library.* A public library that looked way too large for such a small town. The doctor's house, on the other hand, was dark. He must be in the library.

Plunk.

"He's behind us!" Carey shouted.

"I don't see him," Colt said. "It could be debris. Something in the wind. Just hold on."

The wheels left the asphalt driveway and mushed through grass, then back onto pavement. The car lurched to a halt directly in front of the library.

"Get out and keep low," he said.

"This is his house?" Wendy asked. "It's a library."

"Lights at the house are off. He spends half his time here." He spun his head around, looking into the dark. "Just get inside quick."

Colt had his weapon trained down the hill. No shots. He ran around the car in a crouch, stopping to examine the trunk. Two dents showed where debris had struck the car.

His pulse eased. He looked up at the doctor's darkened house a stone's throw up the slope. Nothing that he could see.

He hurried after the others, who were already on the steps that led up to the library's main door. They stumbled up with Nicole through eight-foot double doors. Past the foyer. Into the expansive, double-story library that belonged in a city three times the size of Summerville.

Checkout counter to the right of a twenty-foot arch. Beyond the arch were a dozen cherrywood study tables, each with banker's desk lamps glowing green. Around the perimeter towered the cases, filled with books.

The space above the study tables was open to the second floor, which was rimmed by a railing behind which stood even more bookcases. Three massive wood beams stretched the width of the interior.

Colt stepped forward. "Anyone here?"

His voiced echoed back at him. Nothing else.

"This place looks like a fortress," Wendy said.

"It is," Colt said. "Doc says it would survive a ten-megaton blast. Behind the wood it's all steel and concrete."

"What for?"

"The man's got a survivalist hobby. Built this place and his house to survive the worst."

"Like a tornado," Wendy said.

"Like a tornado." *They should have considered evacuating the town to the library,* he thought.

A terrible gust of wind moaned outside, but the building showed no sign of strain. The power feeding the library failed, though, throwing the huge space into darkness.

No, not throwing; it wasn't that sudden. The lights faded to black over five seconds or so. And smaller night-lights from the receptacles along the wall popped to life—enough wattage to fill the entire library with an eerie amber hue.

"What now?" Carey asked.

A simple but obvious question to which Colt couldn't find an immediate answer. There was a killer on the loose outside. There was a storm battering the town. There was a woman dying from a snake-bite. And there was him, clueless for the moment as to what course of action he should immediately take.

One thing was certain: Doc Hansen wasn't here.

"Follow me."

He led them back to the car, helped Carey ease Nicole into the backseat again, and drove a hundred yards to the doctor's massive Victorian house. Large trees on the east side bent under the howling wind.

They exited the cruiser without speaking this time, storm thundering, rain stinging. Carey turned his face away from the rain and carefully hoisted Nicole to her feet with Wendy's help. Colt would have helped, but they seemed more than capable. And there was no room for him amid the three.

Colt scanned the perimeter as he pushed the doorbell. Nothing but flailing trees and hard rain. High-tension wires on the south side of the lawn bowed with the wind.

"Anyone home?" Wendy asked no one in particular.

Colt beat on the glass, twisted the knob. The wind caught the door and threw it open.

Carey and Wendy dragged Nicole past Colt into a house lit only by the same fluorescent amber emergency lights they'd seen in the library.

"Dr. Hansen!"

But there was no Dr. Hansen.

L et's get her on a couch," Wendy said, eager to be free of the dead-weight under her left arm. Carey seemed so distracted by the prospect of finding no doctor that he'd let Nicole slip a little.

A violent gust shook the house. The whole thing creaked loudly enough to stop all three of them in their tracks.

Nicole moaned.

"Maybe we should have stayed in the library," Carey said.

Colt called out again, then faced them in the ensuing silence. "We should take her back to the police station."

"There's got to be something here," Carey said. "Medicine. She's going to die, man!"

Colt hesitated, then headed into the house, perhaps to look for a medicine cabinet.

Wendy and Carey carried Nicole into the living room and laid her on the couch. The furniture was made of leather, the expensive kind that the good doctor would undoubtedly want to protect from water. But they had no time to concern themselves with such niceties. The house was mostly white, a sanitized bachelor's pad built out of proportion. The walls bore some paintings and mirrors, but the brown leather sofas and cherrywood tables looked sterile and unused.

Carey dropped to one knee, pulled Nicole's hair free from her face, felt her cheeks. "She's burning up again."

Wendy dropped beside him, reached over his arm without touching him, and felt for a pulse.

"She has a pulse. But if we don't get her temperature down, she's not going to make it."

"Get some ice on her," Colt said, entering the room. He tossed her a bottle of Advil. "I can't find anything else. Hold tight. I have to report in and check on the situation."

"What situation?" Carey asked. "This is the situation, right here."

"I understand your concern, and I'm doing my best to help you. But we also have a storm outside, and judging by the way this house is shaking, it's getting worse. Not to mention the fact that there's a gunman on the loose."

Carey just stared at him.

"I'll be back in half an hour."

"Be careful," Wendy said.

Colt nodded. He opened the front door, stepped into the storm, paused with his hand still on the knob for several seconds as if checking something, and then pulled the door closed behind him.

"Now what?"

"I'll get some ice," Wendy said.

"I don't like this. Those pigs never do any good."

Carey's off-color outburst seemed out of character. Pigs? Cops. Then it occured to her: What did she really know about Carey, or his sister for that matter?

Carey turned away. "There has to be an antidote or something around here."

"Do you know what kind of snake bit her?" Wendy asked. "Without that, we don't know what to give her. The wrong one could do more harm than good."

He paced. "Okay . . . Okay, ice."

But ice was not to be, not yet. The door flew open and the cop stepped in, freshly dripping from head to toe. He slammed the door shut behind him and looked at them, gun in palm.

"We have a problem," he said. "I think my cruiser was struck by lightning. It's dead. So is my radio."

"Dead? What do you mean?" Wendy asked.

"I mean it has no power. The computer won't even boot on its own power source. The walkie won't turn on. Neither will my cell phone. I mean dead."

"What about the house phones?" Wendy asked.

Colt crossed to a phone and snatched it off the foyer wall. He listened for a dial tone, then set it back in the cradle.

"Dead," he said.

6

Deputy Luke Preston stood in Cyrus Healy's living room, weapon still drawn, staring at Helen's dead body with a strange mixture of horror and wonder. Steve Wallace stood over the body, looking closer.

"You said Mark Clifton's on his way?" Steve asked, lifting the older woman's gray hair. She was Cyrus Healy's wife of about two years. No one knew too much about the reclusive man other than that he had once been some kind of rocket scientist.

That and the fact that he was on his third wife, who was now clearly dead.

"Don't mess with the evidence, Steve. Yeah, he should be here in a few minutes."

"How did he get here so quickly?"

"He was at the Carlisle Ranch, fishing. Walton's sending two squad cars, too, soon as the road's clear, but at least we got Clifton. Hear he's good. This is messed up, man."

"I think he killed her with a frozen chicken," Steve said, straightening.

"You can't kill someone with a chicken."

"You can when it's frozen solid. What else is it doing on the floor? You don't see any blood, do you?"

"No, but she could have a hole in her spine from a needle for all we know. This guy knows what he's doing. Chicken, yeah right."

"What you want to bet it's the chicken? And what's that on the arm of the couch?"

"What's happening?"

Luke whirled around, gun extended. A large blond man dressed in wet jeans stood by the door, staring at them.

"On the floor!" Steve shouted.

"Take it easy," Luke said.

"You know him?"

"I've seen him around. You're the Healy boy, right?"

"My name is Timothy Healy," the man said, staring now at the woman, who, if Luke was putting things together correctly, was his stepmother. His right hand was doubled over and had been since birth, they said. Useless to him except to move things by nudging them.

Luke glanced at the woman. "This is your mother?"

Timothy Healy stumbled forward, eyes peeled wide. "What's wrong with her?"

Steve stepped up to stop the man. Timothy stopped and gaped. He tried to say something, but no more than a breathy squeak came out.

"I'm sorry about your mother, sir."

"My mom died five years ago. That's my dad's new wife." Timothy looked around, frantic. "Where's my father?"

"We don't know. Don't worry; he'll show up. Right now it would be best if you went home. You live near here?"

"I live on Rivendale Road. Is . . . is my father dead?"

42

"No sir. Please . . ."

"Helen was killed in the head with a chicken?"

Luke looked at Steve, then faced Timothy. "Where'd you hear something like that? You know something we don't?"

"I heard you say that he killed her with a chicken."

"How'd you get in?" Luke asked. "The door's closed. How's that possible?"

"I don't know," Timothy Healy said. "I was just driving by and saw the police car."

"How long ago did you come in?" Steve asked. "A few seconds or a few minutes? He heard me talking about the chicken. That was about a minute ago."

Luke faced the young deputy. They'd been accused of being rednecks from time to time, and it was times like this that Steve made that reputation stick. Even Luke's wife, Marla, who'd known both of them since their wild days in high school, complained that Steve was dragging Luke down with him in the realms of the impress-the-brass department.

'Course, Steve had dropped Marla after high school for Betsy when she'd come back home from college after dropping out in her second year. Jealousy wasn't beyond Marla, by any means. She knew how to kick any man where it hurt, including Luke on occasion. But Luke was man enough to admit that a guy needed kicking now and then. And Marla was the woman to do it.

"Question is," Luke said, "how he got in here without us hearing him."

"I agree. But if he's been standing there for more than five minutes, he might have come in when we were in the kitchen, which could explain why we didn't hear him."

"Just standing there and neither of us seen him when we walk back in the living room? I don't think so."

"Makes as much sense as us not hearing him right here," Steve said.

That much was true. Luke faced the man who was staring past them at the dead body.

"So tell us, Timothy. How long you been standing there?"

"I don't know."

"What do you mean you don't know? You have some sense of time, don't you? Did you come in while we were in here, or did you come in while we were in the kitchen?"

"Maybe you were in the kitchen," the man said.

"What do you mean *maybe*?" Steve asked. "Did you see us or not? Come on, dude, you're killing us here. Just answer the questions straight."

"Go easy, Steve," Luke said. "He's just lost his mother, for crying out loud."

"His stepmother, who he doesn't seem to care for."

Luke faced Timothy and spoke with a calm voice. "Why didn't we see you when we came back in?"

"I was hiding. I heard someone."

Luke shot Steve a look of satisfaction. "See? It's all about asking the right questions. He came in while we were in the kitchen, saw the body, heard us, freaked out, and hid. Where?"

"Behind the curtain."

"Behind the drapes, then. Then he stepped out a minute ago. Mystery solved."

"That's mayonnaise," Timothy said, looking at the creamy blotch on the couch.

"How you know that?" Steve asked.

"Because it looks like mayonnaise."

He didn't look like any retarded person Luke had ever seen. Not short, no weird hand gestures, no large body parts. Just a bit of lummox and the bent hand. Maybe smarter than he looked.

"She got hit in the head with a chicken," Timothy said, as if it were a new revelation.

"That's one theory," Luke said.

"The killer ate some mayonnaise," Timothy said.

"Say what?" Steve asked.

Timothy looked around. "Why isn't my father here?"

Steve caught Luke's eye, then addressed Timothy in a careful voice. "We're sorry, Timothy, but you really should go home until we can figure this out. The storm's not easing any, neither."

Luke held up his hand. "Hold on, Steve. Let him talk. Maybe he knows something we don't."

"He's not—"

"He's got that sixth-sense thing going," Luke interrupted. "You know, like in that *Rain Man* movie. What do you think, Timothy? Tell us what you think happened here."

The house shook with a gust of wind. Luke held up his hand again, grabbed his radio, and toggled the transmitter. "Becky, you copy?"

Static. "Copy. You guys okay?"

"Just waiting. What's the latest on the storm?"

"Same high winds, thunderstorm. The weather service says the three tornadoes they picked up earlier are gone. But more could form. That's all we know."

"Okay. We still have help coming, then."

"That's right. They're on their way. Detective Clifton should be at your location any minute."

"No more sign of the shooter?"

"Nothing I've heard. Can't get Colt on the radio, though."

Steve looked over to Luke. Luke looked back, nodded, not sure what he really meant by it. They were on their own, maybe, but they'd be all right. They'd made it through grade school their own way, hacked their way through high school their own way, and had secured two of the most important positions in Summerville the same way.

Their way.

Luke clipped his radio to his belt. "So how about it, Timothy Healy? What's your theory?"

The man just stared at him, dumbstruck to be asked such a thing. Crippled hand, crippled mind?

Steve cleared his throat.

"It's okay," Luke said. "We have some time. Tell us what you think."

Silence.

"Not that much time," Steve said. "Clifton's on his way."

Maybe the man wasn't as smart or as perceptive as the kind on the shows who could do crazy things. Or maybe he needed specific questions.

"Tell us this, then: how'd the killer get in?"

A light seemed to ignite behind the guy's eyes. "Can I see?"

Luke and Steve exchanged a look. Steve shrugged.

"Why not?" Luke said. "This way."

They led Timothy Healy to the kitchen.

"Here's the kitchen. You see the floor's wet, so we know he was in here—"

"The back door," Timothy said.

"What, you're saying he came in the back door?" Luke asked.

"Yes, the back door."

"Why you say that?"

"There's water on the kitchen floor."

Another glance Steve's way. Okay, so maybe Healy really was an idiot without any special abilities.

"That's good, Tim, real good. Come on, let's—"

"And there was two of them." Timothy's eyes were fear-fired again.

"Two," Steve said. "The killer and the victim."

"Two dead people," Timothy said. His lower lip trembled. "Two . . ."

Okay, so that was new. Crazy, maybe, but new. "What makes you say that?"

"A wet body was dragged to the door. Mrs. Helen doesn't have a wet body."

Luke looked at the floor, trying to see where the whiz kid saw the marks. There were a dozen wet markings, a few of which were clearly footprints, something Clifton would be interested in, but otherwise nothing that screamed "I've been dragged" to him.

"That would mean that the second victim came in out of the rain," Steve said. "Then was killed and dragged back out. That's your theory?"

"That's what happened," Timothy said. "Where's my father?"

"How do you know the killer wasn't dragging a jacket? Or that he slid his feet when he walked? Heck, he could have used a mop in here to clean up some blood, for all we know."

"No, you're wrong," Healy said, rushing toward the back door. He threw it open to the storm and stared out at the black rain. "The killer isn't that stupid. He killed someone here with the same chicken he used on the woman. Then he dragged him out back before returning and celebrating his kill by eating from the refrigerator. That's what happened."

Luke wasn't quite sure he'd heard all this correctly. Was it just him, or had Timothy lost his retardation completely? The man spoke as if he solved this kind of crime every day.

Healy shut the door and faced them. "I'm afraid."

He's beginning to sound more like himself, Luke thought.

"I don't see it," Steve said. "You can't get all that from—"

A hard rap on the door interrupted him.

"That's gonna be Clifton," Luke said, leading them quickly to the living room. *What was Mark Clifton gonna think about them having Timothy Healy in here? Crap.*

Steve opened the door.

A gust of wind hit the door, nearly tearing it out of Steve's hand. The detective from Walton stepped in and shook the rain from his hands. His eyes took in the body, then turned to Timothy.

"What's he doing here?"

"He's the son, er, stepson," Luke said. "We were just questioning him. We're about done with him, right, Steve?"

"We got his statement, yeah."

Timothy Healy drilled Clifton with a stare that might have melted ice. He made no move to leave. "Have you seen my father?"

"I'm sure the detective would tell us if he'd seen your father, Mr. Healy. But you should leave now." Steve took the man's arm and led him to the door, without any resistance. "You'll be okay."

Timothy stared at Clifton. If Luke wasn't nuts, these two men looked at each other as if they'd met in another life and had unfinished business. They even looked somewhat similar: both tall, both blond, both meaty.

Timothy Healy shifted his gaze to Luke. "It's not what you think," he said. "Something's wrong. And there's someone else, just like I said."

"Is that right?" Clifton said, a wry near grin crossing his face. He looked at the body, then stepped over and felt Helen's fingers. "Dead about half an hour. Where were *you* half an hour ago, Mr. Healy?"

Healy nudged his nose with that crippled hand. "My father's not here."

"But you are," Clifton said. "And I don't want you leaving town now. Clear?"

"It's all wrong," Timothy said again. Then he turned and walked out into the gale-force winds and was gone.

"Aw, heck," Luke said. "Maybe we should've let him stay till the weather calms." He paused. "And what if he's right about his father? What if he's stashed out back right now?"

Detective Mark Clifton pulled two surgical gloves out of his soaked jeans pockets and pulled them on with an experienced snap. He'd been on a fishing trip, which explained the army jacket instead of a sport jacket, but no good forensics guy leaves his gloves at home, right?

"One step at a time, Luke." The man looked like he'd been born ready to throw handcuffs on the first bad guy who came within smelling distance. "He killed her with a frozen chicken?"

"What's it with everybody and this chicken thing?" Luke asked. "We got a dead woman and a dead chicken, but it doesn't mean the two are related."

"Interesting way to kill someone," Clifton said, stroking the chicken with one finger.

"Colt says this guy might be after him," Luke said.

The detective's left eye twitched. "A lot of trouble for one man."

"Yeah, that's what I think," Luke said.

Clifton picked up the chicken. He grabbed it by the legs and swung it into his hand. *Smack!*

Then he swung it again, harder. He looked up at them. "We got us one sick puppy, gentlemen."

7

Wendy watched Colt drip in the foyer. The man seemed at a loss. He gave her fleeting glances on occasion but still refused to hold her stare. It occurred to her that he was genuinely unnerved. Not just given the situation, but with her. Maybe he was as uncomfortable around women as she was around men.

Then again, she could be misinterpreting him entirely, prompted by her own hypersensitivity.

"Either of you have a cell phone?" Colt asked.

Carey glanced at her. "You?" He'd left his in the van; they'd already established that much.

"I left it in the Accord," she said. "It had no service anyway. So we don't have any way to call anyone?"

"Not until the phones come back on line. Unless we find a cell phone."

"Then I'm going for help," Carey said.

"No," Colt said, his voice cold. "There's a storm out there."

"I'll take my chances."

"And a killer on the loose."

That gave Carey pause.

Still, to some degree, Wendy could identify with Carey's feeling that Nicole was the one in real danger.

"The killer may be gone," Carey said.

"I don't think so. I think he was just getting started. Soon as this wind lightens up a bit, I'll run down for some help, but the best thing you can do for your sister is stay here and keep her fever down."

Carey stared at the man for a moment, then headed out of the room. "Where's the fridge?"

Colt nodded down the hall. "Kitchen."

Carey left them in a hurry.

The house shuddered under a blast of wind. Colt looked at the rafters.

"You said this guy killed two other cops," said Wendy. "He has a thing for cops?"

"It's possible." Colt avoided her eyes. "He knows my name. He may know more. He calls himself Red."

"So you're suggesting this isn't just random?"

"How would he know my name?"

"Maybe he heard it on one of the radios. Or maybe he's someone you know. Someone from Summerville."

He looked into her eyes, maybe impressed with her reasoning. Or unimpressed with her naïveté, she couldn't tell.

"You saw him?"

"He was too far away to make out any detail. I've never seen anyone around here shoot like that. Other than Mark Clifton."

"What about you?"

He blushed a little.

"I'll take that as a yes," she said. "And for the record, I'm thankful someone here knows how to handle a gun." She looked as Carey walked in with a bag of ice and placed it gently on his sister's forehead.

"Could this Clifton be the killer?" Wendy asked.

"Clifton? No."

"Why not?"

"He was with the FBI for years."

"Sounds like the perfect hiding place."

Colt blinked.

The house shook. "Wind's getting stronger," he said.

She nodded. "So what do we do?"

Colt looked back at the front door again. "If the killer is out there and he knows we're in here, he also knows I'm armed. I set the alarm—it'll work on battery power. As long as we stay inside, we have the advantage. I don't think he could get in without our knowing it."

"We wait it out, then?"

"I have to get back to the station. I'm useless up here."

"Not to us, you're not," Wendy said. She walked back to Nicole and put her arm under the girl's neck. "Help me get her up," she said.

"What are you going to do?" Carey asked, standing from the end of the couch.

"We have to get her back under some cold water. Colt's right—we have to control this fever."

"Out in the rain?"

"In the shower."

They found a large shower in the master bedroom, stripped Nicole to her underwear and bra, and set her on a plastic chair Colt found in the garage.

"Okay, I think you two have this under control," Colt said, looking distinctly uneasy.

Wendy eyed his gun. "You leaving us?"

"I have to check the storm. When it breaks I gotta go. We had some backup coming from Walton, but I have no idea when they'll get here. And my people are probably worried about me by now."

Wendy realized that Colt had probably been close to the officers who were killed tonight. Had she been so insensitive as to ignore some terrible pain he was feeling? She nodded, turned back to Nicole, and cranked the water on. The contact of freezing cold water on Nicole's skin sent the girl into an abrupt spasm. She shook violently, and her teeth chattered loudly.

"Wendy?"

"It's okay, Carey. Hold her. Don't let her fall off the chair."

"You're sure?"

"I'm sure."

Nicole began to cry as she jerked, and Carey joined her with silent tears. The sight tightened Wendy's throat. There was a bond between the two that made her long for such love. Nothing off-color, rather something wholly right and enviable.

Wendy glanced back at Colt and saw that he'd left. Nicole's spasms had subsided. She still shivered, but her fever was back down. Carey rummaged through the medicine cabinet over the sink and came back with a thermometer, which quickly indicated her temperature was 101.

"That's still high," Carey said.

"Not as high as it was. Let the water run a minute longer."

Looking at Nicole in relative calm under the shower, Wendy was struck again by her natural beauty. Had they met under any other circumstance, she might have given the woman a second look with a tinge of envy.

Something was banging on the roof—she could hear it over the shower. No telling how much debris was blowing around out there.

"You think that's enough?" Carey asked.

Wendy looked into his caring eyes and reached for the knob. "She's going to make—"

Bang! The house shook.

Wendy gasped and twisted back to the bathroom door. "What was that?"

Boom! Thunder crashed around them. Someone was screaming at them.

The whole house began to rock as if God himself had picked it up and was shaking it to see what it contained.

The fact that Wendy had her hand on the shower knob, ready to cut the water, saved them all from spilling into the tub.

"Get in the basement!" Colt yelled behind them. His hands suddenly on her shoulders jolted her like an electric current. But just as quickly he was past her, scooping Nicole in his arms and out of the shower and staggering out of the bathroom with her.

"Hurry!" he yelled. "Follow me!"

Carey grabbed Wendy by her arm.

On instinct she yanked herself out of his grip.

He looked confused for a moment. "Okay?"

He went, and she followed down the hall. One word thundered through her mind with the roar that swept over the house. *Tornado.* She'd been in an earthquake once, and it had rumbled, not roared. This was the sound of a jet inside the house.

She was screaming, but she couldn't hear the sound of her own voice.

No wind, though. So far, the house had held up.

So far.

She jerked down the hall to the doorway that Carey had stopped at. He was yelling, mouthing for her to hurry, hand extended to her. She reached him and skirted past without making contact, heedless of what lay beyond.

Not until she was actually airborne over a set of dimly lit stairs descending into darkness did she understand her mistake. Throwing yourself down a flight of stairs is no way to escape falling walls.

Once again, Carey came to her rescue, snatching her shirt from behind and yanking her back with enough force to tear the fabric. She found footing on the stairs, found the railings with both hands, pulled brusquely away again, and raced down before him.

The door behind them slammed shut, and the roar above became a muted rumble.

"Everyone okay?" Colt asked.

Carey nodded wearily.

"I'm okay," Wendy said. And to her surprise, so was Nicole, who seemed to have come alive in a rush of adrenaline.

"Okay," she repeated softly. It was the first word Wendy had heard her utter.

Then Nicole began to cry.

8

he only way Wendy could properly describe the sound of the house's disintegration over their heads was to think of monster trains roaring through the front door with enough force to set off an earthquake under their tracks.

Fortunately, they were in the relative safety of a basement, which, like the rest of the good doctor's house, looked like it had been overengineered.

Then again, Wendy knew next to nothing about building and overbuilding. For all she knew, all basements this size had five steel beams running overhead.

Colt quickly steered them to the far wall, under one of the large steel beams on which the overhead floor joists hung. The door through which they had come was also steel.

"Looks like the doctor was thinking of a root cellar when he built this," Colt said.

"Thank God," Wendy said.

"Or a bunker." Carey held Nicole in his arms; she'd passed out again.

They were silent, powerless beneath the ferocious roar.

The only light came from emergency lights similar to those that lined the halls upstairs.

"How long do you think this thing will last?" Wendy asked. Dust cascaded down like a fine mist.

Colt craned his head, studying the floor above. "I don't know."

"Is it coming apart?"

"I don't know."

"Sure sounds like it to me," Carey said.

"The house was still standing when we came down," Wendy said. "I don't hear any ripping or crashing. Just the roar."

Colt nodded. "If we're lucky, the house is still standing. Windows might be blown out, who knows. Or it could be flattened. Never been through one of these."

There was something irresistible about watching the floor above them. This one system of joists and decking was all that barred the terrible fury from reaching in and ripping them to shreds.

It trembled and it shook and dust sifted down, but for five and then ten and then fifteen minutes the floor held. As did the door at the top of the stairs.

And then, as quickly as the monster had descended upon them, it seemed to move on in search of other houses that needed ravaging.

The wind still blew above them; they could hear it in the distance, a dull and steady rush. But not the full-throated roar of trains and jet engines they'd just heard.

They looked at each other without moving. It seemed to Wendy that none of them really wanted to go up and find out what awaited them.

Carey scanned the floorboards above, as if expecting the tornado to double back and hit them again in case they still had any doubts about its intention. Their eyes met.

Colt had risen to one knee and was listening intently. Sweat glistened on his face, and his T-shirt was covered in a thin layer of wood dust. He faced her, eyes wide, his earlier insecurity now lost to a common need for survival.

"Should we check?" she asked.

He stood and walked toward the staircase. Wendy let him go halfway, suddenly terrified by the prospect of opening that door and facing a black sky with wind howling.

She jumped and ran after him. Together they reached the stairs. Colt stepped aside to let her go first, like a good gentleman, but then thought better of it and held up his hand. "I'll go."

The stairs creaked but otherwise seemed as solid as they should be. Whatever else had been destroyed, the foundation hadn't been touched.

Wendy came up behind him, peered over his shoulder. His back was wet with rain and sweat; she could smell both. The thin cotton lay plastered on hard muscle. She chided herself for noticing at a time like this.

She stepped up beside him on the small landing. "Aren't you going to try it?"

He took the brass handle in his hand, turned it, and gave the door a gentle shove. But it didn't shove so easily.

Colt took one step forward and pushed harder. The latch disengaged easily enough—they could hear it sliding open—but the door would not budge.

"It's blocked," he said and threw all his weight into the door. If it moved at all, it gave only a centimeter before springing back.

She joined him, painfully aware of his proximity. They pushed together, but they might as well have been pushing against a concrete wall.

Wendy stepped back. "It's wedged shut."

Colt ran down the stairs and backpedaled, eyes scanning the floor above.

Carey had rested Nicole on an empty cardboard box they'd found and flattened for her. "What's wrong?" he asked, crossing the basement. "It won't open?"

"It seems the house collapsed on top of us," Colt said.

Wendy banged on the door. "Help!" But she knew there was no one near to help. No one bothered pointing out her folly.

She spun back. "Now what? We're just stuck down here?" She came back down the stairs. "There has to be another way out."

"If I'm right, we have a dozen tons of brick and wood piled on top of us," Colt said. "Let's check the basement for window wells." He pointed to two rooms on each side.

Carey crossed to the nearest. Wendy and Colt hurried to two of the remaining doors. The doorframe around hers must have shifted slightly in all the twisting and tearing above them, because this door was jammed as well. She forced it open with a strong heel kick.

Without thinking, she flipped the switch just inside the door. No power, of course, but she didn't need power. Dr. Hansen had probably paid someone to outfit the house with backup night-lights after tripping over something in the dark or something, and whoever had done the job had been thorough enough to line his pockets. There had to be a hundred of the small glowing lights throughout this house, and one of them lit this room with a dull light.

Just enough light to see a construction blanket on the floor. A closet on one end. Nothing else. Four solid walls without any windows.

"Anybody?" Colt yelled. "Any windows?" He was running to the last room.

"No."

"Nothing."

A little more running and shuffling of feet, and they found themselves back in the middle of the large unfinished space, breathing hard and staring at each other lucklessly. Steel posts rose to steel beams around them. In one corner stood a large white tank that Wendy assumed had something to do with water, judging by all the pipes running up from it.

Nicole lay on the flattened cardboard along one wall. The stairs rose to an immobile door. That was it.

They were trapped.

"No forced-air ducts?" Carey asked.

Colt shook his head. "In-floor heating."

"Geothermal?"

"Does it matter?" Wendy said. "We're trapped."

They faced her.

"Sorry. Sorry, really, I know the male mind tends to think in details like geothermal whatever, but I'm thinking big picture here. Short of a bulldozer coming to our rescue, we may be down here for a while, am I right?"

"Something like that," Colt said.

"There's gotta be at least a grill that allows for ventilation," Carey said.

"You know houses?"

"Summer jobs."

She watched him and Colt as they walked the basement back and forth several times, looking for the supposed vents. Even if they found one, wouldn't it lead to rubble as well? Slowly, any remaining hope faded.

Wendy let them search and went for the construction blanket she'd seen in the otherwise empty room. She took it to their wall, spread it on the concrete floor, and sat down next to Nicole, who slept, oblivious to their plight.

For the first time that night, she felt truly and utterly helpless. Alone. She'd been trapped and alone before, and she didn't like the feeling.

But she wasn't alone, was she? Carey seemed a decent guy. He certainly felt concern for his sister. And Colt, a very shy, very strong man who struck her as deeply principled. And she was with Nicole, whom she knew next to nothing about other than that she was stunningly beautiful.

Yet she felt entirely alone.

Deputy Luke Preston had never worked with the detective from Walton before, but Mark Clifton had a movie-star reputation. You couldn't be in law enforcement and not have heard the guy's name. He'd left the FBI for life in a small town, but everyone knew he could run circles around any of the big dogs in the city. People said that the detective who'd come to Walton from Las Vegas three years earlier was an eccentric man who kept mostly to himself.

Luke wasn't sure if *eccentric* or *just plain strange* said it best, but he gave the benefit of the doubt to *eccentric* because that fit best with the claim that Clifton was also a genius.

True, Luke couldn't say that he'd ever seen an eccentric genius before, but he was quite sure he was looking at one now.

"He said that?" Clifton asked, eyeing the water marks on the kitchen floor.

Steve looked at Luke. "Yup."

"You two bother asking yourself how he came across this information?"

"Well," Luke said, "he said the markings explained it. I'm not saying that he's right, but we couldn't very well not listen to him."

"He wasn't close to his stepmother," Steve said. "And I think Becky said he pretty much hated his father."

"We don't know that his father was killed," Luke said. "Could be anywhere."

"Could be the one drug out the back," Steve said.

Clifton eyed them, brows arched. "There's more than one possible explanation for these marks. You have to ask yourself why he fixated on the one he did. The *why* is what it's all about, not the whats and hows and whens and wheres. The whys."

"The whys," Steve said. "I've heard that."

"Like why Red killed two cops and this poor sap here if Colt's right about him being the target."

"Yeah," Luke agreed. "A lotta trouble for someone after just Colt."

"Then again, revenge can send even the most reasonable killer round the bend."

Luke nodded. Inside, though, he wondered what Clifton meant by a "reasonable killer."

Clifton walked to the refrigerator and scanned the contents. He fanned out his latex-gloved fingers and touched the milk, the caps on some of the fixings. Tasted his finger, smacked his lips.

"Mustard," he said.

"Mustard?"

"This guy likes chickens, mayonnaise, and mustard."

"Seriously?"

Clifton slipped the yellow bottle of mustard he'd tasted and a jar of mayonnaise into his jacket pockets. Two big bulges. He didn't look much like a genius detective now. Wet blue jeans, army jacket, hat hair, pockets full of condiments.

"That's evidence," Steve said.

"That's right," Clifton said. Then he headed out of the kitchen, toward the front door.

Luke hurried after him. "That's it? What about the other body?"

Clifton opened the door and stared out at the roaring wind. "We'll search for the other body after the storm," he said and slammed the door shut behind him.

"Weird," Steve said.

Luke turned back to the one dead body they had on the chair. "So what do we do with this one?"

"We do what he's doing," Steve said. "I can promise you that Bob Buncus isn't coming out in this weather to pack her in ice."

"She won't rot?"

"Not overnight. Where you think Colt is?"

"Last thing he reported was picking up those strangers."

"And what if one of those strangers just happens to be the killer?"

"Kind of unlikely, don't you think? Let's get out of here and find that killer."

It took them about fifteen minutes to secure the room using procedures that Luke suggested they might as well use, considering how rarely they were used. They were set to leave when his radio squawked and filled the room with a terrible scream/roar that made both of them jump. Becky was yelling something. Luke grabbed the walkie off his belt and fumbled with the volume.

"Holy . . ." Her voice came clear. Then broke. ". . . on us. You read me? Come on, answer me!"

"What's that? Say again." Whatever was happening over at the station sounded like a large vacuum sucking at Becky's mic.

"I said take cover right—"

The transmission ended abruptly.

"What?" Steve ran for the door and flew into the wind with Luke hard on his heels to the curb where both of their cruisers were parked. "She say tornado?"

The answer came before Luke could respond. A massive gust of wind, accompanied by a roar so loud that Luke thought a Boeing 747 might be crashing down on them.

But he knew it wasn't a jet. It had to be a tornado, and it seemed to be swallowing the whole town.

As if the storm possessed intelligence and had become aware that one of the humans in its path had guessed its intention, the wind blew a branch that hit Luke broadside. He staggered to his right, feeling for something to hold himself up, and finding nothing, fell headlong.

He was out before he hit the dirt.

9

Nathan Blair turned away from the window that peered into the conference room where the other three task force members sat, discussing the matter in urgent tones. Being with the internal affairs arm of this operation, they had both more power and less power than the rest.

He walked to the desk and picked up a red telephone that gave him direct access to the director. To some of his peers, the scenario unfolding before them might constitute nothing more than one more among a hundred similar scenarios—just one more box on a spreadsheet, another incident in a file, the latest tale forbidden to be told outside these walls.

But from the beginning, Blair'd had his reservations about this case. But nothing could have prepared him for what they now faced. Until the killer had entered Summerville, they'd tracked his movements, waiting for the right moment to pull the plug on his string of murders. Then they'd lost him. How was beyond Blair.

Even worse, all they'd assumed about Sterling Red had been thrown into question. Including his identity. They couldn't assume anything about the killer any longer. He seemed to be able to change his skin like a chameleon. It was almost as if his old identity never existed.

The director's voice answered, soft and silky. "Yes?"

"Anything new on the inside?" Blair asked.

A pause. "Mark Clifton's taken over the investigation on the ground," the director said.

The sensitivity of the operation precluded them from using their own people. The last thing they could afford was an agent with actual knowledge of the situation being compromised and leaking the truth. With any luck Clifton would put an end to this madness before any further interdiction was required. Blair would feed him only enough information to aide in his pursuit of the killer.

"You'd better be praying he finds Red."

The director didn't sound ruffled. "Relax, Mr. Blair. This will all work out, you'll see."

Blair hesitated, knowing his next question was at the very least awkward. "Any word on Cyrus Healy?"

"No."

He glanced back at the others, whose arguments were still muted by the soundproof glass. Silent puppets mouthing.

"Please do me the courtesy of informing me the minute you hear anything. And for the record, I don't like where this is going."

"I understand."

Nathan Blair hung up. There was little more to say. They would have to wait and watch. The case was now in the hands of Detective Mark Clifton.

Or in the mind of Sterling Red, depending on how you looked at it.

10

"o we just wait." Carey was back to holding his sister's head on his lap.

"We just wait," Colt said. "There will be rescue crews out in the morning."

"I doubt this is the only house to get hit. It may be awhile before they get to us, assuming they even know we're here."

"They know I was headed up here," Colt said. "Don't worry; they'll get to us. It may not be at first light, but they'll come."

They sat on the blanket, leaning back on the foundation wall, three abreast with Wendy in the middle. Nicole still slept, still in another world, unaware that they were trapped below a fallen house. Probably unaware of everything but her own need to survive the darkness.

The cold shower had effectively reduced her fever, and the shakes hadn't returned yet. Maybe snakebites were like food poisoning; if you can just survive long enough, the body processes the toxins.

SKIN

No one had thought to grab her clothes from the bathroom as they ran for their lives. Wendy had covered her with part of the blanket. Her steady breathing was now as loud as the sound of the distant wind, the only two sounds in the basement at the moment.

Carey placed his hand on his sister's forehead.

"How is she?" Wendy asked.

"I don't know. Still hot."

Wendy looked at Colt, who sat a few feet to her right, head tilted back, staring at the floor above them. He'd taken his gun out of its holster and placed it on his lap, as if he expected the killer to find them here and duke it out with them, or more likely because it was uncomfortable on his hip in this position.

"You have any brothers or sisters, Colt?"

"No."

"Neither do I. Must be nice, though."

For a moment no one spoke. The more time she spent in Colt's company, the more she found herself liking him. Maybe because he didn't demonstrate any bullheaded confidence despite his obvious strength. Under those muscles he was just another lost child, like most. Only Colt didn't know how to pretend differently, like most.

The silence became uncomfortable.

"Tell us about her, Carey."

He looked at her. "About Nicole?"

"We're not going anywhere soon."

Carey shifted on his seat, and for the first time that night, he seemed truly upbeat. Nicole was his sister, but his affection for her seemed nearly otherworldly. Even strange.

"You're sure?"

"Of course," Wendy said.

He took a deep breath. "She wasn't always who she is today, trust me. We didn't grow up in a . . . good home."

"Join the club," Wendy said.

"From the time Nicole was a year old, we all knew that she was going to be a model or something crazy like that when she grew up. My mother never could lose her extra pounds after she had Nicole, and she screamed at herself all the time for it. Then she stopped screaming at herself and started fussing over Nicole. It was kinda like if she couldn't be beautiful, she was going to be sure Nicole was, you know."

"Don't tell me; I know the rest of the story already," Wendy said.

"I doubt it," Carey said.

It took a moment for him to get going again.

"My mom put Nicole in a beauty pageant when she was six. She was pretty, even without all the makeup and fancy dresses. Nicole could have walked out on that stage at six in the morning, having just climbed out of bed, and walked away with a unanimous decision from the judges. She was that pretty. And we all knew it. Including her."

Carey stroked his sister's cheek. "I think I began hating her for it then, but I was too young myself—eleven or twelve—to realize how it was affecting me."

"Your sister was beautiful, and everyone agreed," Wendy said. "Was that so bad?"

"It wasn't the fact that my sister was beautiful. It was the way my mother treated her. Our whole household revolved around this six-year-old beauty queen. My mom took her to beauty classes every day. Makeup classes, etiquette classes, dancing classes, fashion classes. She had her first nose job when she was eight years old."

"Really?" Wendy leaned forward and looked at Nicole in the dim light.

"Nicole was too young to resist, so I shouldn't have blamed her; but I was too young to know that. She was on a strict diet when she was eight. She had perfect teeth, but that didn't stop my mom from giving her full dental surgery. She was rarely allowed out of the house, and then only with my mom."

"That's horrible. No one tried to stop your mother from doing all of this?"

"No one outside the family really knew. My father was pretty much spineless. Nicole accepted it all in complete silence. She never resisted, never argued. But she was a sad girl. Death warmed over. She had no real childhood."

Carey bit at a fingernail, eyes fixed on some unseen object ahead as he recalled their childhood.

"Nicole was fifteen before my dad finally started to come to his senses. He began to pull my mom away from her. He suggested trips and vacations, all of which my mom refused at first. Eventually they did take a few, but not without endless complaining and fussing from my mom."

"Fussing about what?" Colt asked.

Wendy looked at Colt, who'd crossed his legs and leaned over them, elbows on knees. He was more than casually interested.

"About what trouble Nicole might get into during those few days without her watchful eye. Anyway, that's when it changed. Like I was saying, my father was doing his best to get Mom away from Nicole; small things, not just vacations. Going out for dinner. He'd always wanted to own a Jeep, but every spare penny in our home went to Nicole's 'career.' Which is why he came home all excited when Jeff Bolton said he could borrow his Jeep that Saturday. He insisted that Mom go with him, just the two of them. Just for a few hours. She agreed."

Carey averted his eyes.

"No one knows exactly how the Jeep went over the cliff. The trail was narrow, but not that narrow. Maybe a flat tire forced them off. It fell forty yards straight down and landed on all four wheels, but the force crushed my mom's spine and killed her instantly. My father escaped with bruises and a broken hand."

"That's a long fall," Colt said.

"I'm so sorry."

"I wasn't," Carey said. "Not really. But the accident sent Nicole into a spiral. She changed completely. Stopped eating and had to be hospitalized. I gradually understood how desperate she really was. She didn't know how to live without the fat slob."

"She was your mother," Colt said. "You must have felt some regret."

Carey shrugged. "I guess. As time went by, I missed her a little. But I felt sorry for my dad. He blamed himself for her death. He ended up committing suicide a month to the day after the accident."

Carey's voice tightened, and he had to swallow.

Wendy thought a normal woman might reach out and comfort him with a simple touch. Instead, she repeated that tired old phrase, "I'm so sorry."

Tears suddenly flooded Carey's eyes. "Nicole and I kinda went nuts then. We were taken in by my aunt. I went off to music school and did my own thing. I was really bitter and . . . well, that's another story. Nicole . . . poor Nicole spent her days walking around in a daze and crying every night. She was like a shell of herself. Then she disappeared, and I didn't hear from her for over a year."

"How old was she? Sixteen?"

"Yes. I fell into a depression. I blamed myself for not rescuing her earlier."

"Where did she go?" Colt asked.

Carey looked at him, then at Wendy. "I don't know."

"What do you mean you don't know? She wouldn't tell you?"

His brow wrinkled, but he didn't answer her question. "She found me at my music school. When she walked into the lecture hall, everyone else saw a beautiful stranger in bare feet. But I saw an angel, and she was my sister."

He swallowed again at the memory.

"She was different. So totally changed—not in how she looked, but inside. I asked her where she'd gone, and she'd only say she'd gone to serve the disadvantaged. That's all I know. If she wants to tell me more, she will. Honestly? I don't care where she went."

Now more than before, Wendy thought she would give anything to have someone care for her so much.

"Hmm."

"Hmm, what?" he asked her.

"It's a beautiful story."

He looked at his sister, who seemed to be breathing more easily now. "Remember you said that when she wakes up," Carey said.

"Why wouldn't I?"

"She's . . ." Carey searched for the appropriate word. "Very unique," he said. "Like a child. The purest child I've ever known. Something in her broke."

Colt sat on his haunches, looking away from them. If she wasn't mistaken, he was feeling emotional and embarrassed. He stood and walked across the room. Studied the water heater.

What story are you hiding, Colt? she wanted to ask.

"We'll get through this," she told Carey. "Nicole will be okay. You'll see."

A premonition suggested that was wrong. Something about Nicole's story bothered her. Something, or was it nothing?

*T*hey spent the next hour reviewing exactly what had happened to each of them that night.

Carey explained his encounter with the pickup truck that side-swiped them and forced them off the road. Wendy detailed her own collision with the same truck, her discovery of the van, and their trip to Summerville. Colt told them about encountering the killer who called himself Red and then getting a call from dispatch about a third killing to which he was responding when Wendy waved him down.

"This killer has to deal with this storm too," Wendy said. "Maybe we should be thankful for it."

"With any luck, he took a direct hit," Colt said.

"God's vengeance."

"By morning, this town will be crawling with news and rescue. The real question is, how many were hurt or killed by the storm?"

It was the capstone on a conversation that left little more to be said.

Carey was the first to suggest they get some sleep; then he lay down next to his sister. With nothing more to do than stare at the floor joists, they made themselves as comfortable as possible.

Twenty minutes passed with no more than their own breathing to keep them company. Even the wind had died down outside.

Yet lying there in the darkness, Wendy couldn't shake the fear that their optimism regarding the killer was misplaced. He'd ridden in on the storm; why would it chase him out?

Colt lay several feet to her right, breathing steadily. She wondered what kind of woman might slide over to him for comfort. And whether he would offer any. A gentle word. A hand on hers.

The warmth of his body. The patience a man would need in order to deal with her brokenness.

I'm not what I appear, Colt. I'm a survivor, true, but inside I'm still lying in a ditch, afraid someone will touch me.

"Colt?"

"Yes?"

He was still awake. She immediately regretted speaking his name.

"Do you think we'll be okay?"

He hesitated. "Yes."

Wendy felt so alone, so frail, so worthless in that moment that she couldn't help speaking her mind.

"I'm afraid."

He was silent for a full minute before responding this time. "So am I," he said.

11

Wendy woke suddenly to a ringing silence, as if something had jarred her out of an exhausted sleep, but now, with her fully awake, left nothing but the sounds of breathing.

She rolled onto her back and stared up at the floor joists. The events of last night filled her mind as if a large bucket had dumped them in. They were trapped in a basement.

She turned to see Colt, still sleeping on her right. Was it morning yet? Still no light other than the amber night-lights. She could hear Carey breathing on her left.

She sat up and blinked, questions crowding her mind.

"Hello."

She whirled to the sound of a woman's voice. Nicole stood on Wendy's left, smiling. She was dressed in a man's white dress shirt that hung below her waist.

"Nicole?"

Carey jerked up. "Nicole!" He scrambled to his feet. "You're okay! You're—"

"Where did you get the clothes?" Colt asked, pushing himself up.

"What happened?" Her face was no longer flushed, her hair dried and composed. What Wendy had seen as natural beauty last night had now come fully to life.

"You should sit down," Carey said. "You sure you're okay?"

"Uh, don't I look okay?" Nicole looked around the room. "This wasn't the most comfortable place to sleep, but I'm sure you can explain that." She smiled at them and approached Wendy. "Do I know you?"

A dark light crossed Nicole's eyes, like a ship passing through black space. *There's something wrong with her,* Wendy thought.

Nicole's gaze settled on Wendy, assessing her with such frankness that she felt her heart skip a beat.

"I guess I don't," Nicole said at last.

"Where did you find the shirt?" Colt asked again.

The woman's eyes shifted to Colt. Her expression held a certain innocence, but she also oozed seduction as if it were perfume. Transparency with nothing to hide. *There doesn't seem to be a pretentious bone in this young woman's body,* Wendy thought. *Something's gotta be wrong with her.*

"I found it in a closet in one of the rooms," Nicole said, indicating the shirt. She stepped closer to Colt. "Who are you?"

"I'm Colt Jackson." He hesitated. "Your fever's gone."

She put her hand on his shoulder, brushed off some dust. "Then I owe you my thanks, too, Mr. Jackson."

You're blushing now, but she'll bite you later. Wendy looked at Carey, who winked as if to say, "What did I tell you?"

Nicole stepped back, smiling at them, looking from one to the other. Slowly the smile took on shades of concern.

"Is . . . is everything okay?" she asked. "You all look like you've seen a ghost."

"We have," Carey said. "You can't remember anything from last night?"

"Only that I was bitten by a snake and someone helped us. Why? What happened?"

"We thought for sure you were going to die. We couldn't find a doctor because of the tornado, so we—"

"Tornado?" Nicole looked at him with alarm. "Was anyone hurt?"

"We don't know. But it sure was a crazy ride. That's why we're down here."

Colt looked at his watch. "It's eight o'clock in the morning. Anyone hear anything outside? No light through any cracks." He walked to the concrete wall and placed his ear against it.

Wendy joined him, followed by Carey and then, after some hesitation, Nicole.

"What are we listening for?" Nicole asked.

"Anything," Wendy said.

"I don't hear anything," Nicole said.

Carey took her hand and pulled her back from the wall. The amber lights cast an ethereal glow over both of them. "I was so worried. Do you remember anything else?"

"No." Nicole looked past Wendy to Colt, who subtly avoided eye contact.

Wendy wanted to tell Nicole to leave Colt alone. Her gaze was like a touch, and Colt clearly felt as uncomfortable with such contact as Wendy did. Clearly, though, Nicole was simply expressing her emotions in the only way she knew, albeit in a way utterly foreign to Wendy. Truth be told, she was feeling a twinge of jealousy.

"Where are my clothes?" Nicole asked.

"In the bathroom upstairs," Carey said. "Wet."

"Wet? But I can't walk around in this." She turned and headed for the stairs. "I have to get my clothes in the dryer."

"Dryer? You . . . No, you don't understand. We're trapped down here."

"Why do you say that?"

"The tornado . . ."

"But I found this shirt in the master bedroom." She pointed up.

"That's impossible," Colt said.

For a moment they all looked at each other, dumbstruck by the implications of Nicole's statement.

Colt bounded past her, took the stairs two at a time, grabbed the door at the top, and shoved hard.

It flew wide and banged on the adjacent wall. Light filled the basement.

Colt stood framed by a soft hue, silhouetted like a gunslinger.

Wendy and Carey broke for the stairs at once, passing a stunned Nicole, who followed. "Was the door locked before?" she asked.

She'd been up, and she'd been in the master bedroom. That meant there still was a master bedroom. Wendy reached the top of the stairs at the same moment Colt stepped into the house beyond the door.

And it was just that. A house. Intact. Not a mound of rubble. Just a house standing in silence on a Friday morning. It was Friday, wasn't it?

"I don't understand," Carey said, looking around. A large painting of Napoleon with one of his mastiffs rested on the floor against the hall wall, but otherwise, there was hardly a sign that the house had taken such a shaking the night before.

"So you've been up here?" Colt asked Nicole.

"Yeah, I was wondering what had happened to my clothes and

was looking when I thought I heard someone . . . laughing or chuckling. I found the shirt and came back downstairs."

She paused. "Are you saying that you all thought the house was actually destroyed by the tornado?"

"Uh-huh," Carey said. "Place was a war zone last—"

"But we never *saw* anything fall," Wendy said.

"No, we didn't," Colt agreed. "It sounded like a freight train hit it, but we only assumed it was destroyed." He walked down the hall toward the foyer like a man on a mission. *Back in his comfort zone,* Wendy thought.

"Why couldn't we open the door?" Wendy asked.

"Maybe the painting was blocking it," Nicole said.

Colt turned back. "Painting?"

"It was here on the floor." She pointed to a painting of a dog at the end of the hall. "I moved it up against the wall. But it's wide enough to wedge the door shut."

"But the door wasn't wedged shut this morning," Carey said.

"Wind could have blown it free," Colt said. "After we last tried."

"What wind?" Wendy asked. "Was there any wind in the house? I don't remember any."

A small puff of wind blew past them from Colt's direction, as if it had come from the foyer around the corner. They moved as one toward the source, except Nicole, who clearly didn't share the same concerns as they. She really had no reason to.

To think they'd spent the night in the basement because a painting had become wedged between the steel door and the opposite wall. Amazing. But Wendy knew how much pressure one stick of wood placed lengthwise could withstand. She'd kept the members of the Brotherhood out of a room the day she'd escaped by wedging a one-by-four between the door handle and the wall. They'd banged and shoved and issued a hundred threats while she slowly worked up the courage to slip out the tiny bathroom window.

Another small gust struck her in the face as she rounded the corner. Dust roiled past her. She saw that the large white entry door stood ajar. That explained the wind.

"What a mess," Carey said.

The wind also explained the pile of sand that had blown against one wall during the night. Quite a lot of sand. Light sparkled in reds and blues through the thick prism glass panels on each side of the door. Colt had his hand on the door but had stopped short of pulling it open.

She pulled up behind him, aware of his scent. She felt a brief but strong compulsion to put her hand on his back as any other ordinary woman might do, but instead peered over his shoulder from a safe distance.

She realized then that he had frozen. "What's wrong? Colt?"

He pulled the door through the small ridge of sand that had kept it from blowing open on its own. Wendy squinted at the sunlight. Then stepped up to the door.

At first she wasn't quite sure what she was looking at. She'd never seen Summerville by day. It was a desert town—she knew that much—but she would have expected more than just sand and rock. Shrubs and trees—hadn't she seen both last night in this very—

Wendy instinctively took one step back. Something about the desert landscape in front of her was wrong. Very wrong.

"How far are we from town?" Carey asked behind her. "I thought we were in the town."

"We are," Colt said.

"Where's the town?" Wendy asked.

Colt looked at them, face white. "The town's gone."

12

hat do you mean it's gone?" Wendy said. "That's impossible."
She walked to the porch railing and stared out at the desert.
That's all it was: desert sand and rock that met up with some mesas
on the horizon.

"I mean gone," Colt said.

Except for a square white building nearby to the left, on the same
small hill. The library, if Wendy was right. Not a single other building that she could see. The only indications that there had once
been a town here were some bent steel poles that stuck up from the
ground.

They lined the porch and gawked at the desert in stunned disbelief.
The horizon was red—a sunset or a sunrise, but the sun was high in
the sky.

"There was a town here?" Nicole asked.

"It's buried," Colt said. "This house and the library are a bit
above the rest of the town on this hill. The storm must have—"

"That's crazy," Carey said. "It's not like a tornado can bury an entire town in sand, for crying out loud. The town can't just disappear like that. And it was raining, so wouldn't that keep the dust down?"

"It's gone," Colt said simply. "Do *you* see it?"

No response.

"I'm not saying that I can explain it, but unless the town was blown away by the winds, which is completely absurd, it was buried."

"Wind can do that?" Wendy asked. She was having a hard time imagining a huge dust storm sweeping in with enough force to bury a town.

"Widest tornado on record was in Wilber, Nebraska, a tornado that left a two-and-a-half-mile-wide path of destruction—heard about it on the Weather Channel. This town is only three miles wide. I . . ." He was still stunned. "F5 winds over three hundred miles per hour could, I suppose."

"They can just take everything?"

"Those light poles didn't have lights on them yet. Nothing for the wind to catch," Colt said, jumping down the steps. He ran out to the yard, dropped to one knee, and dug into the sand. A couple inches down at most, and he pulled something out. Grass.

The trees that Wendy had seen the night before were gone except for one on the west side, stripped of leaves and thin on branches, but still rooted in the ground. The house had protected it.

"This isn't possible," Carey said.

"How big was this town?" Nicole asked.

"About seven hundred homes," Colt said, walking down the gentle slope. They followed him through the sand, silenced by the scale of the destruction. It was like stepping into the twilight zone.

"Why's the library still standing?" Wendy asked.

"It's built like a tank. Doc and his engineering. But still . . ."

Colt turned in a circle as he walked. Of them all, only he knew what was missing. He'd lived among homes and businesses and parks that were now simply not here. Wendy craned for a view of anything that might indicate the gas station they'd stopped at last night.

The only sign that there had once been something on the spot was scattered debris, a streetlight lying on one side, the wheel from a tractor, a half-buried washing machine. But even then, not much debris.

"Here," Colt said, stopping and gazing back at what were now the only two clear landmarks: the house and, roughly seventy yards directly east of the house, the library. "Right here there was a brick outbuilding on the doctor's property."

"Brick?" Carey asked.

"Like I said, the doctor was anal about engineering. You'd think he knew something was coming."

Colt began digging in the sand, and Wendy knew his intent. She joined him, scooping up the sand, looking for any sign of anything.

"Why's it so dry?"

"Blowing sand isn't wet. For all we know, it came in from where there was no rain. For that matter, this desert can soak up a lot of water in a hurry and not show it. Anything?"

"No." She scooped up more, like a dog digging for a bone.

"Shouldn't we be talking about how to get out of here?" Carey asked.

"Go ahead, talk," Colt said. "I just want to try to understand what happened here."

"So you're gonna excavate the whole town now?"

Nicole had remained silent, stunned, during all this.

"Dig, Carey," Wendy said.

"I don't see the point—"

"The point is it would be helpful to know if everything is buried by sand, or if everything got blown away. The cars, for example."

"You're going to try to dig up a car?" Nicole spoke for the first time since they'd come outside. "Wouldn't it be better to find a radio or something?"

"It would be," Colt said, eyeing her. "That's a good idea. Except they were fried last night. But—"

"I've got something!" Wendy had bumped into something immovable. She dug around it. Exposed red brick covered with jagged gray mortar. She stood up.

"Gone," Colt said, kneeling over the eighteen-inch-deep hole she'd dug. "But how much of it is gone?"

He dug farther as the other three watched. It didn't take long to reach the bottom, because the concrete floor was only two feet farther down.

Colt stood up, brushed his hands on his jeans. "That's it."

"So right here the base of the town is buried under three feet of sand," Wendy said. "Maybe deeper at lower elevations."

Colt scanned the horizon. He still had his gun and a knife on his belt, but nothing else that would identify him as a cop. His T-shirt covered half of a red rose tattooed on his left arm. She hadn't seen that before.

"A series of tornadoes blasts into town—I mean massive tornadoes—they combine into one massive F5 screamer over three miles wide and rip everything from the ground. Houses, cars, everything. Who knows where it all got dropped. Only thing left behind is sand from the desert and a few steel poles that didn't give the wind anything to grab on to."

"Plus the library and one house."

Colt looked back at the two white structures. "Only because the doctor built the library for something besides holding books. He actually intended it to double as a bomb shelter. Which is why you don't see many windows. That glass is inches thick."

"You think the doctor could be there now?" Wendy asked.

Colt clearly hadn't considered the possibility. "Maybe," he said. "But I kind of doubt it. I think he would have phoned it in to Becky. She didn't say anything when I told her I was headed to his house with you. Besides, his car's gone from the garage."

"So the reason the house made it was because the library pro-tected it from the wind?" Carey said.

"The house was built the same way. Maybe the library helped deflect some wind."

"That's one theory," Wendy said.

Colt walked in a slow circle, hands on hips. "Oh, wow . . . This is absolutely incredible."

"They're all dead, then?" Nicole asked.

Wendy had been so focused on understanding the hows of these seemingly impossible events that she hadn't yet considered the human toll.

"Gone," Colt said.

"That's . . . that's terrible," Nicole said.

Wendy couldn't say how genuine Nicole really was. She was judg-ing, she knew that, but something about this perfect lily who batted her eyes at Colt was driving needles through her skull.

"How many?" Nicole asked.

"Almost two thousand."

"That's awful! Is there's nothing we can do? Could there be survivors?"

"Very few of the houses here have basements. Most are built on slabs. We won't find any survivors. I wouldn't have a clue how to begin searching anyway."

Nicole was still dressed in the oversized shirt, and it flapped as she walked south, away from the house, toward a metal post sticking out of the sand.

"There has to be a way." Suddenly she jumped back, tripped over her own heel, and fell to her seat. "Ouch!"

Wendy hurried forward. "What?"

"I . . . I don't know. There's something here!" She stared at the air directly in front of her. "Felt like I hit a wall."

Carey rushed to his sister's side, followed by Colt in measured stride. "You okay?" Carey asked. "What happened?"

Nicole stood, brushed off her rear end. Wendy stepped past her, took three steps, and felt the leading edge of an electric current jolt through her leading leg.

"Electricity . . ."

"Get back!" Colt snapped.

They retreated ten yards and stared at the sand. "Must be a downed high-voltage line under the sand," Colt said.

"The current's passing through the sand? How's that possible?"

"I'm not an electrician, but it knocked you over, so it's possible. High-voltage lines crossed the south end of the doctor's property, right across town, then south."

"We're trapped?" Wendy asked.

"No. You can see where the line is." He pointed along the small depression in the sand that ran due west. "The current may have melted the sand below. Whatever we do, we stay this side of that line."

"They didn't break?"

"Thin and strong, the one thing that could withstand extreme winds," he said.

They stared in silence, overwhelmed by the vast change in their world.

"So what do we do?" Carey asked. "Why hasn't anyone come yet?"

Colt shaded his eyes from the sun and scanned the eastern horizon. "Good question."

"How widespread do you think this is?" Wendy asked.

They all looked at each other.

"Almost looks more like an atomic blast than a tornado," she said. "I'm not saying it is, but what if whatever happened here had a much larger impact than we realize?"

"Towns all over the desert flattened," Carey said.

"Could be," she said. "It would explain why there's no help yet."

"I can't see it," Colt said. "But a few other towns could have been hit. It takes some time to organize rescue operations. We have food and water in the house," Colt said. "I think the suggestion Nicole made earlier makes the most sense. We should try to find a way to communicate."

A barely audible hum ran through Wendy's ears. It lasted several seconds and then was gone.

"Did anyone else hear that?"

The hum came again, louder.

"What was that?" she asked.

Huummmmm . . .

This time the sound was very loud, and she didn't know whether it seemed to be emanating from the house because she was looking directly at the house or because the sound had actually come from that direction. Either way, a chill touched her spine.

"Okay, what was that?"

"What's that?" Carey asked, pointing up.

A thin streak of black stretched across the sky, as high or higher than jets fly. Not just one streak—at least a dozen, fainter—but there, above the one they could see clearly.

Huummmmm . . .

The sound came again, this time from the sky, it seemed. It reached past Wendy's flesh and swarmed her skull. For a brief moment the world went black.

She gasped, then immediately realized that it wasn't the world but her own vision that had turned black. Pinpricks of light swam on the horizon. She was losing her sight . . .

The darkness faded. Her pulse had nearly doubled.

"What?" Carey asked.

"I . . . Everything went black. Did you see that?"

He glanced at Colt. "No."

Like a panic attack, she thought. Her mind was telling her none of this was possible. She willed her heart to settle.

"Maybe we should leave this place," Nicole whispered.

"They're gone," Carey said.

The black streaks were gone. Or if they were there, they were now so faint that Wendy couldn't identify them.

"Contrails," Colt said.

"Black contrails?" Carey said. "You think they could be missiles?"

"We're not in a nuclear exchange with the Chinese, please," Wendy said. "Forget what I said earlier about a nuclear blast. This was done by a very strong and very freak storm. The noise could have been the wind, and those black streaks up there—I don't know about them, but we've got problems enough here."

It was an emotionally driven diatribe, but Wendy didn't have the nerves to remain calm and collected at the moment. She had the right to say what she wanted.

"I think you're right," Colt said. "The red horizon is from the dust." He walked past her toward the house.

The only reason everyone saw the library door fly open was

because they were all staring at Colt, who seemed to have made up his mind about what should be done next.

The door banged and a tall man dressed in a white shirt came flying out in a flat-out sprint, screaming bloody murder. He saw them and veered toward them, holding one hand as if it was hurt, knees pounding to his chin.

The man, who looked fit and fairly young, ran past before they could warn him, hit the invisible electric field that ran through the sand, jerked spasmodically, and flew back onto his butt, where he stared out at the desert, dumbfounded.

13

His name was Jerry. Jerry Pinkus. And Jerry Pinkus was missing part of his index finger.

He'd come screaming out of the library because he'd woken up with a severed finger, bleeding profusely on the carpet.

That already had him in shock. Discovering the missing town and suffering the high-voltage jolt had added to it.

He made little sense as they hurried him across the sand back to the doctor's house.

Pinkus wore stovepipe jeans, tight around his butt and thighs, emo-style. His shirt was white with tan stripes, tails flapping free. A black belt with silver bullet halves ran around his waist. He had on black boots. Definitely looked like a city type.

Even his close-cropped blond hair was styled aggressively— Wendy could smell the hair product from three feet behind. Strong cologne to boot.

"Is it safe in there?" was the first thing he said that made sense.

"Of course it's safe," Wendy said.

Colt was keeping pressure on Pinkus's finger. Carey was helping him with the injured man.

"Because there's someone in the library."

"I'll get the gauze from the medicine cabinet," Nicole said. They all looked at her. "I saw it in the master bedroom."

Carey and Colt guided the man into the kitchen. Wendy followed.

Jerry's face wrinkled with pain. "I'm telling you, man, he's in the library, and he's gonna kill us all if we don't get out of here."

"Who's in the library?" Colt asked.

"I don't know. But he cut my finger off. For crying out loud, the guy cut my finger off!"

"We went into the library last night. Why didn't you answer our calls?"

"Because I was out, man! Please, guys. I'm bleeding on the floor here."

"Let's get his finger wrapped first," Wendy said.

Nicole ran in with a brown bottle of disinfectant, a roll of gauze, and some kind of ointment—hopefully an antibiotic.

"Let me wrap it," she said. Wendy made no protest.

"Please, Jerry. I need you to focus for a moment," Colt said. "What do you mean 'out'? Did you see this person?"

"I mean out, like knocked out." He felt his head for a bump. "Knocked on the head from behind. I woke up with my finger gone. Can you believe it? He actually cut off my finger!"

"How do you know someone else did it?"

Jerry looked at Colt as if the cop must be an idiot. "You think I'd cut off my own finger? Why? He was in there, man. I heard him. He calls himself Red, and he says nobody's going to escape this time."

"I thought you said he knocked you out from behind?"

"After he talked on the intercom and said nobody escapes this time."

"This time?" Wendy asked. "What's he mean, this time?"

"Heck if I know . . ." Pinkus looked at his hand being wrapped. "Can you believe he did that?"

"Jerry," Colt said. "I need your help. I know you're hurt, but if what you're saying is true—"

"Of course it's true."

"Someone who calls himself Red killed two policemen and an old woman in Summerville last night. If there's a killer named Red in the library—"

"There's no *if* about it," Pinkus said, his face ashen. "He's there, and he's after all of us. No one's gonna escape this time. That's what he said."

Colt turned to Carey. "Carey, get over by the door and keep an eye on the library."

"Serious?"

"Yes."

"What if this guy has a rifle?"

"Stay under cover, but I want eyes on the library. I'll be right there."

"What if—"

"Go!" Colt snapped.

Carey nodded and went.

"Tell me everything," Colt said.

"Wait." Nicole disappeared toward the bathroom and returned with her jeans, shoes, shirt, and a bottle of Advil. She started to pull on the clothes. "Sorry."

Jerry swallowed the pain pills and spoke quickly, explaining how he'd agreed to meet a guy named John Potter between Vegas and Carson City, in Summerville. Like Pinkus, Potter was a gamer. A professional computer gamer, and one of the best in the world. By the sound of it, guys like Jerry and his friend pretty much ate, slept, and breathed games. And in rare cases actually earned a decent living doing so.

Without bragging, Pinkus claimed to have an IQ well north of 150. He'd been weaned on computers, PlayStations, and the like. That's what made his injury so terrible, he said. The killer had severed his "mouse" finger.

Anyway, Potter was supposed to meet him at the library in Summerville, but the storm must have kept him away.

That was when a man who called himself Red spoke to him over the speakers. The guy somehow knew he was a gamer. Even knew his name. Then *smack!* The next thing he knew he was waking up without a mouse finger.

Jerry grew silent for the first time since flying out of the library.

"That's it?" Colt said.

"That's it? He cut off my flipping mouse finger," Pinkus said. "That's my stinkin' life!"

"I'm sorry. I just meant, that's all that happened, the end of the story?" Colt wasn't being mean; he was just pressing, like any good cop.

"What does he mean, no one escapes?" Nicole asked. "You really think he's after all of us?"

"What do you call this?" Pinkus shrugged at his bloody stump.

"But he let you live."

Colt paced and absently fiddled with his gun. "More like he's toying with us." For the first time he told them about the painted message. Payback time.

"Neither of you have a clue who he is?" Wendy asked. "Or why he might be after you?"

"No. I've been beating my head against this," Colt said. "I don't have the slightest idea."

"Me either," Pinkus said.

"We should barricade ourselves in until help gets here," Wendy said. "This killer survived the storm? He actually found the one place in this whole town that would stay standing and he survived with us?"

"So the rest of the town really did blow away?" Pinkus asked. "I hoped I was just tripping or something."

"He obviously knows this town," Colt said, returning to the subject of Red. "Someone who grew up here, maybe. Or nearby. Knows enough to know about the library and take shelter there. You said you came from Vegas," he said to the gamer. "You live there?"

"Henderson, on the south side."

"I used to live there too. He knows both our names."

"I think we should leave," Pinkus said.

"Leave to where?" Wendy asked. "There is no there."

"*He's* here!" Pinkus shouted. "Don't you people get it?"

Carey walked into the kitchen. "What's happening?"

"You call that covering the door?" Colt said.

"I have the door locked. What's happening?"

"We're trying to decide whether to let some killer named Red come and kill us in our sleep or make a break for it and let him pick us off like chickens," Pinkus said, standing up shakily. "I have to take a leak."

The gamer disappeared down the hall.

"You serious?" Carey said.

"Nothing up front?" Colt asked him.

"No. The library's just sitting there."

Colt pulled open a cupboard door and was showered with some plates that crashed on the floor. He shut the door. "Anyone have a pen?"

"Pen? What for?" Carey asked.

"So that if we do decide to leave, you'll know where to go."

Why Colt was looking for a pen in the cupboard was beyond Wendy—he was a bit of a shut-in in some ways. And very intelligent in others.

She retrieved a pencil from the desk and tossed it to him.

"Paper?"

"That would be in the same place as the pencil," she said.

He nodded, crossed to the kitchen desk, and came back with a napkin, which he slapped on the counter.

"I'm not sure we should try to get to safety, but in case anything happens, you should all know the lay of the land around here." He put his gun next to the napkin. "We're here." He marked the napkin as he spoke. "Two closest ranches are here and here. One about five miles east, one roughly the same west. This one is in a small valley, and this one in a smaller depression, mostly just flat ground. It's possible that one or both escaped the full force of the wind. If we run into trouble, you head for one of the ranches. The east ranch or the west ranch, you got that? Stratford Ranch and the Bridges Ranch."

"Go alone?"

"Go however you have to. If you get lost, go north and you eventually hit the highway."

"And then what?"

"Then I don't know. Either way you go, it's a few days walk to the nearest town. Hopefully, you get picked up."

They stood there quietly, coming to terms with such a trek. "In the meantime?" Wendy asked.

Colt picked up his gun and absently thumbed the hammer. "In the meantime, we have a choice to make."

"Guys?" Jerry Pinkus stood in the hall, face white with shock.

"What is it?" Nicole asked.

Pinkus looked to his right. "Did you say you locked the front door?"

"Yes," Carey said.

"It's not locked now. It's open."

Despite his height, Pinkus suddenly looked very small.

"He's in the house."

14

veryone froze.

Colt stopped thumbing the hammer of his gun.

Carey stopped talking.

Wendy stopped breathing.

The only person who didn't stop was Pinkus, who'd already shocked them but seemed to have more to say. "He's—"

Colt silenced him with a flat hand. They listened.

A voice came low and breathy, but from where, Wendy couldn't tell.

"Payback time . . ."

She fought a sudden impulse to run, realizing she didn't even know where the back door was!

"Colt?" she whispered so softly she could barely hear herself.

His eyes engaged hers, wide pools of blue, and he mouthed something that she missed because she was so focused on his eyes. Then he mouthed the same thing to the others, and she caught it.

"Follow me. Quiet." Again: "Follow me."

He glided more than walked or tiptoed across the kitchen floor. Through a small breakfast nook. Through a side door that led to the empty garage.

He gently shepherded the rest of them past him and eased the door shut. Standing momentarily silent in the dark garage, they heard a thump from somewhere deep in the house.

"This way." Colt led them out a back door, then shut it behind them.

"Okay, we have to move." He spoke in a quick, hushed tone. "Every second counts. He'll realize we've left, and if he catches us out here in the open, we're toast."

He handed the napkin to Wendy. "Carey, Wendy, Jerry . . . I need you to run west, toward the Bridges Ranch I drew on this napkin. Just head west toward the bluff." He pointed to a bluff on the horizon. "You see the dip in it?"

"Yes," Wendy said.

"Stay north of where the power line was. Once you take off, you'll be in the open, so move as fast as you can. The power lines head south at the west end of town; you can cut to the southwest then. The ranch is about five miles out."

"What about you?" Wendy asked.

"I'm going east with Nicole. It's harder to find—"

"We're splitting up?" Carey said.

"Yes. To double your chance of getting away."

"Why can't I go with Nicole?"

"We need a balance. Strongest with weakest. And you three together."

"Why—"

"Please. If anything happens, head north to the highway."

"Wait—"

Nicole stepped up to her brother, kissed him on the forehead, and touched his cheek. "It's okay. Go."

Wendy almost spoke her mistrust of Nicole then, but she had nothing besides her intuition to offer as a reason. Still the thought of Colt going out alone with Nicole made her jittery. Even angry.

You're jealous, Wendy.

No, that was ridiculous. She hardly knew Colt.

"Let's go," Wendy told Carey. "We don't have time for this."

The fact that Colt didn't see her as the weakest in the group wasn't lost on her, but she wasn't sure she believed it. Just because she'd survived the Brotherhood didn't mean she had the first clue how to survive being hunted by a killer in this forsaken desert.

They reached the corner of the house, and Wendy looked back. Colt had waited, and he now gave her an all-okay sign. She made a circle with her thumb and forefinger.

Nicole took Colt's hand with both of hers—an image that made Wendy envious and ashamed. Then they disappeared around the corner, headed toward the library.

"Let's go." She started off.

"I can't," Pinkus said.

"What? I thought . . ."

"I've lost a lot of blood. I can't run. I can barely move. Especially out there in this heat. Look," he said, engaging each of them eye to eye. "It's as safe back here as out there once he goes after you."

"He's right," Carey said. "Someone should stay in case help comes anyway."

Wendy made the quick decision that she couldn't out-argue Pinkus over this. And she certainly wouldn't drag an unwilling party through the Nevada desert.

"Okay," she said. "Good luck." She faced the west. "Ready, Carey?"

"Not really," Carey said.

Without a backward glance, they sprinted onto the flat desert, giving the power line a wide berth.

Colt found the sand surprisingly well compacted, littered with hundreds of stones, not smooth as he would have expected. The air was hot and smelled of burning rubber, from where he had no clue.

He tried not to think of the woman who was holding on to him. Trusting him.

Or of the madman behind him who'd killed his mother.

Or of his own childhood, which had hammered him into an insecure mess. The fact returned that without a shred of doubt the most beautiful and sensuous and kind woman he'd ever met was now holding tightly on to his hand.

It had been many years since he'd held a woman's hand. Her hands, though, had clutched him instinctively, without hesitation. She needed him.

He hoped her faith in him was well-founded. It should be. The one skill Colt had mastered was being a cop. As long as he focused on the job at hand, he was fine. At the moment, Red was his job. Stop Red. Save Nicole. Nicole was his job.

He grunted.

"What?" she whispered.

"Run," he said.

They ran out into the desert, keeping the library between them and the house. He fought a quick mental battle over whether to release her hand. Judging by her grip, she seemed uninterested in doing so. But he knew they could run faster with free hands, so he finally opened his. She let go and kept pace.

Focus, Colt.

Yes, focus, Colt. How could any sane man be thinking about a girl in the middle of a harrowing situation like this? Colt Jackson. So was Colt Jackson a twisted, scarred mess who'd managed to survive more than his fair share of challenges up to this point? Yes.

A stinkin' freak, as someone like Pinkus might say. *Two* stinkin' freaks from Las Vegas.

Focus!

They ran roughly two hundred yards before Colt slowed to a fast jog. He wouldn't be satisfied until they had a good thousand yards on the library, but they'd never get there in a full sprint.

"You okay?" He breathed hard.

"Yes."

He glanced back. Saw two small forms racing in the opposite direction. Two? One had stayed behind, then.

Nicole followed his look and pulled up, panting. "There's only two. They're out in the open."

"And so are we. Wendy probably left Pinkus because of his hand. Don't worry; he may be the safe one now. We can't stop—come on."

"Do you think they'll be okay?" Nicole panted. "They seem so exposed."

"With any luck, Red's still in the house."

"What's to keep him from taking off after them?"

Or us. She didn't say that. Her mind was on them, he guessed. They were now the outcasts, the ones with a disadvantage because they didn't have the library to block their escape. Or the cop and his gun with them.

"He entered the house and left the door open," Colt said to Nicole. "Meaning he wanted us to know he was there. As soon as we went silent, he knew he'd engaged us. But he also knows that I have a gun,

so he can't just march around playing hide-and-seek. He had something else in mind."

He stopped to let them catch their breath. "But we ran, and we
ran quickly. He has to move slowly because he can't know we ran.
Which is why we ran."

She was silent for a moment. "Your mind really works like that?"

He looked at her and saw that her eyes were round and sincere.

"You thought all of that in the few seconds before we ran?"

He wasn't used to this kind of talk from a woman. "Pretty much."
He got them moving again.

"I've watched you," Nicole said. "You're a strong man, but I didn't
realize how smart you are. I think they'll be fine."

"Red's strong too. More important, he's faster than me. And he's
probably smarter than me."

That gave her pause. "We'll see."

They ran past the thousand-yard mark in his mind, and he slowed
them to a fast walk. They were both panting hard. Sweaty. She walked
very close to him. Unnaturally close, considering all the empty desert
around them.

But that was the Nicole he was quickly coming to know.

"Has anyone besides Jerry Pinkus been confronted by Red?" she
asked out of the blue.

"I have. Why?"

But he didn't need her to explain why. She was asking about Pinkus,
not Red.

"You're wondering if Pinkus could be Red."

"Just a crazy thought," she said.

"He cut his own finger off?"

"I can't imagine that," she said. "But it was Pinkus who found the
door open, and it looks like Pinkus stayed behind. We heard the killer's

voice, but Pinkus wasn't next to us, was he? I don't know, it just seems . . ." She didn't finish.

"I don't think so." But he couldn't explain the conclusion to himself, much less to Nicole. He'd seen Red in the dark from a distance. Could be the same person. Roughly the same height as Pinkus, though heavier. The entire library story could be a fabrication. "Either way, he's behind us, right?"

She nodded. "Right." But somehow he thought she took more comfort in him than in his answer.

15

Wendy and Carey slowed to a walk when they couldn't run any farther, which had to be after about half a mile.

"Makes me wish I'd majored in track instead of music," Carey said. "You think he saw us?"

"If he did, he's not shooting at us. But he'll come after us. He'll find the tracks headed east and west and come after one of us."

Wendy glanced back. Still nothing. They'd caught a glimpse of Colt and Nicole once, but for the most part, the library blocked the couple. Then they were gone, too small to see.

"I don't see anything. I think we made it," she said.

Carey looked around them, then above. "I can't believe there aren't any helicopters searching for survivors. How could this have happened to us?"

"Your sister was bitten by a snake, remember? That's how it all started."

"So if she hadn't been bitten, we'd still be in the hills, safe from this crap."

"And I wouldn't have stopped to pick you up. I'd be well on my way."

"Blame it on the snake."

"Blame it on the snake," she agreed.

"But a wacko nutjob psychopath named Red? Both in the same night? You don't find that just a bit crazy?"

"Start jogging; we have to get to that ranch," she said.

He did.

"You know what they say about freak storms," she said.

"No, what?"

"They bring out the freaks."

"Really?"

"No, but a full moon does. Supposedly. Either way, it's not our fault."

He considered her comment. "It's the snake's fault. Without the snakebite, we wouldn't have gone to the doctor's house and survived the storm only to have a wacko nutjob psychopath after us."

"Blame it on the snake."

"Right." He chuckled. "And wasn't the snake ultimately defeated?"

She looked at him. "You mean in a spiritual sense? I don't know; I'm not really a spiritual person."

"How's that?"

She hesitated. "I grew up in a cult. Bad experience."

"Oh. I'm sorry."

"Don't be. I'm over it."

"Really?"

"Yes, really."

"'Cause I don't think we ever really get over our childhood. It's always there, waiting."

"Like a snake," she said.

"Like a snake." He paused. "I was into the occult once. Pretty heavily. After Nicole disappeared."

It seemed as if Carey had confused *a cult* with *occult*, but Wendy didn't care to correct him.

They knew they were close when they reached the canyon Colt had mentioned, which was now hardly more than a depression.

"What if it's buried?" Carey said.

For all of her positive patter, she was feeling no more hopeful than he was.

They jogged on for another ten minutes.

"He said five miles, right?" Wendy panted, completely out of breath. "How long to jog that?"

"Don't know. An hour?"

The blackness hit her again, nearly dropping her to her knees. Stars danced through her eyes.

The air thickened. Her head swam.

And then it passed as it had before.

"You okay?"

Only then did Wendy realize that Carey had placed his hand on her shoulder.

For a moment she didn't know what to do. She never quite knew what to do.

He let his hand run closer to her neck and squeezed her muscles gently. "You okay?"

She slapped his arm away with enough force to send a clear message.

"Come on." Wendy started jogging again.

"Hey," he said. "What was that about?"

She pretended not to hear him, too humiliated to answer, staying ahead of him on the sand.

Finally, she slowed, then stopped. "We've been going longer than an hour. What if we missed it?"

Carey looked around, then up at the sun. "West, right?" He pointed west.

"But we could easily miss a few buildings in these hills."

"I think the point was the bluffs may have protected the ranch," he said. "In a canyon or valley, right?"

Movement on Wendy's right caught her attention. Something on the hill had just vanished over the other side. "Did you see that?"

"See what?"

"I could have sworn I just saw a horse on that sand dune."

"Anyone on it?"

She started up the incline, trying to decide what she really had seen. "I don't know. Maybe a kid. I just caught a glimpse from the corner of my eye. Come on!"

She ran the last twenty yards and pulled up sharply at the crest.

Wendy didn't know which was more surprising: the absence of any horse, or the sight of a ranch house on the valley floor, about three hundred yards ahead.

A wooden outbuilding stood on a small incline halfway down to the house. Otherwise, only the ranch house and a large barn set fifty yards off of it.

"See anyone?"

She studied the lone ranch house. A fence ran around a corral, but no animals. And no cars. If the ranch had escaped the full brunt of the storm, where were the signs of life?

Carey must have noted the same. "It's abandoned."

"Looks that way. Doesn't make sense. The horse must have taken off, scared."

"Come on."

They ran on and were halfway down when Carey veered toward the outbuilding.

"Carey?"

"Just one look."

They circled the small barn and found the front door. "It's probably nothing but a utility shed," she said.

"The kind of place ranchers park four-wheelers and old tractors. Worth a look." He put his hand on the handle and pulled.

"It's been opened," Wendy said, stepping back. "There's marks in the sand where the door opened."

He already had the door halfway open, but he paused, looked at the brush marks under his feet, then glanced up at her. Okay, so someone had been here since the storm. Her pulse began to race.

Carey faced the barn. Eased the door wide. They stared into a dark interior.

He was right. An old green tractor stood encased in the shadows, one of those kinds with an enclosed cab. Wendy wasn't even sure what they used tractors for in these parts, but with the heat of summer, air-conditioning would be a must. Nothing else except old tools against each wall.

"Let's go."

"No, wait." Carey grabbed her shoulder and stared at the cab with wide eyes. "Is someone in there?"

She squinted in the dim light, suddenly petrified by the idea. People don't hang out in tractor cabs at ten in the morning.

Carey walked up and yanked the door open. He took one look

inside and jumped back with a cry loud enough to flood Wendy's veins with more adrenaline than they could handle.

She screamed and recoiled.

Carey had crashed into the wall behind him but was oblivious to it. He stared ahead into the cab.

"What?"

"It's a man," he said.

"What do you mean a man?" Her pulse pounded in her ears.

"I think he's dead."

Wendy forced herself forward and peered into the cab. A man knelt on the seat, arms tied behind, bent at the waist as if bowing, but his head was pulled back obscenely with some clamps fixed to his hair. His Adam's apple stuck out like a large knot.

His eyes were open.

She lifted a hand to her chest and for a moment thought she might throw up. A piece of white cardboard on which the killer had scrawled a few words hung from the dead man's neck.

Her head began to swim. She had no idea how any sane person could do such a thing. Any person, for that matter. She'd never seen anything remotely as disturbing. Staring at the contorted body in the tractor seat, everything she'd learned about life seemed at once pointless.

"You think that's Bridges?" Carey asked. "When do you think he did this?"

The killer had anticipated their coming here. He probably killed the rancher after the storm last night, Wendy thought. But the words didn't come.

Carey stepped forward. "What's it say?"

But Wendy didn't care what the note said. She spun and ran out into the sun, gulping at the fresh air.

SKIN

Something in the barn fell with a clang, and Carey swore. He hurried out, holding the note. Scrawled letters glared red in the sunlight.

Payback time baby
Remember me?
Get your skins back to the library or the others die.
P.S. Have you figured out how many of you are on my side yet?

"He's gonna kill them," Carey breathed.

"Payback? Does he mean us?"

A voice cried on the wind, indiscernible, but clearly from below them.

Carey ran to the corner and peered around, then quickly motioned for Wendy to join him. She looked down at the ranch house.

Someone dressed in a yellow shirt stood between the house and the barn, arms spread, yelling something. The man saw them and frantically waved for them to come.

He turned and ran into the ranch house.

"He's alive!" Wendy said.

"Clearly."

"He needs our help."

She took off in a fast run.

"Wait, what if it's *him*?"

"That look like a killer to you?"

"They never do."

"That's a survivor, and for all we know, he has a way to get out."

With a grunt, Carey followed. Together they flew down the hill toward the ranch house.

16

That's it," Colt said, staring at the ranch house, now just a dot on the horizon. "At least the house made it."

He scanned the desert. Here, a couple miles from town, the terrain had changed less, for obvious reasons. There was no town to wipe out. Still, he half expected to see more reshaping of the landscape. New gullies, flattened rises.

Instead, even the ranch house had escaped the tornadoes. They must have touched down within a mile of town before destroying everything in their path.

"So that's good, right?" Nicole asked.

"It means there are probably other survivors. The Smith place is a mile south of here. We may want to head down there if we can find some transportation."

She touched his elbow. "It's safe, right?"

"We'll find out."

He pulled his gun from its holster as they walked and spun the weapon in his hand once before letting the cool steel butt smack into his palm.

"Nice." Nicole grinned.

He immediately regretted the display. In fact, he had no clue what had possessed him to do something so uncharacteristic. Not any need to impress Nicole. In fact, he'd rather have been strung up naked from a tree than do something as juvenile as spinning his gun to impress a woman.

And yet he knew he'd just done precisely that.

"Let's go," he said, feeling his face flush bright red.

He started forward again and had taken about ten steps when he felt her hand on his elbow. He found he could live with the distraction. In fact, he might have been disappointed if she hadn't touched him.

It took them another ten minutes at a steady pace to reach the ranch house. No cars, no animals, no sign of Gene Stratford, who rarely left home. Odd.

"Gene!" He called out several times, with no response.

"Wait out here," he said. He handed Nicole his knife.

"What's this for?"

"It's a weapon. You should always be armed."

She looked at it. "Even if I knew how to use it, I don't think I could."

"Then pretend. It'll slow them down until they realize you don't know how to use it."

"Slow who down?"

"Please, just hold it." She shrugged and squatted down, knife in hand.

Colt mounted the porch and put his hand on the door, gun easy by his right ear. Door was unlocked. He glanced back, saw Nicole staring at him from her crouch twenty yards from the house, where he'd left her, and shoved the door wide, gun extended.

No lights, no power, shades drawn, teacup on the table, remote control on the floor, bathroom door cracked. But his subconscious picked up these details.

His higher-level consciousness was drawn to Gene Stratford, who sat in his recliner with a small lamp sticking out of his mouth.

His right hand was missing, severed at the wrist, and a piece of cardboard was tacked to his chest.

Payback time baby
Remember me?
Get your skins back to the library or the others die.
P.S. Have you figured out how many of you are on my side yet?

Colt stepped backward and slammed the door shut. He spun around and faced Nicole.

She stood slowly. "What?"

Everything had just changed, that's what. Whoever Red was, he or she or they had planned this with meticulous precision. And he wasn't after Colt alone.

All of their hands were being forced.

Colt walked toward Nicole. "We have to go back."

"What are you talking about? The *killer's* back there."

"The killer killed this rancher and left a note saying he'll kill Carey and Wendy if we don't go back to the library."

Nicole lifted both hands to her mouth as realization crashed down on her. Her fingers began to tremble.

"They're in trouble," she said.

"Come on."

Wendy was so desperate to find another living person, so repelled by what she'd seen in the barn, so single-minded in her desire to be rescued, that she didn't consider the possibility that running straight into the house could be a mistake until it was too late.

She crashed through the front door and stared around at the dim interior, momentarily disoriented. That was when the thought came. But it left as quickly as it had come, because there was nothing wrong here.

Brown shag carpet. An amber-resin chandelier over a large dark oaken dining table. Log timbers ran the length of the room.

"Hello?"

Carey stood behind her, panting. "Where are they?"

"Hello?" Wendy called again, louder this time. "Anyone here?"

Still no answer.

"He just ran in," Carey said. "He has to be in here."

"Okay, check the phones. Look for a gun. The garage." Wendy was already on the move. She snatched the phone off the wall.

Dead.

"I'm checking down the hall."

Carey brushed past her and entered the kitchen.

She ran down the hall, checking doors. A bathroom. Master bedroom. "Hello?"

She thought she heard a grunt from somewhere in the house.

"Anyone there?"

The bathroom off the master bedroom was small, not a five-piece like most modern homes had. Yellow striped wallpaper covered the four walls. Strange, but she could swear she'd seen this very wallpaper in a bathroom before. The bathroom she'd locked herself in when she'd escaped the Brotherhood.

For a moment Wendy just stared at it, surprised by the feelings of nostalgia. And fear.

"Wendy!"

She broke her stare and ran back the way she'd come.

"Wendy? In here."

She knew by the sound of Carey's voice that it was bad. Knew that whatever hope they'd found in seeing another survivor was now dashed. Knew that she shouldn't go into the kitchen.

"What is it?"

"He's . . . he's in here."

Red?

She stepped back, suddenly trembling. How could . . .

"Wendy, get in here, right now!"

Wendy stepped forward and turned into the kitchen. The man in the yellow shirt whom they had seen a few minutes earlier lay on the kitchen table, throat cut. There was a line of blood flowing from the table to the floor, where it pooled.

He'd just been killed. Another cardboard note, this one pinned to his chest with the same knife that had presumably cut his throat.

This makes seven. Now we can start.
I'm waiting.

Wendy looked at Carey, aghast. "He was just *here?*"

She could see his mind spinning behind those round eyes. His hands were bloody, as if he'd tried to stop the bleeding or something.

"How's that possible?" she demanded. "We left him back at the town."

Carey grabbed a towel and wiped frantically at his hands. "He got here faster than we did. Or someone else did it."

Wendy walked back into the living room, sat hard on the black leather sofa, and squeezed her forehead.

Carey ran into the room, still wiping at his hands with that towel. "We have to go back!"

Yes, Wendy thought. But it was a little more complicated than that.

"We have to get back now!"

"Hold on, we—"

"He's going to kill Nicole." Carey headed for the door.

"Stop it!" The tone of her voice surprised even her. She stood. "Just calm down. We have to think this through."

"Like what? Like if he was just here, he might be out there right now?"

"For starters, yes. But if he wanted us dead out here, he could have killed us. He doesn't want us dead. He wants us back at the library."

"And if we don't, he's going to kill Nicole," Carey said.

"He wants us *all* back at the library. That's why he let Jerry live. He wants us alive in the library."

"He's saying he's killed seven?" Carey asked.

"Two cops, two here, at least one other in town . . . For all we know, Colt's run into something. That has to be what it means."

"But Nicole's—"

"With Colt. You think she'd be safer with you?"

No answer.

She reached over and pulled back the shade. No movement of any kind. "Just settle yourself." She was talking to herself perhaps more than to him, but she didn't bother confessing.

Carey paced. "We can't just wait here."

"No, he probably wouldn't react too well to that."

"He'd probably kill one of us just to force his way."

"He probably would."

"So we either have to go get help or go back."

"Going to get help would upset him even more, assuming we had a clue where to go to get help."

"South, Colt said. We can't go south. There's no one there, or they'd be here looking for survivors."

She nodded. "Which leaves us with going back."

"Exactly."

"Into the path of a psychopath."

Carey looked at the door, then at the floor, thinking. "We're already in it."

If she was right, Red had at least one accomplice—someone they knew. Was it possible that Carey was working with Red? She couldn't imagine it. Colt? Not a chance. Nicole? Please. Pinkus? Possible. For that matter, what if Pinkus *was* Red?

Unlikely. She hoped.

"Okay." Wendy took a deep breath. "Search the house for any weapon you can find. He didn't say no weapons. Look for a gun."

"We have to hurry."

"Then let's get started."

17

Wendy couldn't shake a terrible premonition that there was far more than met the eye here. All glass-half-full thoughts aside, she now had no illusions about their quick salvation from what had suddenly become a nightmare.

She and Carey walked into a soft wind for over an hour, silent except for heavy breathing. They hadn't found the rancher's weapons, maybe because the killer had removed them. No vehicles. Nothing that the doctor's house couldn't give them.

"There they are again," Carey said, pointing at several long black trails high in the afternoon sky. "That's got to be some kind of jet, right? Don't they see us?"

"I've never seen black contrails," Wendy said. "We'd be like specks to them."

Twice they saw a thin curtain of sand rising from the desert to the north. Wind, Carey said. Thank God for the wind, which blew softly in their faces.

She stopped at the top of a small rise and studied the shimmering desert ahead. The library and the doctor's house looked like two small adobe building blocks on a bed of sand.

She could just make out the small dip in the sand formed by a high-voltage line buried beneath. They would have to stay north of the line, north of the town itself.

Carey stared at the horizon with her. "There's gotta be a mistake. This can't be happening. How could the killer get from the ranch back to the town ahead of us? You think he did that?"

"Maybe the dust we saw was coming from a truck, not wind. You think of that?"

"That's what you thought? Why didn't you say something?"

"Just a thought," she said. *And he's not working alone,* she didn't say. The thought made her nervous. Crazy as it sounded, what if Carey was the killer? What if he'd snuck out of the basement last night, gone down to the ranch they'd just come from, and killed the man they'd found in the tractor? Unlikely, but not impossible. And what if he'd cut the yellow-shirted man's throat while Wendy was in the master bedroom? Again, unlikely, but not impossible.

"Come on."

The worst part of going back to the town was knowing that unless Colt had run into a similar note from Red, he was gone. The thought of doing any of this without him struck her as impossible. Terrifying.

They stopped about two hundred yards from the house and library. It was almost impossible to imagine the foundations of buildings buried in sand several feet beneath them at this very moment.

"Do you see anyone?" Carey asked. "Pinkus?"

"No." Dust devils danced. "Keep your voice down."

"Why?"

"I think we should go to the house and try to think things through."

"He said go to the library."

"I'd rather go with Colt and Nicole."

"What if they're already in the library?"

"We'll take that chance."

She walked toward the house, followed quickly by Carey on her right and just behind.

The door was open as they'd left it, or as Red had left it. Still no sign of Pinkus. Wendy's gut knotted tightly. She looked around before lightly mounting the steps to the porch.

"You sure about this?" Carey whispered.

No, she wasn't.

She eased past the door and stared at the empty house. "Hello?"

Still no sign of anyone. What if Red had found and killed Pinkus? Unless Pinkus was Red. She doubted he would have killed himself.

Wendy walked into the kitchen. "Colt?"

"They're not here," Carey said. "He said to go to the library. Nicole could be there. We should go to the library."

"Hold on. You can't just waltz in there on your own, asking some crazed killer if he wants to take your finger off! We should wait for Colt."

"Who said anything about taking my finger off? We don't have a clue if Colt's coming."

"If Colt doesn't come back, then neither does Nicole."

Carey hesitated, looked back at the door. "Then you stay here in case they come here. I'll . . ." He stopped, reconsidering what he'd been about to suggest.

"Go there by yourself?"

"Yes." He turned, walked back to the door, and was gone.

She didn't quite understand his resolve to head to the library—it seemed a bit foolish to her. But it made sense that they should at least check out the library, and if he was willing, she wouldn't stop him.

Silence engulfed the house once again. The painting that had wedged them in last night sat against the wall now. Napoleon stared at her stoically. She considered their reasoning for returning to the town. A threat made by a faceless killer named Red had forced them back. A threat backed up by the brutal slaying of two ranchers.

But why was the killer after them in the first place? And how many of them did he know?

A scream suddenly carried through the front door. Carey. She couldn't understand what he was trying to say, but something had just happened.

Wendy ran from the house, leapt off the porch, and sprinted toward the library. Door was open. Another yell emanated from within.

"Wendy!"

She was halfway to the door when two people raced around the building's corner. Colt and Nicole.

Relief flooded her veins. At that moment she just might have thrown caution to the wind and embraced the man, so thankful was she that he'd come back.

They met at the front door, panting. Colt had his gun out and went inside first, giving a grim nod. They both knew why the others were here—Red had forced them all back.

Wendy ran into the library ahead of Nicole. Light from a skylight in the ceiling filled the large room. Cherrywood tables with banker's lamps in the center, surrounded by bookcases.

Carey had found Jerry Pinkus, who stood trembling by the closest of those tables. There was something on the table, a mess of something, and it took Wendy a few seconds to recognize a finger that had been mutilated. Presumably the finger that Red had taken from Jerry Pinkus's hand last night.

Then she saw the blood on his mouth, and she knew what had happened. Jerry had taken a bite out of his own finger.

Carey had a hand on Jerry's shoulder—a feeble attempt to comfort the man.

"He made me chew it," Pinkus said, sobbing. "He forced it into my mouth—"

"When?" Colt asked, scanning the room.

"Now. Just now, man. I was in here, waiting, and the sicko—"

"Did you see him?"

"No."

Colt stepped around, eyes peeled for the dark corners. "How could you not see someone who stuffed your own finger in your mouth?"

"Because he came up behind me. You don't believe me? You try chewing on your own finger after someone's cut it off."

"He was lying facedown on the ground when I found him," Carey said.

Colt cast him a glance, then slowly lowered his gun. "What did he say?"

Pinkus looked at Carey, then the others. "He said that if we don't do exactly what he says, he's gonna start cutting."

"The question is," Colt said, "cutting what?"

Colt brushed past the skinny gamer, eyes still scanning the shadows. As he'd suspected, Red had forced Wendy and Carey back to the library, which probably meant they'd found a dead body as well.

Which in turn meant that the killer or killers had planned this with surprising precision. If this killer named Red had wanted him dead, why hadn't he just killed him in Vegas in the alley? He held his revolver snug, eyes peeled, and let the question circle his mind like a hungry buzzard.

As far as he could see, nothing had changed here. Still a dozen empty study tables surrounded by bookshelves packed with books. Above the tables, two stories high, several thick wood beams for ceiling support. A railing ran the perimeter of the second floor. No sign of a killer.

He faced the others. "You found a body?"

"Two," Wendy said.

"And a note."

"'It's payback time. Remember me? Get back to the library, or the others die. P.S. Have you figured out how many of you are on my side yet?' Something like that."

He nodded. "So now we know he's involved all of us. Which probably means we all have something in common."

A voice suddenly crackled over the intercom. "Thank you, thank you, thank you so much for coming. If you move, I'll put a slug in your head. Please walk to separate corners and close your eyes. Open your eyes, and I'll put a slug in your head. And trust me, I'm loaded for bear. Leave your weapons on the table." His breathing came, three breaths. "Now."

They stood motionless.

"There's five of us," Nicole whispered. "Only one of him."

She slid her hand over his, looking for comfort. Colt wasn't sure how to respond with the others' eyes on them. Out in the desert without an audience, he'd accepted her shows of affection despite his discomfort. On the way back to Doc Hansen's, they'd stopped three times to catch their wind and scout, and each time she'd leaned against him or taken his hand in both of hers for reassurance. Each time he'd grown more comfortable with it, almost forgetting the situation they were in.

"I don't see a choice," he said quietly. "I've seen him shoot." Colt moved to put his gun on the table, forcing Nicole to release him.

"We can't," Wendy whispered. "There has to be something we can do."

"For all we know, he's got a gun on our backs as we speak. We play along and wait for the right opportunity. If he just wanted us dead, he'd have killed us."

They stared at each other in silence as the logic sank in.

"Okay?" he asked.

She nodded reluctantly.

"We just go and wait?" Nicole asked, looking around with furtive glances.

He looked around at the towering bookcases. They were being watched; he could feel the stare on the back of his neck. "Just go and wait. Now."

Colt walked toward the west wall, to a bookcase next to the counter that offered good coverage in the event he decided to take Wendy up on her suggestion to do something.

Something like dive for cover; run for the gun with desperate, misguided hopes of actually reaching it before a bullet took him out; and take Red on, head to head.

Something like suicide.

With one last look around, he closed his eyes.

Completely powerless. Humiliated.

He had no choice. None of them did.

*S*terling Red thought about stalking around the library, passing within inches of each, smelling them, breathing in their ears, maybe even touching them and making them jump.

He thought about forcing them all to undress to bare skin for no other purpose than to show his complete dominance over them.

He thought about taking off his own clothes and walking among them to show his utter confidence in his own skin. His own power.

He thought about marching them outside blindfolded and forcing them to dig holes in the sand into which they could then place their heads to be covered. This particular thought was actually very tempting, not because it was juvenile as some might conclude, but because it was so perfectly representative of what was happening here.

All through the night he'd thought about many exhilarating paths he could force them down, but in the end he'd decided to stick to his original plan. He didn't have unlimited time. After what they'd done to him, Red savored his dominating position. Their fate was already decided, of course, but it was less their fate than the means to their fate that he was most interested in. The library had grown satisfactorily silent. Red walked down an aisle, drawing his fingers along the spines of the books as he passed.

"Colt?" Nicole's voice echoed softly in the quiet, tight and laced with fear, as if she expected Colt to save her from the silence.

Red silenced any response. "Shhh . . . shhh . . . shhh." And again, because he liked the way the sound echoed around the library. "Shhh . . . shhh . . . shhh." A third time for good measure. "Shhh . . . shhh . . . shhh."

He walked to the large desk he'd selected for its vantage point, lifted a plastic bottle of mustard he'd taken from the house's refrigerator, and sucked on the tip. A satisfying quantity of tangy mustard filled his mouth, and he swallowed it.

He set the bottle down and donned his baseball cap, picked up the megaphone, and pressed the talk button. He'd chosen the megaphone because it was loud and disturbing and had the added benefit of distorting his voice.

He pressed his lips against the mouthpiece. "Thank you," he said, then waited a moment. He could smell the mustard on his own breath. His arms started to shake, and he stilled them without too much effort.

"How does it feel? Being ganged up on like this?"

"What—"

"Shut up," he said. "You've all had so much to say today; now it's my turn." He watched them all, standing like good puppets, facing away from him, blind to the world.

What he had to say now would only take him a minute, and he found himself regretting this oversight in his planning. There was no reason not to relish his superiority during opportunities such as this.

"They say that beauty is in the eye of the beholder," he began. "Love is blind, all that nonsense. We all know that's a lie. The only thing I hate more than people who say they love me is people who are ugly. And I'm not the only one. If you all dig deep in your hearts, you'll realize that you too hate the ugly. Hate ugliness. If only you'd admit it."

He let that set in for a moment.

"I'm going to play the part you all think I was born to play. I'm going to kill lots and lots of people. Seven so far—no one's found the old man I stuffed in the lady's shed. Seven because it's the number of perfection and beauty."

A shake ran down his back. He stilled it.

"I'm here for payback, and if you will simply kill the person here who's the ugliest, then I will consider myself repaid in full."

A slight movement came from Pinkus's direction.

"I'm going to give you six hours to choose the particular person I have in mind. Six because it's the number of evil, which you clearly think I am. Fail, and I start to kill again."

He lifted the mustard bottle and supplied himself with another helping.

"I know how difficult this choice will be, so I've come up with a solution. The two women will each spend fifteen minutes of quality time alone with each fellow. Then they will each choose their preferred man. You will then reconvene and hang the man who was not chosen with the rope I've provided. The ugliest of the batch."

Red picked up the mustard bottle. "And then," he said, walking over to retrieve the gun and knife from the table, "you'd better pray that I agree."

18

Sweat trickled down Wendy's forehead. A steady quiver had taken over her fingers. There was something about keeping your eyes shut while a distorted voice told you it was going to kill you that frayed the nerves.

But it was a single thought that kept drumming through her mind that sickened Wendy more than an imminent fear of death. *He's insane. He's completely mad. He's gone so far off the deep end that he doesn't know terra firma still exists.*

She tried to listen for a note of familiarity in his voice, but apart from the obvious fact that the voice was male, she couldn't place it. Could it be one of them? Carey? Pinkus? Even Colt, for that matter? Enough time had passed for any one of them to slink off, grab a hidden megaphone, and speak to them all. Why else had Red insisted they shut their eyes?

"Is he gone?" Nicole voiced the question on her mind.

For a moment, the rest were evidently as reluctant as Wendy was to respond.

Then someone was walking across the library. "He's gone," Colt said.

Wendy opened her eyes and ran for the center, dodging tables and scanning the bookcases as she went.

"So's your gun," Pinkus said.

"What do we do now?" asked Carey.

"For starters, get out of this library."

Nicole had stepped up next to Colt and placed her hand on his elbow. She might have Colt convinced she was innocent as some reborn dove, but Wendy couldn't shake her irritation. In fact, it seemed to be growing.

"Why do we do that?" Nicole asked Colt.

He hesitated. "Because in here, we're cows in a slaughter pen."

"And how do we know he isn't one of you?" Carey asked.

There. It was out on the table.

"What do you mean?" Nicole asked.

"I mean we all had our eyes shut. How do we know that wasn't Colt or Pinkus talking?"

"Uh, because I'm not a killer?" Pinkus said. "What do we know about you?"

"You guys coming, or are you going to stay here and argue the obvious?" Colt asked.

"What's obvious?" asked Nicole.

"That technically speaking, Red or those he's working with, assuming he is working with someone, could be anyone in here. He's messing with us. He has us trapped and he's poking around, after something else. Testing with a few jabs and hooks like a boxer feeling out his opponent."

Colt didn't wait for them this time. He just pulled away from Nicole and walked out the front door.

He led them out to the hole that revealed the buried foundation, then pulled up and paced. Wendy glanced around at the horizon. A red haze rose from the hot desert, distorting an otherwise blue sky. No sign of life.

"Let's establish what we know about this guy," Colt said.

"What if he gets bored with our discussion about what we know about him?" Carey asked, looking around. "The clock's running, right?"

Colt ignored the comment. "From the shooting yesterday, we know he's extremely efficient with a gun."

Natural for him to think of guns first, Wendy thought. Somehow it made her feel safer.

"He likes killing to make a point," Wendy said. "The rancher we found on the tractor was brutally murdered."

"He's motivated by control and power," Colt said. "And he's fixated on eliminating that which is ugly."

"Or making himself beautiful," Wendy said. "Maybe he hates ugliness because he's so obsessed with being beautiful that any kind of ugliness disturbs him."

"Fine," Pinkus said. "This isn't getting us anywhere."

"If we don't do as he says, he'll keep his word," Colt said.

"Unless we can stop him first," Wendy said.

"That's right. And that's our only choice at this point."

"What?" Pinkus shouted. "Are you nuts? You can't stop him."

Colt walked over to Pinkus and took him by the hand, deliberately close to his wounded finger, and said, "This is the last time I'm saying this. Keep your voice down. You're endangering us all."

He released the gamer, who blinked in shock.

"I don't think I could choose one of you to die." Wendy looked over at Nicole, who blinked and quickly agreed. *Too quickly,* Wendy thought.

"No, of course not. That's ridiculous. She's right."

"Technically, he didn't ask you to choose someone to die," Carey said. "Just pointing that out."

"Why don't we just walk out," Wendy said. "Seriously, what's to keep us from heading north on foot? All together, so he can't force us back like he did last time?"

Colt didn't immediately respond, which meant he couldn't find a reason to disagree. Could it be that simple?

"He'd come after us," Pinkus said, keeping his voice low with an effort. "You said he could shoot. He'd take us out like target practice."

Colt studied the doctor's house, thinking.

Nicole stepped up to Colt and put her hand on his back. "What is it? Tell us you have a plan." She caressed his back gently.

She'd virtually claimed the man in the space of a few hours. Wasn't Wendy right to be annoyed? And why didn't Colt push her off, for heaven's sake?

Because he was as wounded as she. *But not deceptive,* Wendy thought. He's as pure as they come. But Nicole? Wendy wasn't buying it. Never mind that she was the least qualified person on earth to determine appropriate behavior.

Still, one thing she did know: *I don't like this woman. I don't like her at all.*

"You two are getting just a bit cozy, aren't you?" The moment the words came out, she cursed herself for having spoken them. The others had undoubtedly heard jealousy dripping from each word.

Nicole shot her a quick glare, removed her hand, then resumed her innocent act without a word. Colt blushed a shade of pink and pretended not to have heard.

"There might be a way," Colt said, eyes still fixed on the house. He faced them and now moved subtly away from Nicole. "It's risky. Pinkus is right: it could get us all killed. But it could work."

"What?" Carey asked.

Colt averted his eyes. "You'll have to trust me."

"How can we do that if we don't know what to trust you with?" Pinkus asked.

"Unfortunately, I don't have a choice."

Because he knows Red could be standing here at this very moment, Wendy thought, *and he can't risk giving him advance warning. Smart man.*

"I agree," she said.

Nicole looked at Wendy. "I do too."

"Is this really that practical?" Carey asked. "This guy's demonstrated that he can kill at will. If we don't do what he wants, he may kill us all. If we do what he said, only one dies. I'm not saying that's an easy choice, but we have to at least think about it."

"You volunteering?" Colt asked.

"There's no guarantee that we pick the person he wants us to pick," Wendy said. "Is it that obvious?" Meaning, is it that obvious who's the ugliest here? She would have to say Colt. Maybe Pinkus. But she suspected that Red wanted them to kill Colt because Colt was their best hope for survival—and the only real threat to Red.

She pushed the thought away. "And then we would have to kill that person. We can't just deliberately kill someone; we've already established that."

Carey held up his hands. "I'm just making sure we know what we're getting into."

"We're wasting time," Colt said. "Are we all agreed?"

Pinkus nodded reluctantly. Surely he'd concluded that if they were forced to choose, he was a good candidate for execution.

Carey nodded. *Considering that he was clearly the most beautiful man among them, he deserved some credit,* Wendy thought.

"Follow me to the house," Colt said, "and do exactly what I say."

19

The house loomed ahead, battered by the previous night's storm but structurally undamaged as far as Wendy could see. Amazing. Behind them the library rose like a huge mausoleum.

Wendy touched Nicole's arm. "Can I talk to you a minute?"

Nicole's eyes widened, but she stepped aside willingly. "Yes?"

The others glanced back, and Wendy avoided their questioning looks. This wouldn't take long. "What are you trying to do with Colt?"

"What do you mean?"

"You know what I mean. You're leading him around like a puppy. We need him, and we need him thinking straight. Maybe you should back off."

"Back off?" There was a hint of panic in Nicole's voice. "I . . . I don't understand."

"Look at him," Wendy whispered. "He doesn't know what to do about you. You're hitting on him, and he's falling hard."

"He is?"

"Your hands are on him every chance you get."

"They are?"

"Please, this isn't funny anymore. Leave him alone, for all of our sakes."

"But . . . I'm not trying to hurt him. Really . . ." A tear snaked down Nicole's cheek.

Wendy wanted to slap the woman.

Then again, what if Nicole really had somehow been shocked into a state of innocence by her mother's death? What if she was like Wendy, desperate for love and finding it in the reassurance of physical contact? But even more innocent than Wendy. A child trapped in a woman's body.

They were approaching the house, and their time was short. Wendy couldn't leave it alone. "You're saying there's nothing sexual in your advances?"

"No!" Nicole whispered. "Of course not."

Her tone of voice, the look in her face and eyes—none of it suggested anything but complete sincerity.

"But you like him?"

A beat. "Yes."

Wendy didn't believe a word of it. But rather than call her on it, Wendy said the only thing she could. "Okay."

They entered the garage through the same door they'd last left it, in the back. Colt opened a large closet that he was obviously familiar with.

The good doctor was a bit of a survivalist in the never-can-be-too-safe way. He'd built a house and a library that could withstand more than any other structure in town. And he'd stocked this closet with canned foods, water, and an assortment of camping items, including two tents, three sleeping bags, a spade, nylon rope, lightweight rain gear, a brown backpack, and hiking boots.

But it wasn't the camping gear that interested Colt. It was the two bulletproof vests with the camouflaged clothing that he went for.

"That's it?" Pinkus said. "There's five of us."

"Wendy, make sure no one's carrying any weapons," he said.

He wanted her to frisk them.

"I'll frisk Nicole; you get Carey and Pinkus," she said.

Their eyes met, and she silently told him to stop staying so close to Nicole. But he didn't get it.

"Just frisk them."

So she did, starting with Nicole, then Pinkus and Carey, quickly, lightly, and on edge. *Mind over matter*, she told herself. For heaven's sake, there wasn't a romantic thought in her mind directed at any of them.

"Why wouldn't you want us to have any guns?" Carey demanded as she awkwardly patted his sides.

"In case one of us is working with Red." Wendy finished and stepped back.

"So now we have a no-guns policy?"

Pinkus held up one of the vests. "What are you going to do with this? It's not going to work."

"You're starting to bother me with your negativity," Nicole said with a bite. "Please stop."

You go, girl.

Two minutes later, they'd lined up front to back by the rear entrance as instructed by Colt. Wendy first, then Carey, then Pinkus, then Nicole, then Colt at the rear. He'd put one of the vests on and held the other in his hands.

"Keep the formation as tight as possible. If he's still watching from the library, it will block his view. We should be able to get some distance on him before he knows we're gone. Stay directly in front of me, single file. Anyone takes a bullet, it'll be me, and I'll have the vests. Any questions?"

Pinkus had a comment. "This is nuts."

"So is going back," Wendy said. "Let's go."

Colt swung the second vest over his head and held on to it as if it were a towel around his neck. "Northwest of the draw, Wendy. Keep the house between us and the library."

She nodded. "Ready?"

"Let's go."

Wendy took off at a fast walk, with Carey breathing down her neck, literally. They bumped toes and heels and nearly tripped a few times in the first fifty yards, but they found a cadence.

Like a centipede with body armor, they moved steadily into the desert.

"What's happening?" Pinkus asked. "Is he following us?"

"Shut up and walk," Colt whispered.

Their shoes shuffled through the sand, they breathed heavily under the hot sun, and sweat quickly darkened their shirts. But they made it a hundred yards without a peep from behind. Then two hundred.

Then three hundred yards.

"Are we far enough?" Pinkus wanted to know.

"Shut up and walk," Colt said again.

Four hundred yards and not one sign of pursuit.

Wendy had kept her eyes fixed on a slight rise in the rocky sand dead ahead, knowing that if they could get over that rise and into the depression that followed it, they actually stood a chance.

They were now less than a hundred yards from that crest, and she was tempted to break into a run. She picked up her pace.

The others seemed to understand her reasoning and followed suit. Fifty yards.

They were going to make it. At least to this first dip.

Thirty yards.

From there they would head southwest along the draw at a run, without need of armor.

Wendy broke into a run as she crested the lip of the draw, heart hammering with hope. "Run!" she shouted in a hoarse whisper.

No one objected. They broke file and ran. Over the crest. Down the other side.

Directly toward the black truck parked at the bottom of the draw.

Wendy cried out in surprise and slid to a stop. At first she thought it might be a good thing—stumbling into a black Dodge Ram with dark tinted windows that had escaped the storm. It could take them to freedom!

But this thought was immediately and forcefully shoved back down by the wisps of black diesel smoke that rose from its tailpipes. The truck was running, which meant it was inhabited. Out here, that could only mean this black truck was anything but good news.

They stopped abreast, panting, staring ahead. Stunned.

"Red," Carey said.

"Something like that," Colt said.

The truck faced them at an angle, wide tires shiny black around chrome wheels. It crept forward a few feet with a soft rumble, then stopped again, like a bull daring them to enter its ring.

Wendy took an instinctive step back. "Now what?"

"How'd he get here?" Pinkus asked.

Carey cast him a side-glance. "You don't know?"

"Stop it, Carey," Nicole said. "What do we do?"

Pinkus glared at Carey. "How should I know?"

"That truck belongs to the ranch Wendy and Carey went to," Colt said. "They took it from the barn and hid it back here. He saw us leaving and cut us off. It doesn't matter at this point. Back up."

"They?" Wendy said.

"Back to the house?" Nicole asked in a thin, unbelieving voice.

"We don't have a choice," Colt said.

The truck's window silently slid down a few inches.

"Back. Get back!" Colt warned.

Nicole screamed and grabbed her face. The sand at their feet sprayed up as several silenced slugs struck the ground.

They spun and ran as one up the slope, over the crest, toward the house.

Nicole was running silently, but her right hand was still covering part of her face. Colt glanced at her, then rounded Nicole and ran backward.

"Show me. Slow down. He's not going to shoot us. Show me."

She slowed to a fast walk, as did they all. Then she removed her hand. Blood brightened her right jaw, but it wasn't flowing. She'd been grazed by a bullet, but no worse.

Colt put his hand on her good cheek, still walking backward. "It's just a scratch. You'll be okay."

Wendy knew by the way he said those seven words that Colt Jackson felt deeply for this beautiful woman who was now a little less beautiful.

He wiped some of her blood away. "It'll be fine, I promise."

The black truck rumbled behind them. Nosed over the crest, then stopped like a guard dog.

"Back to the house," Colt said.

The next time Wendy looked over her shoulder, the truck was gone.

20

olt ran for the medicine cabinet, grabbed the same disinfectant and gauze Nicole had used on Pinkus's severed finger, and headed back toward the kitchen, desperate to do this one small thing for Nicole. Her being shot was his fault.

He stopped halfway into the kitchen. Wendy held a piece of paper in her hands. Another note from Red.

"What is it?"

She turned it around for him to read.

Do you think I'm beautiful now?

Colt splashed disinfectant on a patch of gauze and tenderly wiped away the blood on Nicole's jaw and neck. The bullet had split the skin, deep enough to warrant stitches by any estimation. She'd have a scar if they didn't get her to a doctor to sew the wound up properly.

"What's he so obsessed with beauty for?" Wendy asked. "Are we supposed to know this guy?"

"We must," Colt said, quickly fashioning a bandage for Nicole's jaw. "Something ties us all together. Maybe each of us has done something to tick him off. Each or all."

Wendy looked at Colt with sadness in her eyes. If they did what Red wanted, Colt would be the loser. He knew that as well as any of them.

"We can't do this," Nicole said, touching his cheek.

"We have to," Carey said. "He just shot you. And we know she's not the ugliest, so he'll still want us to choose someone else." He paced frantically. "We have to at least make a show like we're playing along."

Pinkus stayed uncharacteristically silent.

There had to be a way around this, but Colt's mind refused to give him any alternatives. He finished the bandage and stepped away from Nicole, afraid to look in her eyes. "We're running out of time."

No one disagreed. They all knew. They had to play along, and they had to do it now.

Colt turned around and walked out of the house. He didn't look back, but he could hear them following him to the library. The sun was already dipping into a red western horizon. It was now obvious the storm had ravaged far more than Summerville. It was the only explanation for the absence of rescue teams a full day after the tornado's passing.

The same long, faint sound they'd heard earlier filtered into his ears. He lifted his head. More dark contrails. Nothing else.

"What was that?" Pinkus asked from behind.

"We heard it before," Carey said. "The wind or something."

One of them was Red, Colt thought. Either Pinkus or Carey was working with Red, or worse, was Red. The pieces fit.

Then again, he could be wrong, and therein lay the problem. The pieces did fit, but not perfectly. He'd given the matter careful thought, and certain inconsistencies still nagged at him. Simple questions about who was where when. Most of these inconsistencies could be overcome with some creative thinking, but some would have required an accomplice, which Red's note at the ranch suggested he had.

The largest of these inconsistencies lay with Carey, who had been driving toward Summerville with Wendy when Red had shot up the town. But that didn't mean Carey wasn't working with Red.

And Pinkus . . . an even more likely candidate.

Still, they could both be innocent. Victims like the rest of them. All of the evidence remained circumstantial, at best.

Colt motioned for Wendy to step aside with him for a moment. "You'll be talking to them, if we do what he wants. Try to find an inconsistency in Pinkus's story. Where he was the night of the murders. Anything."

She added a little distance between them. Colt wondered if she felt intimidated by his presence, or his proximity. Now that he thought about it, she'd stayed clear of them all. Expressed concern when he'd asked her to frisk Carey and Pinkus. Maybe she had issues with men? Maybe not so unlike his own problems with women.

"I don't trust her, Colt," Wendy said, glancing in Nicole's direction.

"She's not with Red, I'm sure of it."

"Maybe not, but I still don't trust her. I'm just telling you that."

Jealousy, Colt thought, then rejected the notion. No woman had ever been jealous of anything about him.

"Just find out what you can," he said.

When they joined the others, they were met with scattered stares and an accusation from Pinkus. "What was that all about?"

Colt ignored the man and walked into the library. Red had given them explicit instructions. It was now clear that they had to follow them precisely.

He stopped at the first set of tables and faced the others. "Okay, we do it exactly how he said. Wendy and Nicole will spend fifteen minutes each with myself, Carey, and Jerry in separate rooms."

"Doing what?" Pinkus asked.

"Whatever they want to do."

"And what are we supposed to do, sit there with our thumbs—"

"You're supposed to be trying to convince her to let you live," Carey said. "Don't you have a switch for that thing?" Meaning his mouth, Colt thought.

Pinkus had no comeback.

Colt glanced at the two women. "Remember, you're not picking the person who you might want to live. You're choosing the person who you think Red would choose. He's looking for the ugliest, in his eyes, something he claims isn't a factor because beauty isn't in the eye of the beholder."

"What's that supposed to mean?" Wendy asked.

Colt shrugged. "That the opinion shouldn't vary from one person to another. That it's obvious."

"It's so juvenile," she said.

"Well, he's making it real."

"Are you sure there's no other way?" Nicole asked.

"Yeah, I'm sure."

She approached him. "Then I'll start with you."

"And I'll start with Carey," Wendy said.

Colt felt like he imagined a cow might feel, being led to the slaughter. As far as he could see, Red's challenge offered him no hope. The sum of the matter was quite simple: Red wanted him out of the way, so he was forcing the others to kill him. If they didn't—or if they chose the wrong person—say Pinkus, who wasn't as ugly as Colt was— then they would pay an even higher price.

Nicole must have sensed his misery, because she smiled gently and squeezed his hand.

They entered a small room with a table in the center and brown over-stuffed chairs in two corners. Beige walls, green carpet, no windows. Emergency lighting similar to that in the doctor's house glowed amber.

Nicole locked the door behind him, then guided him to one of the chairs with purpose. "Sit down," she said.

He sat.

She pulled a chair from the table and eased down in front of him. For a moment, neither of them spoke. She stared at him, but he couldn't hold her eyes.

"How do you feel?" she asked.

"Like a death-row inmate receiving last rites," he said.

She didn't laugh or even smile. "Carey told me that he told you my story," she said. "He doesn't know everything, of course. But I'm sure he got enough right. How does it make you feel about me?"

What parts might Carey have been wrong about? Colt wondered.

"I . . . It made me want to cry," he said.

His world crashed in around him with his own words. The hope-lessness of his predicament, his inability to help any of them, the loss of the chief and the town, countless dead, the staggering scope of it all—it swallowed him whole. But there was more, and Nicole was drilling down to it.

A lump grew in his throat, and he had to bring his full effort to bear to keep from throwing himself at her and weeping in her arms.

The wave of anguish that he felt came not from Nicole's story but from his own. The one he'd fought so long to bury. The one he no longer even considered his own. But now, stretched so thin by this conundrum, he didn't know how strong he could be for them all.

Her eyes glistened with tears—this without hearing a word. She reached out and touched his chin. "I knew from the moment I saw you that you were special. We share some sort of bond, don't we?"

His eyes flooded with tears.

"Tell me. Tell me your story."

Never in a million years could he have imagined that a woman would speak those words to him. In this locked room with Nicole, he felt like he could say anything to her. And so he did.

"I had a rough childhood. I think Red might know it."

"Tell me."

"My parents divorced when I was seven," he said. "We lived in Las Vegas. My mother dropped me off at the bus station and told me to buy a ticket to Albuquerque, New Mexico, because my father lived there and wanted me. She said that her boyfriend didn't like me. He was actually her pimp. When I tried to buy the ticket, they said I was too young. It took me two days to find my way back home, because I couldn't remember how the cab had gone."

"But your mother didn't take you back," Nicole said.

"They shut the door on me. Her boyfriend told me he'd beat me up if he ever saw me again. But I didn't know where to go, so I waited in the hall outside the apartment. I could hear them talking and laughing inside."

"What were they saying?"

"My mother's boyfriend said I was the ugliest kid he'd ever seen and that maybe they should make a deal with the circus. My mother didn't argue with that. I almost knocked on the door a hundred times that night, and I think that if I had he might have killed me."

"What did you do? What *could* you do?"

"I was on the street."

"At age seven?"

"I finally managed to get on that bus to Albuquerque. The kindness of strangers and all that. When I found my father a week later, he beat me. He said he'd told my mother he'd beat me if she ever tried to unload me on him."

"That's horrible."

"Anyway, I made it back to Vegas on the same bus, and this time I went to the strip club where my mother worked and made a deal with the manager. If he'd give me food, I'd do whatever he wanted. He agreed to let me scrub the floors backstage and wash the costumes once a week. It was the biggest mistake I ever made, but I didn't know what else to do. I just wanted to be near my mother."

"Did she allow it?"

"She didn't have a choice, but she didn't make it easier for me. All the women made fun of me. They said I was ugly. They called me the Turd."

"All of them?"

He nodded. "I wasn't the best-looking kid."

Nicole placed her fingers on her lips, eyes wide. "How long did this last?"

"Until I was a teenager."

"You . . . So you knew nothing about women except humiliation. From women that other men desired and sought after. You grew up thinking desirable women were disgusted by you. And you still feel that way."

No one had ever said it quite so plainly.

Colt sat back and sank into the upholstery. "Let's fast-forward a bit. Three months before I left Vegas, a man told me he was going to kill my mother because she was as ugly as I was. They found her with her wrists cut two nights later. I think he's the same killer who's doing this to us. He wants me dead."

The revelation seemed to surprise her. "Why?"

Colt couldn't say what was on his mind. Not because it made no sense, but because his throat had suddenly swelled in pain.

"Because you're ugly? Because he hates ugly people and for some reason you came into his line of sight."

Sorrow rose from within his bowels and flooded his chest.

"You became an officer because you don't believe you have any intrinsic worth," she said softly, placing both hands on his knees. "Since you have no value, you have to serve others to justify your existence?"

He hated the fact that tears kept flowing, but he couldn't stop them. And Nicole refused to let him off the hook.

"So then if you're put in a position where you can't help others, such as this one, what does that make you?"

Worthless. She had it right. But he didn't have the courage to be so brutally honest, even now.

Nicole slid to her knees and put her head against his chest. She began to cry with him. Then harder than he was. Weeping and weeping, so much that Colt wondered if she might hurt herself.

She clung to him tightly and wet his shirt with her tears. Only then did it occur to him that she was a woman in his arms, needing him, being comforted by him. To Nicole, he wasn't worthless.

She had turned the tables on him.

Colt put his arms around her body and held her awkwardly. "Shh . . . shh, it's okay," he said. He'd never done anything like this.

Slowly Nicole settled.

"I guess we do have something in common," she said, still leaning against his chest. She pulled back and looked into his eyes. "When

I was seven, my mother told me I was the most beautiful girl in the world." She traced his lip with one finger. "When you were seven, you believed you were the ugliest. They say that opposites attract . . ." She sniffled and then gave him a smile.

"You're still the most beautiful creature in the world," he said. And then Colt did something he'd done only twice before in his life, neither time very successfully. He leaned forward and kissed a woman on her lips.

She pulled him tight and hungrily returned the kiss. Whatever he may have thought about her tendency to use touch in purely platonic ways no longer mattered. This kiss was as passionate and romantic as he imagined they came.

Nicole broke it off first. She was breathing hard, and he could smell her breath, musky like lipstick even though she wore none.

She stood and walked to the door, then back. "I have to choose," she said.

Colt gathered himself. Ran both hands through his hair. He'd lost his hat in the storm last night, and his head was a mess of tangles. A ridiculous thought crossed his mind. An image of waking in bed next to a wife with his hair tangled.

He knew Red had other ideas, but if Nicole chose him over her brother, he might be able to save her. All of them. It was a ridiculous line of thought, but even so, Colt suddenly wanted to live. Not only because of his own survival instinct, but because he'd found something in the room that begged for him to live.

"You do," he said.

"Who do you think Wendy will pick?" she asked, staring at the door.

"Carey," he said. Unless she concluded that Carey was working for Red.

"Not you?"

The question stumped him. "She could, I guess."

"Doesn't it strike you as strange that we're all being so clinical about this?"

"We're going through the motions because we have no choice. Your jaw's evidence of that. I don't think it will stay . . . clinical . . . for long."

"Everything seems so safe in this room." She walked to him and put her head on his chest again. Wrapped her arms around his waist. "It seems so safe in here."

"I know what you mean. But beyond that door the danger is real. And I have a feeling that it's going to become even more real in a few minutes."

21

Wendy dutifully spent fifteen minutes with Carey and then Pinkus, during which time she learned nothing new about Carey and only a little new about Pinkus. Now she was with Colt, and she was learning plenty.

She wasn't sure why Red had insisted that they spend the time together—if he really wanted them to pick the ugliest person, they just as easily could have made that determination without all this talk.

The only thing she could figure was that Red wanted them even more emotionally entangled than they were, making the whole ordeal even more agonizing than it already was.

And it's working, she thought.

She hadn't learned anything new about Carey, because Carey spent most of his fifteen minutes rehearsing the logic of exactly what was happening to them and why. So much so that Wendy began to wonder if he was doing it to mislead her.

If Carey was Red or was working with Red, which she had a

hard time imagining, then wouldn't he do just this? Wouldn't he try to prove he *wasn't* Red by seeming determined to expose Red?

Carey did chant a few lines from a poem about evil and good, which seemed odd to her. He had a beautiful deep voice, but she had little idea what was going on inside his skull.

As for Pinkus, she got mostly a series of assertive and high-strung arguments that she absolutely had to pick him because they both knew he wasn't as dog-ugly as Colt, the cop. No offense, but this was a matter of life and death for all of them, and if they didn't do exactly what Red wanted, they would all end up dead. He'd proven that, hadn't he? Maybe Pinkus was right when he said he was closer to that realization than the rest of them. Like he said, having your finger removed and then being forced to chew on it had a way of driving points like this home.

"You know Nicole's going to choose her brother. So let her. That means you have to choose me. If you choose Colt, Red's gonna freak. If this was about some inner-beauty crap, you might have some kind of argument, but it's more obvious than that and you know it."

"Do I?"

But she had to admit that his logic was strong. It put a lead weight in her gut. Pinkus left the room the same person as when he'd entered it, part suspect and part gamer punk who was thin on empathy and strong on logic.

Colt, on the other hand, seemed to have found plenty of empathy during his fifteen minutes with Nicole. There was a light in his eyes that she supposed involved more than a sense of mutual understanding.

He certainly didn't look like a man about to face the gallows. The weight in Wendy's gut rose to her chest.

Then he told her the same story he said he'd told Nicole. Her heart broke for him. How any sane mother could treat a child so cruelly was a mystery to her. The only way she could understand it was to equate life in a brothel to life in a cult. People who sacrificed their children on self-serving altars as Colt's mother had done were motivated by a profound ideology much like that of a cult.

Or perhaps more accurately, a profound *lack* of ideology. Complete vacancy in heart and soul.

Wendy was about to tell him how similar their stories were when he told her about Nicole's unique bond with him.

"What bond?" she asked.

"When she was seven, she was the most beautiful child in the world. When I was seven, I was the ugliest." He said it as if the confession was a badge of honor.

"She said that?"

"It's true. Then she wept in my arms. I know it's hard to imagine, but that's never happened to me before."

"With your past, no, it's not hard to imagine. But there's no truth to it. You do realize that, don't you?"

"What do you mean?"

"You weren't the ugliest boy in the world at age seven. You were only told that lie."

He seemed to consider her point, then dismissed it. "That's not how Red sees it."

"Really? How so?"

"He knows me." Colt approached her, and she feared he might reach out to touch her. "He knows my whole story, and he's using it against me. Red wants me dead."

"But now you think Nicole is going to choose you."

"I think so. You should pick one of the others."

"What if she picks her brother?"

Colt stared at her. "I don't think she will."

"She's close to him."

"Carey's not ugly. She knows that you'll pick him now."

"Why would I pick him over you?

"Because you now know that she'll pick me," he said.

His reasoning is flawed, she thought. Skewed by this new emotion Nicole had introduced him to. But no amount of reasoning would save any of them at this point.

A knock sounded on the door, followed by Carey's voice. "You done in there?"

"Let's go," Colt said, then led her from the room.

Pinkus, Carey, and Nicole stood around a cherrywood study table in the middle of the library, eyeing them silently as they approached. Dusk was turning the place dark. *Absurd,* Wendy thought. *It's all surreal.*

Surreal or not, she and Colt took up places to form a rough circle around the table. Judge, jury, and execution squad. One of them had placed two pads of white lined paper and pencils on the table.

Carey nodded. "This is it. We have to do this. We all know that. Six hours is almost up."

"Do we?" Wendy said, not because she thought they had a choice, but just to break the surrealism they'd entered.

"For all we know, there could be a gun lined up on one of us at this very moment," Carey said. "Yes, we do all know that. Each of you can write your answers on the paper."

Wendy frowned. "Just like that? As if it's just another tribal council at the end of a *Survivor* episode?"

"Don't make this harder than it has to be, Wendy," he said. "If you have a better suggestion, fine. If not, I suggest yes, we just do this as if it's another tribal council. We don't have a choice." He bit the last sentence off, exaggerating his pronunciation of each word.

Nicole reached for a pencil and one of the pads. Wendy followed suit.

Pinkus put both hands together as if he were praying and addressed them with one last appeal. "Please, do the right thing. If you get this wrong, he starts killing again, just remember that. This isn't about what you think, it's—"

"Shut up, Jerry," Nicole said.

Wendy agreed. "Yes, shut up, Jerry."

And then Nicole pulled her pad close and wrote a name on it.

It took a moment for Wendy to actually begin writing after her pencil made contact with the page. She'd never before been forced to do something so asinine, so cruel, and so hideous as what she was doing now. Worse, the whole thing seemed like a meaningless exercise to her. She had no plans to kill anyone, regardless of what names turned up on the page.

But she knew Carey was right. The killer was watching them, taking pleasure in their dilemma.

"Done? Toss the pads on the table," Carey said.

Nicole looked at Colt with round, kind eyes. She slid her tablet onto the table. On it was written one name.

Carey.

Colt blinked. His eyes darted up to meet Nicole's.

Pinkus drilled Wendy with a stare, but it took Colt a few moments to avert his eyes from Nicole and look her way.

Wendy dropped her tablet on the table.

Colt.

"What?" Pinkus cried. "What?"

Colt fixed her with a glazed stare. She shrugged. *I tried to tell you, Colt. You know nothing about how a woman's heart works.*

She wasn't sure herself what she meant by that, only that she was compelled to show him she believed in him, not some strategy that might get him killed. Nicole, no doubt, had guessed that Wendy would choose Colt, so she'd chosen to save her brother rather than Pinkus.

Pinkus took a step back. "You're wrong, you know." His eyes skipped around the library. "He's gonna fry you, man. For not being honest. And he's gonna kill Colt anyway."

They all just looked at him.

He turned to Wendy. "Why did you do it?"

"Because I guessed that Nicole would choose Carey," she said. "And because I don't think either Carey or Colt is capable of killing an innocent human being. You, on the other hand, might."

She let her logic sink in.

"You see, Jerry? You're safe. I really don't think anyone here will kill you."

She looked at Carey, whose eyes darted to his sister. She wasn't so sure about her judgment of his character, but it was now out of her hands.

"What . . . what if he just kills all of us?" Carey stammered. "He said he'd start killing again if we didn't kill the ugliest. If we don't kill him, the killer will kill us."

"If you kill Pinkus, then you become a killer," Wendy said.

Colt spoke for the first time since the vote. "In all honesty, I think he meant me when he said ugliest. So kill me, then."

Carey looked from one to the other, stumped. She was right; he didn't have the resolve to kill. But he wasn't happy about the prospect of being hunted, either.

Wendy pulled out a chair, sat down, and crossed her arms. "Then let him kill all of us."

"You're crazy," Pinkus said. But his voice lacked conviction. He swallowed deeply, grabbed a chair, and sat. As did Colt and Nicole. Then Carey.

For a minute, no one spoke. Nicole was staring at Colt with remorseful eyes, but he wouldn't engage her. He'd become a cop again out of necessity. The Nicole fantasy was over.

Pinkus and Carey both scanned the library for any sign of an attack, and when none came, Pinkus spoke up. "So what do we do?"

"We wait," Colt said.

"Just wait? It's been six hours."

"Then kill me."

"He's gonna come for us all."

"He's probably watching us now," Colt said. "For all we know, he's in this room. Either way, this isn't the day for alternatives."

Pinkus glanced at the doors. "It's getting dark outside. Maybe we could make another break for it."

"He's not that stupid. One of two things happens here: either a rescue team finally comes and gets us out of here, or Red makes his next move and we do what we have to do at that time. In the meantime, we're stuck here."

"Guys, I don't think—"

Colt slammed his palm on the table. They all jumped. "Will you please shut up? We wait."

Pinkus looked back at the door. "I was going to say something else."

"What?" Colt demanded. "What can you possibly have to say that will help us now?"

"It is getting dark, isn't it? I mean, I thought it was, and it should be. But is it just me, or does it seem lighter now?"

Wendy sat up in her chair. *The thick glass panels should be black by now,* she thought. They weren't.

In fact, they were filled with light. She stood up.

Colt stood with her, staring. "It was getting dark."

"How's that possible?" Carey demanded.

They were all on their feet now, walking toward the front door.

Far away a dog barked. They all froze as one.

"Was that a dog?"

Colt ran first, around the checkout counter and straight for the front door.

"Rescue dogs," Carey cried. "They're here!"

It had to be! And it would explain why the killer hadn't killed as promised. He'd been shut down by the approach of rescue workers.

Colt was only a yard ahead of Wendy when he grabbed the large brass handle of the library's thick door and pulled it open.

Light flooded the atrium. So much light.

But she could have sworn that it had been growing dark. The dog barked again, far away.

They spilled out of the library in a mob and pulled up, rooted to the marble entryway. Gaping at the scene before them.

The blood drained from Wendy's face. How . . . how was this possible?

"It's back?" Pinkus said. But it couldn't be a question, because the answer was far too plain.

The town was back.

All of it.

22

The red phone on Nathan Blair's desk rang shrilly. He was receiving all his updates through that phone rather than in the situation room with the others. Rest would be good about now. An hour or two catnap to clear his mind, but so much was happening every hour now that missing even a single call could ruin him.

According to Longhorn, Clifton had confirmed that a second victim had indeed been killed in the house and then dragged outside as suggested by Timothy Healy. They'd found the body in the shed, stuffed in a barrel. Cyrus Healy, Timothy Healy's father, had been found.

He snatched up the phone. "Yes?"

"Colt Jackson and the others are at the police station," Beth Longhorn said.

"So Clifton found them?"

"No, they just walked in."

"Meaning what?"

"Meaning they seem to be cooperating with Clifton. He's in a position to break them down."

"That's good. They still have no clear leads on Red's identity?"

"Not yet. But it'll only be a matter of time. Clifton's sharp. With any luck he'll flush Red out and we can all put this behind us."

"We don't have that much time," Blair said. "We've seen how fast Red can work. And the fact that he's murdered Cyrus Healy can't be a coincidence. He knows exactly what happened, and he's in Summerville to clean house. If the killing continues, I think we should consider an intervention. I don't trust them. And I'm not convinced the director's telling me everything."

"I understand, sir, but an intervention could blow the whole thing wide open. It could be . . . dangerous. You sure you're willing to risk that? I really think we should give Clifton a chance on this."

Blair sighed. "Are you sure we can trust Clifton?"

The answered lagged a few seconds. "No, but he's our best shot. Isn't he?"

23

"What do you mean the town was wiped out by the tornado?" Steve's voice crackled on the radio.

"I don't know," Luke said, keying his transmitter. "That's what Becky said they said. Kinda nuts, huh? Evidently Colt's lost it. And it ain't just him. I'm on my way to pick up Timothy Healy now. I'll see you down at the station."

"Copy that."

Luke dropped the radio on the passenger seat and steered the cruiser down Fourth, headed back out to the same small neighborhood he'd spent half the night in. *The small town had seen more action in the last two days than it had in the previous twenty years,* he thought.

He passed the house Cyrus and Helen Healy had been killed in. The old man had been found stuffed in a barrel in the shed. Why the killer had seen fit to lug Cyrus's body out of the house was still a mystery.

They'd taken both bodies to the morgue the morning after the big storm. Branches littered the front lawn, including the one that had knocked him out for a few seconds before Steve had come to his aid.

One heck of a storm, that was for sure. The tornado had never actually touched down, but it had evidently passed right over the Healy house. Damage around town was significant, but no one had been hurt by the winds. No, only their serial killer had managed to kill anyone.

They still had a half dozen extra officers posted around town in case the killer showed back up, but yesterday had been quiet.

There was more than one theory about what had happened. Could be that some roving maniac had come into town with guns blazing under cover of the storm, then moved on. Storms bring out the craziness in some people, they said.

Seemed a bit coincidental to Luke, and if he read Detective Clifton's eyes right, to him as well. And it didn't explain how Colt had gone missing after going up to the doctor's house.

Prevailing wisdom—meaning what Detective Clifton believed, if Luke was reading him right, which was awful hard with how close the guy held his cards to his chest—was that the killer was still here, waiting. Maybe even someone they knew.

Luke pulled up to Timothy Healy's house and honked his horn. The Healy boy, as they called him, even though he was in his early twenties, was taking the death of his father and stepmother quite well. Very well. Not surprising since his father, Cyrus, had kicked him out of the house when he was eighteen, despite his handicap, and his stepmother, Helen, had evidently disliked him.

Gave him a motive, Clifton said. But after spending an hour with Healy, he'd dismissed him. They'd keep their eyes on the kid, but he didn't smell like a killer to the detective. More like an idiot savant.

Timothy came out a minute later. Seeing him walk down any street, you'd never guess he wasn't all copacetic upstairs. Looked as normal as they came. Sturdy, if a little pale. Only his bent hand showed anything abnormal. And maybe, if you looked hard, you could see that he held his mouth a little slack, but that might have been Luke's imagination.

Luke cleared the passenger seat and motioned Timothy to sit up front with him.

"Thank you, sir." The young man slid in. "Thank you." He protected his bad hand by keeping it close to him.

"Thank you for coming down. Like I said on the phone, the detective just wants to talk to you for a few minutes. You okay?"

Timothy looked at him a little cockeyed. "No, I don't think so."

"I'm sorry. Losing your father—"

"Not about that. I'm sad about my dad's death, sure. But . . . you know we were never so close."

"Still . . ." Luke could tell the poor kid was more torn up than he let on. Probably still in shock.

"You wouldn't hurt your father, right, Timothy? I mean, I know he wasn't nice to you—"

"No, he wasn't," Timothy said, turning back. "He wasn't nice at all. But you don't just hurt people because they hurt you. What kind of world would we be in if that happened all the time, huh?"

"Right. That's what I think. I know Detective Clifton already asked you all this, but I had to ask. For me."

"My dad was very mean to me. And I didn't like him so much. But how could I hurt him?"

"Exactly."

Luke backed out of the driveway, eyes on the mirror.

"They found Colt Jackson?" Timothy asked.

"How'd you know about him?"

"I knew it, Luke. I knew he was back."

"Back from where?"

"I don't know where, but I knew he was gone. And I know that you need him. You need him bad."

"You operating on some kind of premonition or something? Because that's twice now you mentioned things that you have no reason to know. Once the other night in your father's house about what the killer did, and now about Colt's sudden appearance."

"I don't know."

The thing that made Timothy so interesting to Luke was that he pretty much talked and acted like an ordinary man. Then suddenly he'd turn weird.

"You should tell this to the detective. Okay?"

"Sure," Timothy said. "Sure thing."

When they pulled into the station ten minutes later, two Walton police cruisers were in the lot. Steve was still out on patrol. They'd recovered Colt Jackson's cruiser from the doctor's driveway the morning after the storm, electronics fried by what seemed to have been a lightning strike.

*I*nside, Mark Clifton had set up shop in the chief's office—not because he seemed to give a rip about seniority, but because it was the station's only private space. At the moment he sat on the edge of a desk in the main room, arms crossed, staring at Colt and four strangers who all looked like they'd been through a war.

Clifton nodded at Timothy. "What's he doing here?"

"You told me to bring him in for more questioning."

"You're talking to ghosts, Luke. I said evidence, not questioning.

Last thing I need on my hands at the moment is a half-wit. Or two of them, for that matter. Just get his fingerprints, Luke."

"If you say so." There was no way Luke was going to give Clifton a "Yes, sir," especially after that crack.

Timothy was staring at Colt Jackson with a cold calculation that made Luke look twice. The room was suddenly silent.

"He won't stop until you're all dead," Timothy said.

"Luke?" Clifton stood. "Now. Please."

"Come on, Timothy." Luke took his arm.

"Did you see them in the sky?"

"Luke!"

"There's more." Timothy again.

"More what?"

"The whole sky is black," Timothy said.

"Let's go, Timothy," Luke said.

"Like a black sea." Then Timothy turned to the door and let Luke lead him out to the lobby and collect his fingerprints using one of the kits from the storage room. He gave Timothy some hand wipes and took him to the car before addressing him.

"Now what in tarnation was that all about? You were talking nonsense in there."

Timothy just stared ahead, eyes fixed on some distant object.

"Timothy?"

"Can you take me to the library, Luke?"

"I think you should go home."

"But can we stop by the library first?"

Luke paused, considering the phone call on his cell that requested he pick up Timothy Healy and deliver him to the station right away for a second round of questioning. Actually, it could have been anybody. He had assumed the number on the caller ID was Clifton's cell phone, but he really didn't know.

"Do I look like a cab service?"

"Please, Luke. It's important. I just need a few minutes in the library."

"What for?"

"There's something I need to see. Something strange in there."

There's something mighty strange right here, boy. What was weird was that Luke liked the guy. He wasn't sure why, but he really did.

"That's crap."

Timothy looked at him. "He's going to kill again," he said, as matter-of-fact as a parson announcing a potluck. "He's not finished by a long shot. And he's not in this alone. There's enough of them to wipe out this town with a single scream from their unholy throats. You don't know what you're dealing with here."

"But *you* do? Why you talking so crazy?"

"I know."

"Which makes the detective right about you being a suspect. Come on, man, you talking all crazy like this makes even me nervous, and I like you." He paused, considering his own words. Fact was, Timothy Healy could very well be their best suspect. Maybe he shouldn't like the kid so much. Maybe it was all an act, and under this gentle-looking package Timothy was a brutal killer.

He had an idea. Slowly, so as not to bring too much attention, he reached for the gun in his holster. "So what you say, Timothy? We don't have any reason to be afraid of you, do we?"

"You should be afraid of the truth."

Luke hardly heard the response, because he was too focused on his own maneuver. Knowing the safety was on, he tossed the gun at

Timothy as soon as it cleared his holster. The gun hit him in the gut and fell to the mat. Timothy looked down at the weapon.

Luke swallowed. "Oops. Sorry about that. I was just checking to make sure it was cool." *Cool? Crap, if Steve had seen that stunt, he'd be on the floor.*

Timothy blinked at him, then handed him the weapon. "Can we go to the library?"

"Okay. But just for a minute."

24

Wendy watched Timothy Healy being led from the room, thinking the man with the crippled hand was the only one aside from Colt whom she really trusted.

They'd stumbled out of the library and found the town exactly where it had been the day before, littered with branches from a bad storm but all there. And then they'd rushed down the hill to some pedestrian Colt called Stewart and learned that everyone had been looking for them since the storm had passed through. Figured they were dead.

A nurse had cleaned the cut on Nicole's face and applied more antibiotic ointment, but Pinkus still wore his old bandage.

None of them were very talkative. Including Pinkus, who kept pacing and scratching his head with his good hand. They were tired, they were hungry, and they were shell-shocked. But even worse, they were confused.

Detective Clifton, on the other hand, seemed to be taking their sudden reappearance with surprising calm and deliberation. He'd listened to their tale without expression except for a frown when Colt told him about his mother's death and the threat preceding it. But in the end, none of it seemed to impress him.

He walked over to a green chalkboard when they'd finished. "You're going to have to help me here, because I'm not understanding everything." He drew a line on the board, and a large circle over it. "This is the highway in; this is Summerville. Here is the doctor's house." He marked the spot with an X. "Are you saying that all this, including the highway in, was just gone?"

"I'm just telling you what we saw," Colt said. "Or thought we saw, or whatever. We came out the morning after the storm, and it was all gone. Which leads to the obvious question—"

"Except for the doctor's house and the library, where Jerry here came from," Clifton interrupted. "Right?"

"Right. But we saw what we saw. Or thought we saw what we saw. We had to have been drugged or something. You should be drawing our blood, not grilling us like suspects!"

"Suspects? Who said anything about suspects." Clifton glanced up at one the men he'd called in from his own town. "Get that nurse back down here and have her draw their blood."

"Yes, sir."

Pinkus waved his bloodied bandage in the air. "You think *this* is a figment of my imagination? Is that what you're trying to say? You want me to take the bandage off, man? He made me chew on it."

Clifton offered him a shallow smile. "I'm sure it's all been very traumatic. And I'm just here to uncover the truth. Catch a killer. Put the creep in the deep. No need to freak, Jerry."

The man was like no detective Wendy had ever seen, either in real life or in the movies. For all she knew, *he* was the killer. The only downside to finding that the town hadn't been wiped out was that it left a hundred times as many possible Reds walking around.

She caught herself. On the other hand, maybe there was no Red.

"Fair enough?" Clifton asked, drilling Pinkus with a stare.

"I need this thing changed," Pinkus said.

"I'll take that as agreement." He addressed them all now. "The fact of the matter is, I believe you. Not all of you, mind you. There's more than one lie floating around this place at the moment, but I do believe that some of you really do believe you woke up with the town gone, exactly as you say you did."

"Why wouldn't we all believe that?" Wendy asked.

"Because you don't need to believe that if you know what really happened."

"Which is?"

"What I'm trying to figure out."

"But what we think happened, didn't," Colt pressed. "That's obvious."

"That's right. It happened up here." Clifton tapped his skull. "I can assure you that the town wasn't wiped out by a huge tornado and buried in sand. What did happen was that a killer who calls himself Red came into town apparently gunning for Colt and killed four people in the space of one hour before going quiet. My job is to find him, and the only interest I have in you is to that end. You all apparently disappeared for a day. I think the two could be connected. Don't you?"

The nurse came in, set up a tray as they watched, and began the blood-drawing with Colt, who eagerly offered his arm.

"Which four did he kill?" Wendy asked. If everything had been imagined yesterday, maybe the murders at the ranches had been as well. "The truck driver?"

"We found the driver of the pickup truck shot through the shoulder but alive on Route 99 near his truck—"

"That was us," Carey blurted. "That's how we got here. My sister was bitten by a snake, and we were coming to find a doctor when the truck sideswiped us and took our van out. Wendy found us and brought us. That was us! Where's the van?"

Clifton eyed Carey and Nicole. "We had it towed. Snakebite, huh? I suppose you still have those marks."

Nicole lifted her foot, peeled off her shoe and sock. "Here. See, these two red marks." She pointed to the two pinpricks that had caused so much trouble the night before.

"Camping?"

"Yes. How did you know that?"

"Some campers west of here reported a brother and sister missing yesterday."

Carey stood. "Bob and Demitri. We have to tell them we're okay."

"Sit down. They'll be told."

"But we're free to go, right? No offense, but we didn't really come looking for a holiday in this dump. The sooner we get out of here, the better."

"You'll go when I'm done with you. Sit . . . down!"

Carey slowly sat.

Wendy thought Carey had a point. They all had lives to get on with. She'd lost not one but two days on her road trip to meet with her mother. Her car was still at the gas station, they said.

The nurse moved on to Pinkus, who eyed the needle but didn't argue.

"How long *do* you plan to keep us?" she asked as politely as possible. "I was on my way to Utah when this happened. I have family expecting me."

"Then I suggest you give them a call. I still have a few more questions."

"Why us?" Colt asked, crossing to what appeared to be his desk or at least one he shared. "And how did he get to us? For that matter, how is it even possible for all of us to share the same experience if it wasn't real?"

"Sit down, Mr. Jackson."

Colt looked at him, taken aback by the detective's cold tone. He leaned against his desk and folded his arms.

"Thank you. Now back to the question as to how many Red has killed." He paced as he fed them the information. "The shots to the pickup were consistent with those to Colt's windshield. We still don't know how he got into town." Clifton glanced across them all, and Wendy knew that in his mind they were all suspects. "He went on foot down First Street, shooting up the town, and when the chief responded, he was killed. Then Eli. After his exchange with Mr. Jackson, he escaped through the back alley and went straight to Cyrus and Helen Healy's house, where he reported his latest murder to dispatch. Helen Healy was subsequently found dead with several blows to her head."

"Blows to the head?" Pinkus said. "What about Cyrus Healy? How was he killed?"

"Did I say he was killed?"

Pinkus glanced at Colt. "I'm just saying . . ."

"We haven't released that information. How do you know he was killed?"

"We all know," Colt said. "Red told us he killed an old man and stashed his body in the shed."

"Red didn't actually talk to you yesterday, Mr. Jackson. Remember? None of that happened. So I have to ask myself, how do you all know things you have no business knowing?"

"You don't think we had anything to do with it, surely," Nicole said.

"That's what I'm here to find out."

"That's ridiculous," Colt said.

"What's ridiculous is this story you've laid on me."

Colt's face darkened. "I'm telling you, you're going to find drugs in our blood. Something happened to us. We may have imagined the town gone, but Jerry Pinkus lost his finger and Nicole's cheek is cut—none of that's in our minds. Red threatened us."

"Drugs. A strong pyschotropic like Fentanyl maybe . . . Could make sense. Doesn't really answer the question. Just raises more."

"What question?"

"Who did it? Why he did it? How he's doing it? How did he get the drugs into your system, for starters."

The nurse finished up with Wendy and moved to Nicole.

"That's where you should start," Colt said. "I'm telling you, you're going to find something in that blood."

"So start. Where could he have gotten to all of you at the same time?"

"House. Library."

"Both are being given a full forensic work-up as we speak. Anywhere else?"

"The ranches," Carey said.

Pinkus shook his head. "I wasn't at either ranch."

"Or the gas station," Colt offered.

"Right," Wendy said.

"Come to think of it, the gas station struck me wrong," Colt said. "There was a smell about the place."

Wendy nodded in agreement, remembering the same.

Clifton made some notes, then talked into a walkie phone. "Jim, get a team out to the Diamond Shamrock station. Sample the air, the surfaces. Get it all."

Wendy's mind was still tracking with the detective's body count. "That's four bodies."

"So far. But I don't think he's done."

Colt gave her a stoic look. It was hard to imagine that just a few hours ago, in their timeline, this man had been weeping on Nicole's shoulder. The stark difference between what had happened in the library and the plain reality about them here was unfathomable.

"Four bodies," she said.

"Unless you know of more." She let it go.

"Do you?"

"I think she's referring to the Stratford Ranch," Colt said.

"You're saying there's another dead body at the Stratford Ranch?"

"I don't know. It all depends if it all happened up here." Colt tapped his head. "If Stratford is dead, he's been killed with a lamp."

Clifton held Colt's stare.

"And there's the two bodies at the other ranch," Carey said.

"Two more?"

They told him.

"Wait here." Clifton stepped into the foyer, where the dispatcher worked, spoke to Becky, then returned.

"Highway patrol's a mile from the Stratford Ranch on Route 56. We'll hear something in a couple minutes."

If Clifton were Red, he wouldn't have to do that, Wendy thought. On the other hand, it's precisely what he would do to throw off any suspicion. If the detective had the right to suspect her, she had the right to suspect him.

He dismissed the nurse with orders to fly the blood to the lab in Vegas for mass spectral analysis immediately. They were looking for any evidence of any hallucinogenic and/or psychotropic drug. He wanted results within the hour.

"So what if they do find the bodies?" Pinkus said. "What does that say? Everything we imagined really happened? This is nuts, man, just plain nuts!"

"Did I say freak, Jerry?" Clifton asked. "No. Do you like mustard, Jerry?"

"I guess."

"What about mayonnaise?"

"What's that supposed to mean?"

"It's a question. I'm trying to get you to focus. So focus!" Clifton yelled the last word, and they started. "Do . . . you . . . like . . . mayonnaise?"

"Sure," Pinkus replied quickly.

"I thought so."

"What's that supposed to mean?"

"I think Pinkus is making a good point," Wendy said. "What happens if they do find those bodies?"

"Then we have to ask ourselves who killed those people."

The door swung open, and Becky stood in the frame. "They found Stratford in his living room," she said. "He's dead. His right hand is missing."

Clifton nodded. "Okay."

Becky stared at him, as if she expected more.

"You have something on the other ranch?" he asked.

"Um . . . no."

"Okay then."

She pulled the door closed behind her.

"As I was saying, now we have to ask ourselves who killed those folks."

"You can't seriously think we had anything to do with it," Wendy said. "We were just passing through this dump when that storm hit us. After what we've been through you want to pull this crap? And don't tell me not to freak."

"Pig."

Wendy wasn't sure she'd heard correctly. She looked at Carey, who'd said the word. Carey looked at the detective without showing any sign that he was either satisfied or regretful as a result of making the comment. Maybe he hadn't.

Clifton grinned. He walked over to the refrigerator, withdrew a sack, and walked toward them. He suddenly pulled a white object from the bag, swung it over his head, and smashed it down on a small wooden writing desk several feet from them.

Crack! The desk split.

Something cold sprayed Wendy's face, and she jerked back. The white lump on the desk rested on a thin crack that ran its length.

"What's that?" Pinkus asked. "A chicken?"

"The frozen chicken that killed two of the seven dead bodies we now have on our hands," Clifton said.

"Why'd you do that?"

"You like chickens, Jerry?"

"Was there a note on the body?" Colt asked.

They all looked at him.

"Red left us a large note that forced us back to the library. He also claimed to have accomplices. Did they find the note?"

The door opened, and two men in dark suits walked in. They nodded at Clifton, then eyed the rest of them.

"Find anything?" Clifton asked them.

"Yes, sir. We found the doctor. His body is hog-tied in a tractor at the Bridges Ranch, west of here."

Clifton frowned at Colt.

"There's more, sir," one of the suits said. "I suggest you see this for yourself. Maybe Mr. Pinkus would care to accompany us as well."

"Me? Why?"

The agent kept looking at Clifton without answering Pinkus.

Although both men were dressed and groomed like superiors from the big city, they seemed to report to Clifton. Or at least respected him.

"When did the FBI get here?" Colt asked.

Clifton ignored the question. "We're up to seven. I want full forensic workups at both scenes."

The tall, dark-haired man nodded. "That'll stretch us pretty thin."

"Then tell Bill to chopper more men down. I want this done by the end of day." He picked up the half-frozen chicken by its legs.

"Yes, sir. The press—"

"Tell the press to go put their heads where the sun don't shine."

"It's not just the press. The governor's office is screaming for something."

"You expect anything different?"

"It's not just the multiple homicides," the man said. He glanced at Colt and the others as if unsure he should continue.

"Say it," Clifton said.

"It's the fact that Cyrus Healy was killed. The man evidently has a past."

"Past?"

"No one's talking."

Clifton stared at them for a moment, none too pleased, then walked forward, chicken dangling from his right hand. He faced Colt. "You have anything in your trunk that doesn't belong there, Colt?"

"Like what?"

"Just asking."

"No."

Strange question. But then Clifton was a strange man.

"Take your car to the doctor's house and meet me there," the detective said.

To Wendy, Nicole, and Carey: "You're all dismissed. For now. Don't leave town."

To Pinkus: "Go with Colt and follow me."

"Why can't we leave town?" Carey protested.

"Shut up or I'll put you in a holding cell. You hear me? Don't. Leave. Town."

Wendy was regretting talking back to Clifton already. Whoever he was, he held far more power and respect than any small-town detective could possibly have. They said that very powerful or very smart people often tended to the eccentric side. Clifton fit the bill.

As the detective passed the taller agent, he dropped the chicken into his hands. "Give the governor's office this. Tell them it's a critical clue and to guard it carefully."

Colt followed them.

With a quick glance at the others, Wendy followed Colt.

"Pig."

This time it sounded like Nicole. Or was that a door hinge squeaking?

25

Pinkus dutifully followed Colt into his car. Clifton didn't react when he glanced over and saw Wendy climb into the cruiser. She darn sure preferred to go with Colt rather than with any of the others.

They all knew they would be going their own ways as soon as Clifton was satisfied that they weren't the killers here. Carey and Nicole would continue their strange relationship, Pinkus would go hide behind his computer in Vegas, and Wendy would head out to find her mother.

Colt fired the car. No sign of Nicole and Carey.

"Radio's broken, but at least the car works," Colt said.

"Who was that person who walked in?" Wendy asked.

"That's the Healy boy. I've never met him personally, but they say he's similar to a savant. Slow but very intelligent."

"He was saying he saw what we saw."

"Sounded like it. The fact that his father was one of Red's victims is what gets me. And the fact that the authorities seemed to draw some significance from it."

"You're saying the old man they found in the barrel was his father?"

"Yes."

Wendy didn't know what to make of that. The son of one of Red's victims had evidently seen the black streaks in the sky. Yet one more crazy thing to make her head hurt.

"Red isn't finished," Pinkus said. "That's what all this means."

"Not until we have him behind bars, he's not."

"At least we know he's not infallible," Wendy said. "We called his bluff and walked out alive."

"True." Colt frowned.

They drove in silence, gazing out at the town. Painted buildings with American flags waving at half-mast for the chief and Eli, streets lined with some grass but mostly scrub oak and desert rock, leaning telephone poles with birds lining the wires, little brick houses for you and me. Just another small Western town. But very much here, unchanged—as it had been last year, and the year before that, and the year she had been born.

They passed the gas station with her Honda Accord and now Carey's van parked along one side. A team of investigators, some in white suits, were there already. Clifton and company weren't messing around. Whatever was happening had someone bothered enough to go after Red hard.

"Surreal, isn't it?" Colt asked.

Wendy nodded absently. "I could have sworn this was all gone yesterday," she said. "I mean, if I fell over and knocked my head and woke up thinking I'd visited Mars, that would be one thing. But nothing like that happened."

"I know. I know, but . . ." He didn't finish. Evidently he didn't know but what.

"Five of us, Colt. We all saw the same thing. What's that called? Mass hysteria?"

"Maybe. We're all seeing the town now, right? Is *this* mass hysteria?"

"A thousand other people are also seeing this," she said.

"Exactly—that's my point. Only five of us saw the town gone yesterday. The other thousand saw the town not gone. So our minds were what? Fried?"

"Evidently."

"Right. End of story."

"No, not end of story. Not until we know why we saw what we saw."

"Mass hysteria," he said. "Like in one of those doomsday cults."

"Like one of those." He didn't know she'd grown up in a cult, but now that he'd surfaced the idea, she wondered if he was onto something. She considered it.

"Something just occurred to me," Wendy said. "We're a unique group. I mean all five of us shared similar experiences."

"Really? You think I'm unique?" He grinned.

"We all seem to have had terrible mothers."

"Speak for yourself," said Pinkus.

"What about you?" Colt asked her.

Here it was. She quickly decided to tell him the shortest of all possible versions.

"Me? I grew up in a cult that believed in strict isolation. I was severely beaten whenever I touched anyone outside the tribe, regardless of the reason. Cleanliness is next to godliness, but you can't see God unless you're clean. Oh, and the cult leader is pretty much God. Plenty of touching allowed there."

Colt looked at her, shocked. "How can anyone allow that?"

"How do they allow your mom to do what she did to you? My point is, all five of us were products of profound ideology, or the lack thereof. Extremes—parental extremes—that molded us into what we are."

"Which is?"

"People capable of seeing what isn't there."

"Or is there," Colt said.

"I remember plenty of times when the whole tribe 'saw' something together. A light from the sky, a dove, a horse once."

"Did you see it?"

"I thought I did back then."

"So you think this could all have been some kind of mass hysteria shared by a group of freaks with terrible childhoods."

That's where she was headed, but it didn't sound right.

"Too many holes, huh?"

"I don't know. I don't know much anymore. But we didn't imagine those dead bodies, and we didn't imagine Red. Hopefully whatever happened yesterday is past us."

Ahead, the doctor's house loomed. The black car carrying Clifton and the FBI agents pulled to a stop in the driveway. The detective got out and slammed the door.

"Talk about strange people," Wendy said.

Colt followed her stare. "The detective?"

"Mr. Chicken. Maybe it's him."

"Now you're talking," Pinkus said.

"Let's not jump to any conclusions," Colt said. "Given his reputation, it's hard to imagine him as Red."

"But it gives him the perfect cover. He's . . ." Pinpricks of light swarmed Wendy's vision. The world faded slowly to black. She sat perfectly still in the sudden darkness, willing herself not to panic. It would pass. This was the third time her mind had started to shut down on her, a condition probably brought on by stress.

But this time her breathing seemed to be directly affected. She felt smothered. As if she were in a claustrophobic cocoon. Her fingers tingled; her chest tightened.

She blinked. With that blink the day returned.

Colt glanced at her. "You okay?"

"That was weird. Everything went dark." Her voice wavered. "It's like . . . it's like I'm losing my vision."

They stayed quiet for a moment before he offered the only comfort he could.

"We're all under a lot of stress," he said.

"Yeah." Mass hysteria and all that. "You could say that."

*T*hey climbed out and followed the detective into the house, where a man with a thin nose and bushy eyebrows met them. He peeled off latex gloves and shoved them into the pocket of his white lab coat.

"Brent Chambers," he said, extending his hand. "Bill thought we could use some psychology on this and brought me in."

Clifton took his hand briefly and dropped it without shaking. "I know; I asked him to do it." His eyes were already scanning the house.

Chambers offered Wendy his hand, and she took it dutifully without making eye contact, Colt noticed.

Chambers waved them on. "This way."

Yellow tape cordoned off the hall with the stairs that led to the basement. The painting of Napoleon that had supposedly wedged the basement door shut was now on the wall—Wendy doubted it had ever fallen.

"At first look, it seems like any other unfinished basement," Chambers was saying, leading them down the stairs. Several technicians were gathered along the wall to their left. No sign of the blanket they'd slept on.

"They missed the room when they searched yesterday, but today we found a false door in one of the closets."

They entered one of the rooms Carey had searched for a window well during the storm. There still was no window well. But the closet was open, and the back wall had been pushed in to reveal a small room. Chambers ducked through and led them into what he called "the office."

No windows. Black-paneled walls with embedded speakers. A desk sat against the far wall, and on the desk a computer monitor. The chair was one of those ergonomic nylon mesh types designed for comfort at a high price.

Other than a computer tower that hugged the desk, there were no other fixtures in the room.

"A computer room?" Colt asked.

"A gaming room," Pinkus said. "The doctor was a gamer?"

He gawked at the desk, right side. Colt saw then what had stopped him.

A human finger perched delicately atop the wireless mouse, poised to press the mouse button. But this finger wouldn't be doing any pushing soon. It was severed at the knuckle.

"Is . . . is that . . . ?"

"Your finger?" Clifton finished. "You tell us."

Pinkus walked halfway to the desk, then halted, swallowing. "That's my stinkin' finger!" He whirled to Clifton. "We gotta sew it back on!"

"I think it's a bit too late for that," Chambers said. "You're sure it's yours?"

Pinkus looked at his bandaged hand. "It has to be."

Clifton stepped past Pinkus and withdrew a book from among ten or twelve that lined the computer desk's single shelf. *Dominating World of Warcraft: The Definitive Guide.* By Jerry Pinkus.

Colt scanned the other books on the shelf and saw that at least half of them were gaming guides written by none other than Jerry.

"You wrote those books?" Wendy asked. "So you are all that, huh?"

"I told you I was a gamer."

"You didn't say you were the definitive voice on gaming," Colt said.

"So what?"

"So judging by the mouse and your missing finger, the killer knows more about you than we do. What haven't you told us?"

"I told you, I'm world-class."

"Why would the good doctor here be interested in a gamer?" Clifton asked.

"Anybody seriously into gaming would have a book or two of mine." Pinkus shrugged. "I don't know. Maybe he knows about my medical connection."

Clifton's brow arched. "Medical connection?"

But Pinkus didn't appear eager to spill the beans.

"Way I read all this," Clifton said, motioning to the mouse and the finger, "you're now a prime suspect. This ties you directly to the doctor. We need a motive, but we'll find it. I suggest you start talking."

Pinkus shoved his bandaged hand at the desk. "My finger's there. You think I cut off my own finger?"

"Possibly."

Silence, ghost silence.

"Fine. I'll tell you," Pinkus said, "but you'd better keep your traps shut, 'cause I don't want this out."

Clifton's frown promised no such thing.

"Until about seven years ago, I really wasn't much of a gamer at all. I played, of course, but not anywhere near the level I play at now. I had frontal lobe epilepsy, FLE, a condition that wasn't conducive to extended game play, as you can imagine. But when I was eighteen, my parents, who were pretty much washouts—I won't bore you with all the details—volunteered me for a clinical study run by a research laboratory under the condition that they get fifty thousand dollars, which they did. Anyway, the test took care of the epilepsy."

He seemed finished.

"Frontal lobe epilepsy," Chambers offered. "That sometimes leads to interictal psychosis and schizophrenia. Dissociative behavior. You're saying that has something to do with your ability to . . . play games?"

"Maybe. They hooked me up to the world's most sophisticated interactive gaming environment, complete with electrodes on my skull, a visor with built-in 3-D screens, sensation pads on my fingers— you name it, they had it covered. I was totally immersed in the environment, a different world entirely. We're talking virtual reality on steroids. But it was the stimulation of the frontal lobe through microwave pulses that did it."

"Did what?" Wendy asked.

"Put me in, man. I mean *really* put me in." His eyes grew round, making him look like a kid at the fair for the first time. "They didn't expect it to cure the epilepsy. They were trying to find a way to induce a fully immersive hypnotic state in which the subject, me in this case, fully entered the gaming environment. They'd figured out that subjects with conditions like frontal lobe epilepsy could more easily disassociate if properly stimulated."

"This was how long ago?"

"Seven years."

"And it worked?" Colt asked.

"I spent six days under, if that's what you mean. The game and I were one. Something happened to me during that time, 'cause when I came out, I was a natural. I mean a serious natural. It's like I know what a game is going to do before it does it." He shrugged again. "I guess it worked."

Clifton walked to the severed finger, stroked it lightly, from nail to knuckle. "So you being some kind of epileptic computer-game prodigy clears you. Hmm? Is that what you think?"

"I didn't say that. It's not like I asked for any of this. All I know is that my parents were $50K richer and I came out of the experiment a natural game player."

"Without epilepsy," Chambers said.

"Pretty much. I have small seizures now and then, but they're in my control for the most part. Frankly, I don't mind them so much. I see them as a reminder of the conflict that we all face."

"What conflict?"

Pinkus hesitated. "Between worlds, you know. Everything. The old and the new. What tastes good and what doesn't. What's real and what's not." He looked at them each, as if unsure whether to expose himself any more. "Everything."

"How did you eat?" Wendy asked. "You were really in some computer game for six days without knowing it wasn't real?"

"They fed me intravenously."

"Interesting way to facilitate disassociation," Chambers said, more to himself than to any of them. There was a twinkle in his eyes, as if the lights had come on. "Find a subject prone to psychosis marked by ideas of reference, paranoid delusions, hallucinations—such as a subject with frontal lobe epilepsy—and stimulate the section of the brain from which the seizures originate, thereby triggering, rather than limiting, the synapses that fire to create a normal epileptic episode. Control the physical effects, the seizure, and harness the delusion."

He faced them. "It might work."

"Except how many people do you know who have frontal lobe epilepsy?" Pinkus asked. "Not too practical, if you ask me."

"But no complications?"

Pinkus hesitated. "No. Do I look like a complication?"

Colt thought he could argue to the affirmative.

Clifton set the book on the desk. "I want the room dusted for matches with the suspects. Anything from the library?"

Chambers shook his head. "We're just wrapping up inside. Nothing besides their prints, some hair. A few shoe marks that match. Clean."

"Suspects?" Colt asked.

"All of you."

"What about this being the same guy who threatened me in Vegas?" Colt asked.

"What of it? He's after you for being ugly in Vegas? He killed your mother then as a foretaste of what he planned on now? Is that the depth of your deductive powers? That doesn't help us determine *why* he wants you. And it certainly doesn't clear you."

"I realize you're some kind of genius, Mr. Clifton," Wendy snapped, "but I'm tired of your abrasiveness. We aren't killers, you know. Colt's right; this is impossible!"

"No," he said. "Instead, you woke up in a desert without a town. How stupid of me."

He turned for the door. "Please cooperate with the technicians. Don't leave town. I have some business to attend to and will be back early afternoon."

He left with a nod at Brent Chambers, who instructed Pinkus to stay put for additional questioning. "Please don't touch anything. I'll be right back." The man left.

"That went over well," Colt said.

"Not too smart, huh? I tried to keep to myself, I really did. But he's just so pigheaded."

Colt studied the finger. "None of this explains why we all saw the desert."

"Maybe it does," Pinkus said. "Mass hysteria you were talking about? It's a proven phenomenon. Maybe he did give us some kind of psychotropic drug that made us see—"

"That wouldn't explain how we all saw the same thing," Wendy said.

"Actually, the whole point of mass hysteria is the mass part. All seeing the same thing. And there are a number of hallucinogenic drugs that present common stimuli in everyone who takes them."

"Looks to me like he's after you more than us," Colt said, nodding at the finger "Some maniac you beat in a Call of Duty game?"

Pinkus chuckled nervously but didn't immediately dismiss the possibility.

Wendy walked to the desk, eyes fixed on the black monitor. "Do you think it's possible?"

"That we all saw the same thing?" Colt asked. "It's not just possible, it happened."

"No, worse. That we did something out there."

"At this point, anything's possible. Something happened while we were out there. We found the bodies Red killed; that wasn't mass hysteria. At least it's over."

"You're sure about that?"

"As sure as I can be," he said.

"And how can we be sure?"

"We find what got into us," he said, turning for the door. "Then we find Red."

26

It was noon, and Sterling Red was shaking again, worse than the last time; but then, it always felt worse than the last time.

He needed to stop shaking because he needed to slip in the back door of this yellow house he'd selected at random, do the nasty, and then slip away before they figured out who he was.

He paused by the back door and stretched his fingers inside the gloves, willing them to calm. The shakes were a bit like urination, he thought. You can only hold it so long in public, and when you finally get alone to let it go, the longer you've held it, the harder you go.

The shakes were a bit like hell, he also thought. Everybody deserves a little. Or a lot.

Blue-collar theology.

One of the players was actually starting to figure things out; that was both good and bad. What was shocking was that the rest were so clueless.

Most people were trapped in such a mundane understanding of all things small that they missed the greatest elements of reality. Not that he blamed them. If they knew reality the way he did, they would all have the shakes too.

That's why Sterling Red liked to eat mustard. The sharp taste grounded him, stung him, and reminded him not to become too comfortable like all the slugs around him.

This is what he knew about people: few ever set aside their sweet helpings of self-delusion to taste the bitter paste of truth.

He knew that most people deserved to rot in hell.

Not him, of course, he'd risen above them all. The world was simply jealous of his higher status and therefore banned his kind from fixing the rest or putting them out of their misery if need be. Indeed, he hardly belonged to this world any longer, which is why he had the shakes. Why he was so miserable. And why he loved to eat large quantities of the bitter yellow paste that he hated so much.

The fact that he was so witty about his own misery in no way lessened the bitter truth of it.

But he had hopes of helping these few who had betrayed him to face their own misery.

Red let one final terrible tremor shake his body; then he stilled his hands with practiced control. He found the door locked, but this didn't stop him or slow him down. He smashed the window with his elbow, reached inside for the dead bolt, and let himself into what appeared to be a laundry room.

He'd hoped for an alarm to add some excitement, but whoever owned this house evidently had consumed so many helpings of self-delusion that the thought of being a crime victim was no longer conceivable.

There were a dozen or maybe five dozen ways to take a life, and Red knew them all. But this wasn't about the way he killed. It was about *why* he killed.

It really was too bad that there was no alarm. If there had been an alarm, then the speed of the kill, not its inventiveness, would have been his challenge.

Red decided then to pretend that an alarm had gone off. Or better yet, to raise an alarm of his own. His pulse began to pound.

The shakes were gone.

Red marched into the home, making no attempt at stealth. Alarm first, that was the deal. That was the way he would show them it wasn't over, had hardly begun. That was the ugly truth he would cram down their throats.

The phone sat on the wall, one of those old ones connected to a cord. A yellow phone. He snatched the receiver off the wall and punched in 911.

"Emergency services, may I help you?"

"Yes, you may, Honey Pie. This is Sterling Red. I'm the one who's terrorizing Summerville. I'm at an old yellow house on Stitches Street, which incidentally is a bad name for a street. I chose this street because I thought it might be nice to stitch someone up, but now that I'm giving you the alarm, I won't have time for that. And tell them they'll find seven again, just like last time."

He paused. Took a long breath, flooded with the excitement of knowing that she was probably already on a second line raising the alarm.

"Did you get all of that?"

"I'm—"

He set the receiver back in its cradle.

It was a small house. An empty living room with an unused fireplace. An empty guest room with a sewing machine that was in the process of hemming some old jeans. A master bedroom with doilies on the dresser and lace for a bed skirt. A bathroom with a man and a woman hiding behind a shower curtain.

He killed them each with one blow.

Red walked; he refused to run. He couldn't leave without completing his ritual—must remind himself of how bitter it all was.

The mustard was in one of those glass jars, not the new plastic squeeze bottles that make getting the bitter paste out easy. Furthermore, the refrigerator was too cold, which made the condiment thick.

He leaned his head back and shook the bottle at his mouth, but the mustard refused to fall out.

They were coming. But he, like that stubborn mustard, refused to compromise an otherwise perfectly executed move. If they came before he left, he would have to kill them. He had said he would kill seven—he hadn't said only seven.

The mustard came out in a rush, flooding his mouth with a sour bitterness that filled him with satisfaction. He swallowed once but found his mouth still nearly full. For a moment he thought he might gag.

He dropped the glass jar on the floor, where it shattered. Then he spat the rest of the mustard out. Having lost his appetite, he decided that he would forgo any other condiments. Unlike the mustard, their sole purpose was for his pleasure anyway.

The sound of tires braking too hard reached him. They were here.

Red walked out the back, around the corner, hopped over the hedge, walked along the adjacent house, and peered into the street.

The first cop on the scene was Luke Preston, and Luke Preston had left his car running. It was an unexpected and delightful treat.

The shakes returned as soon as he slid behind the wheel and eased the door closed. The windows were tinted and no one would notice, so he let them ravage his muscles for a few seconds before leaving the yellow house on Stitches Street behind.

He would kill five more ugly citizens of Summerville after he dealt with Nicole.

Sweet, tender Nicole.

27

Nicole sat in the coffee shop, alone except for Daisy, the fiftyish waitress who talked more than she waited. But Nicole welcomed the distraction with a levity that had Daisy smiling. She'd had never felt so glad to be alive, so thrilled over a simple cup of coffee, so eager to take on the worst of life as she did now, having survived such a dreadful ordeal.

With nothing better to do after being swabbed by the FBI, she and Carey had found the coffee shop several hours ago and talked quietly while they ate.

Only two others had entered the shop all morning. Daisy talked nonstop about the crazy happenings around town that had all the folks scared to go out and live regular lives. That's what that scum of the earth wanted, she claimed. To terrify all the good folks into hiding out in their basements. Well, she'd die before she would give in to any psycho.

But Nicole knew Daisy was the kind of woman who would melt into tears if such a psycho walked into the shop.

A call from the police had found them about an hour ago, asking that Carey go down to meet with one of the laboratory technicians about some irregularities in his blood work or something.

Should've been back by now.

"Another cup, child?" Daisy asked, lifting the pot for her to see.

"No thanks. Any more and I'll drown."

"I hear you. So when you and your brother leaving? Roads are clear now."

"Hopefully this afternoon, but we have to get the van fixed."

"Shouldn't be too hard. You try Mike's Auto Repair? Known Mike Almond all his life."

"The police towed it to the Diamond Shamrock station. Carey's taking care of it."

She'd told Daisy about the snakebite and their van being side-swiped, but nothing about disappearing for a day. She didn't want to think about, much less talk about, all that craziness; she didn't care if it was denial.

"Well, if they don't get to it, you tell them you want it hauled over to Mike's. I could give Mike a call."

A fist pounded on the back door. Daisy wiped her hands on her apron. Tires squealed outside.

"Deliveries," she said. "Wasn't expecting the truck till later."

She walked through the kitchen toward the back. A black-and-white cruiser pulled up on the front curb and honked the horn.

Thank goodness, Carey was back.

Through the cruiser's front passenger window a hand motioned for her to come out.

Nicole dropped a ten-dollar bill on the counter for Daisy and hurried outside to the police car, now waiting with passenger door open. She didn't think twice about sliding into the seat and slamming the door closed. She just did it.

Then she looked at the officer and thought twice. The second thought was like a fist to the face. The man behind the wheel wasn't an officer—not unless officers in this town wore panty hose over their faces and dressed in jeans.

But Nicole didn't have time to understand who this was or what he was doing, because he hit her head with enough force to make the light fade. She felt her temples throbbing and her world slipping.

A strong odor slowly pulled Nicole from a nightmare about a man with panty hose stretched over his face. The image of his face was fleeting, and she couldn't see who he was behind the hose. Only those freaky eyes hidden in shadow.

She opened her eyes, immediately grateful that it had been a nightmare. The room was dimly lit. Yellow light. She sat up, head pounding.

"Carey?"

"Hello, Nicole."

She turned to the soft voice. Her abductor was sitting in an overstuffed chair, one leg folded over the other and swinging slowly. He twirled a knife in his hand—she could see that—but there wasn't enough light to make out his face beyond the hose.

Then she knew that the nightmare had actually happened to her. Red had taken her in a police car and knocked her out.

Fear came to her in a rush. Heat spread through her body. She tried to get up, but her head was spinning and pounding and she didn't seem capable of enough leverage to lift herself to her knees.

"Sit down, Honey Pie. You're not going anywhere for a while."

"What's happening?" she cried. "What are you doing?"

He stopped twirling the knife. "Don't tell me you still don't know."

"Know what?" she yelled, on the verge of tears.

"It's payback time. I thought I'd made that clear. And don't pretend you're not the worst of the lot. You make even me sick."

She looked around. Some boxes were stacked along one wall. A storage room?

"Are you still confused about that?" he asked.

"What do you want?"

"Let's start with what I *don't* want. I don't want a whining woman who asks me what I want when she knows good and well exactly what I want."

"But I *don't* know!"

"I want you to fess up. Play your part. You may have the rest of them fooled, but nothing slips by Sterling Red."

He suddenly grunted and began to shake. "See what you do to me?"

"Who are you?"

"I'm the beast, remember? Or have you changed your mind? Do you like mustard?"

For a moment she thought he sounded familiar, but then she remembered that the detective had asked Pinkus that question. She was drawing an association.

"I don't have much time, so I'll just get down to it. You failed to kill the ugliest, so I killed seven more. That means round two goes to me. I suppose round one went to you, which is why I'm here. But winning round one does not mean that you were clever or cute or anything but very stupid. Are you getting all of this?"

She didn't know what to say.

"Say yes."

"Yes."

"Good. As the winner of round two, I get to up the ante, so I have a little surprise for you in particular, just to show my appreciation for your beauty. Fair enough?"

"Why are you doing this?"

"Don't be so blonde. You know exactly why I'm doing all of this. Maybe I should wash your mouth out with mustard. You think I don't know what happened in your dear, sweet family?"

He knew?

"Maybe later," he said. "Tell them all that if they don't do what I've asked in another six hours, I'm going to up the damage. Seven more people will die in this lovely little town. And I won't quit until you do."

"You . . . you can't just walk around killing innocent people because you have some grudge."

"Grudge? Oh, it's much more than a grudge."

He took a steady breath. "Because you're so beautiful, I've decided to give you a break. I'm recruiting you. As my faithful recruit, you will destroy the ugly cop. Chew him up and spit him out and see to it that he remains dead."

"That's . . ."

He interrupted her. "Because you may find that the honor of being my recruit doesn't provide enough motivation to carry out that demand, I'm arming you with a lesser but often more powerful motivation. If you don't do what I've asked, I'm going to destroy your face and make you one ugly whore."

Nicole sat frozen.

"I thought that would get your attention." The man stood and walked toward the door.

"You . . . you can't do that," Nicole said.

"Won't, not can't," he said, opening the door. "Learn your words. I won't because you will. And if you won't, then I will. Do your face, that is."

"I won't!"

"Then I will," he said. Then he stuck the knife into the wall and bolted the door behind him.

28

olt was in Cyrus Healy's shed when the screen door into the house slapped shut and a Walton cop he'd never seen before hurried across the lawn toward them.

"Colt Jackson?"

"Yes."

"I have a call for you, sir." The man held out a walkie. "Luke Preston's been trying to reach you."

His radio was still out, and he hadn't brought a cell phone. Dispatch knew he'd brought Wendy out to the house.

He took the radio and saw that it was on a private channel. "What's up, Luke?"

"We found two more bodies," Luke said. "He told Becky we'd find a total of seven. I've been trying to reach someone who knows what the heck is happening, but you're gone, the detective is gone—"

"Slow down! Two more, are you sure? Where?"

"'Course I'm sure. I'm in the house, man! I've been here where he did 'em half an hour."

"Where?"

Luke told him. Colt felt his world spinning.

"The FBI are there. You called them, right?"

"Detective Clifton's here now. There's mustard all over the kitchen floor. The killer called the murders in himself."

"I'll be over in five minutes." Colt started to walk.

"He wants to talk to you," Luke said.

Detective Mark Clifton spoke in the familiar drawl that kept Colt guessing as to his intentions. "Mr. Jackson?"

"Yes, sir."

"Who's with you?"

"Wendy."

"I'm going to need you two love birds to have a full medical exam, immediately."

"Why? You found something?"

"A couple dead bodies," Clifton said.

"I mean in our blood. What did you find?"

"The mass spectrum analysis found a molecule that doesn't exist in the Aldrich Catalogue."

"I . . . I'm sorry, what does that mean? All of us?"

"All of your blood samples contained significant traces of an unknown drug that has the technicians in a bit of an eager state. It's a psychotropic. A hallucinogenic drug that is somewhat similar in parts to the molecule that forms LSD."

"The *drug* LSD?"

"Similar to LSD, but quite different."

"Which means what?"

"A drug of this kind would influence your perceptions."

"That's it, then." Colt stared at Wendy. "We were drugged."

"That's not really it, no," Clifton said. "It doesn't explain how all five of you had the same perceptions. It doesn't explain how the drug was introduced into your system. It doesn't give us a motive. It doesn't bring any of the dead bodies back to life."

Colt had been around his kind long enough to know suspicion when he heard it. "You can't seriously be suggesting that this implicates us."

"It certainly doesn't clear you. Would you be more likely to kill under the influence of a drug or stone sober?"

"That's not the point."

"He thinks we did it?" Wendy demanded. "Were we all drugged?"

Colt nodded at her. To Clifton: "Then keep us under lock and key and see what happens. Those two victims you have now are the result of us not following Red's demands. You lock us up and more will die. We may have been drugged, but this killer is real, Detective. He's following through on his threats."

No response.

Colt took a deep breath. At least they were making some headway, however impossible the idea of them being drugged sounded.

"So now what?"

"We look for a source. The library came back clean. So did the house. We're focusing on the gas station and the ranch houses. We need you examined."

"Fine. We'll meet you at the station."

"That would be acceptable."

Colt cut the connection. "Well, there you go. We're loony as a toon."

"I know what I saw, Colt. It was real."

"Was it? Then where is it now?"

She turned away.

"Come on."

They ran out to the front, slid into the cruiser, and left the curb with a squeal of tires. Took the next corner, then left onto Locus Street.

"He's killing others because of us," Wendy said. "And he isn't going to stop."

Her meaning settled on him like a black fog. "Because we are unwilling to kill the ugliest, he's killing others. Not us."

She didn't answer. That ugliest was him. They both knew it.

He wasn't sure which was worse—the rage he felt at Red's manipulation, or the hopelessness of his own predicament.

He took the car up to eighty and screeched through the turn onto First Street, where Sterling Red had first made his intentions clear.

"Colt?"

She was talking about his speed, he thought, but Colt's attention was immediately drawn to the police cruiser headed straight toward them two blocks away and flying fast like a suicidal magpie.

"Colt!"

He corrected his slide and swung back into his own lane.

The approaching cruiser swerved into the same lane, now on a collision course.

This time Wendy yelled. "Colt!"

"What's he doing?"

"It's him!"

He saw that the man wore a stocking over his head, and his first instinct was to speed up. Take Red head-on. Nothing made more sense to him.

His second instinct was the opposite. He had to save Wendy. The maniac was trying to kill them both in one swoop.

Colt locked up, torn between these competing impulses.

"Get over!" Wendy screamed. "Get over!"

She got his attention. He held the throttle down a moment longer, until the two cars were only fifty feet apart; then he jerked the wheel to his left. The other car did not flinch.

They passed in a blur, inches from scraping, but Colt saw the masked face staring blankly at them through its lowered window, as if the whole near miss had happened in slow motion.

He slammed on the brakes and slid half a block before jerking to a halt at an angle. Behind them, rubber squealed. Red was turning around.

"Why'd you stop?" Wendy demanded.

He couldn't tell her exactly why. His instinct was piloting them down this torrent of adrenaline.

Colt cranked the wheel and dug for his gun as the car spun around. Rubber smoke rose around them.

The police radio on the dashboard burped to life. "Come on, Ugly. You know you wanna do it. One more time."

Red was on the radio, the same private channel Luke had called him on five minutes ago.

The two cars faced each other a block apart, like two jousting champions, but riding about three hundred horses of raw power each rather than a single mount.

"Colt Jackson, you turn this car around right now," Wendy said as calmly as she could manage. "He's going to kill us."

"I don't think so. Can you trust me?"

She considered, knuckles white on the armrest. "What are you going to do?"

"Show him that two can play this game."

"What game?"

"Trust me."

204

White smoke suddenly boiled off the rear wheels on Red's cruiser. He was coming.

"I have a message for Carey," the voice on the radio crackled.

Colt shoved the accelerator to the floor. Wendy lowered her face into her hands and whimpered. The two black-and-whites roared for a head-on.

"Tell him that if he doesn't place a five-inch gash on his sister's left cheek, I'm going to permanently disfigure her. You have seven minutes to find her and sixty minutes to complete the operation."

Colt didn't so much swerve into the opposite lane as brake into it. He spun the wheels as hard as he could to the right and locked up the emergency brake when he was still thirty yards from the approaching missile. The maneuver would kill them all if poorly executed, but Colt didn't know how to do it poorly.

The back end of the cruiser swung left into the opposite lane. Colt released the brake and slammed down the gas again. The wheels continued their slide, all the way around so that the car now faced the same direction as Red's cruiser.

He surged forward. Then Red's cruiser caught them, doing twenty miles an hour their better. But twenty miles an hour didn't make for an impossible shot, and Colt had his gun ready when the other cockpit roared by.

"Stay down!"

Wendy needed no encouragement.

They shot as one, he into Red, Red into him, two shots each—*boom-boom, boom-boom*—the sight of Red in the freaky stocking, a black baseball cap backward, emblazoning itself into Colt's mind.

Twenty miles an hour doesn't make for an impossible shot. Twenty miles an hour at a cannon throwing lead back at you does.

They both missed.

Red slammed on the brakes and Colt shot by, already up to fifty miles an hour.

The radio crackled. "Five minutes, Ugly. In the library, no weapons, no other cops, no FBI. Nicole has the knife. Her brother's on the way."

Colt braked hard. Spun the car around. But the other cruiser was already two blocks away, flying in a direction that would take them farther from the library.

Wendy sat shell-shocked beside him.

Colt swore and pulled the car back around.

"I just told you I don't trust her, Colt. We should call this in."

He glanced at her. Maybe not quite as shell-shocked as he'd imagined.

"He'll kill her," he said. "We have to get to the library."

29

he citizens of Summerville had evidently heard of the bodies dis-covered today, Wendy thought, because the streets were empty, and it wasn't due to any approaching storm.

"We have three more minutes," Colt said. He was more frazzled than Wendy had seen. Understandable—she was as horrified as he by Red's threat to disfigure Nicole.

"Isn't this like giving into the terrorists?" Wendy asked. "Surely you can't be thinking that Carey should actually cut her."

"You suggesting Red do the job?"

"No. But . . ." But what? They both knew that Red would fol-low through. A cut was one thing. Whatever Red had in mind for disfigurement would be something far worse.

"So we were drugged. But everything we saw happened, actually happened. That's what you're saying?"

"Yes. We did what we did, just not the way we saw it . . ." He shook his head. "I don't know, it's crazy. All I know is that Red is real and when he cuts it's for real."

"At least it's over."

"The town's back. Red isn't over."

No other cars were parked on the street in front of the library when they roared by. Same with Doc Hansen's house. Deserted.

They drove around to the back and climbed out.

"Is it always this empty?" Wendy asked.

"He's probably already cleared it out; God only knows how. An evacuation order from the station. Seems to have access to whatever he wants."

"We don't know where she is."

"Come on!"

The front doors were locked, but Colt ran on to the north side, where a stairwell led to a green metal door. Open.

The library's basement was lit by the familiar amber lights they'd spent so much time with earlier. Piles of boxes and cages filled with newspapers ran along both sides.

Carey stood in the dim light, panting. "Nicole!"

A muffled cry came from their left. Then another cry farther down: "In here!"

Footsteps slapped on the concrete behind them, and Pinkus ran in, winded. He pulled up, staring at all three. "You're here!"

"Where'd you come from?" Colt demanded.

"He pulled up beside me in a police cruiser and said I had five minutes to get my butt here or he'd put a bullet through my head. I'd just finished with the cops."

Colt took in this new piece of information on the fly and hurried toward the sound of Nicole's voice. "Nicole?"

"Colt!" She was sobbing behind the door.

He flung open a dead bolt on one of the side storage rooms. Nicole flew out and threw her arms around him.

"It's okay." He patted her back awkwardly.

"I'm so sorry, Colt."

"Shh, it's okay."

"He told me to tell you that he won round two. And if we don't do it this time, he's going to kill seven more."

Wendy felt the blood drain from her face. "Oh no!"

Colt paced. "Round two?"

"We won round one," she said. "I . . . I don't know what he meant, but it's not over." She paced, nibbling a fingernail, eyes darting absently.

"We can't let that happen," Colt said. "As soon as we regroup, we're going out and we're getting as far away from this town as humanly possible. If we're not here to play his asinine game, he can't play it."

Wendy thought the idea actually made sense. As soon as Carey cut Nicole. She wondered when Colt was going to tell her.

"You're crazy," Pinkus said. "When are you going to figure out that you can't run from this guy? You go to the ranch and, *bam*, dead people. You take us out with those flak jackets and, *bam*, black truck. You refuse to do what he demands and, *bam*, seven more dead people. You can't run!"

"That last *bam* was you, Pinkus," Wendy said. "We refused to kill you. You're saying that was stupid?"

"No, but you can't just say we're splitting, for Pete's sake."

"Then what?"

"I don't know."

Thank you, Pinkus.

"I think we can make it," Colt said. "I think he thrives on the face-off. He didn't have to play chicken with us, Wendy. He could have just delivered his message over the radio without exposing himself. So what happens if you take the challenge away from him?"

"He gets super ticked and kills fifty people," Pinkus said.

"I think Colt's right," Wendy said. "He's toying with us. This is all for retribution. Revenge."

"But why?" Nicole asked.

"Because he's a psycho," Pinkus said.

"Because one or more of us did something to him, obviously," Colt said.

"Something none of us know about," Wendy said. "Or are unwilling to confess. Meanwhile, we're running out of time."

She exchanged looks with Colt in the dim light.

"He said we have six hours," Nicole said.

That was news. But Wendy was more concerned with the sixty minutes at the moment.

Colt broke the news to Nicole. "He told us that if Carey doesn't make a five-inch cut on your face with a knife he left, he's going to disfigure you himself."

Her mouth slowly opened in shock. "The knife?"

"He gave us sixty minutes."

"I won't do it," Carey said, walking in.

"Cut my face?" Her eyes glazed over. She reached up and touched her cheek. Slowly her look changed from one stunned into shock to one trembling with anger.

She swore bitterly. "That pig, that . . ." She caught herself, but the tone she'd used for those few words was filled with hatred that brought a chill to Wendy's neck.

"I won't do it," Carey protested. He crossed to Nicole and hugged her. "I can't."

Nicole put her hand on his shoulder, eyes distant. "Don't be a fool, Carey. You have no choice."

Watching this torment wrung Wendy's nerves. She felt violated.

"We can't allow this, Colt."

"You're right. But . . ."

That *but* again. But what? What alternative did they have?

"Why don't we run now? We have a car outside; we'll all fit."

"The last time we used that logic, we got people killed," Pinkus said.

"Stop it!" Wendy cried. "*You* stay and face him."

"And you run like a coward."

"Your bravery is at the expense of Colt's life!" She hated saying it out loud, but she couldn't stand this man whom she now thought must be tied in with Red. "I'll tell you what, why don't we finish the game we started? I'm sure Red would appreciate that. We'll kill the person we condemned last night, which would be you, Pinkus. Are you still so eager?"

She didn't wait for him to respond, because he wouldn't. She marched to the exit and grabbed the handle, knowing she looked foolish and not caring now. The door was locked.

She spun around. "You have a key, Colt?"

"It's locked?" He ran over and tried the door. "It's locked."

"What did I say?"

"Shut up, Pinkus," Colt snapped. He ran up a flight of stairs that led to the upper floor and tried the door. "It's locked."

"There's no other way out of here?"

"No." Colt swore.

"Pinkus is right," Nicole said. "You have to cut my face, Carey."

"I don't have to do any such thing. I won't."

"Then *he* will," she snapped. "You want that? I don't."

"We're fighting for our lives here," Wendy said. "Forget him."

"You said that before too." Nicole said. "But it's not you he's gonna disfigure."

She was right. But it still infuriated Wendy.

Nicole walked into the storage room and returned with a knife. She stuck it out toward her brother.

"Cut me, Carey."

"Nicole . . ."

"Take the knife. Just one cut, like he said."

"Nicole . . ."

"Cut me!" she screamed.

"We have time."

"Do it before I lose my nerve. Just the skin. Do it!"

Carey took the knife with a trembling hand. Wendy turned away, holding back waves of rage. Colt had vanished into the darkness. Pinkus sat with his knees pulled up under his chin. For a long time no one spoke.

When she looked back over her shoulder, Carey held the knife at his sister's cheek, shaking. Nicole was crying silent sobs, eyes clenched. Wendy averted her eyes again. The sobs suddenly grew to moans of horror, and Wendy thought Nicole had been cut.

"I can't, I can't!" Nicole wailed. "I'm sorry, I just can't."

Wendy turned around. Nicole backed into the wall. "Don't let him do it!" she screeched, hands on her face. Her cry was robbed of air, and she sank to her seat along the wall.

Colt hurried in from wherever he'd been hiding and slid to his knees beside her. With one hand he smoothed her hair; with the other he touched her cheek.

"Listen to me, Nicole. Just take a deep breath and listen to me. Everything's going to be okay. I promise you."

In the dim light Wendy could only see Colt from behind, none of his features. Watching him touch her so tenderly, speak so gently, she felt torn. Furious and empathetic at once.

Nicole leaned back and quieted.

Colt spoke again, very quietly. "We won't let anyone ruin your face. One cut will heal like you said. You'll be as beautiful as you always have been. One cut will hurt for a minute, but the pain will fade."

She made no objection.

"I'm so sorry, Nicole. I'm so sorry."

Red was right about one thing: Beauty wasn't simply in the eye of the beholder. It had a universal quality recognized by all, and Nicole had it. This was the beauty that Colt was speaking of. And by doing so he was honoring her.

"Okay," Nicole said.

"Okay?"

She nodded. "Yes, okay. Please hurry, Carey. Be strong for me. Just cut my cheek and let me cry."

Carey hesitated, then stepped forward with Colt's encouragement. She didn't move when he placed the blade against her cheek. He drew it down and she winced. Trembling, Carey dropped the knife and stepped back.

Colt pressed a white cloth against Nicole's cheek to stop the bleeding.

And then it was finished.

For a long moment no one spoke.

"Hey, guys?"

Pinkus was at the top of the stairs, bathed in light. Before him, the door into the library was open.

"I sprung the lock," he said. "I swear, I sprung the lock with a credit card."

Wendy felt her heart jump. "Let's go!"

Colt looked over at her. He seemed in agreement. Pinkus looked out the door, then down the stairs. "Okay. So where do we go?"

"To Vegas. We all get in my car, and we haul out of here before he knows we're gone." Colt faced Nicole. "What do you think, Nicole? Are you up for this? They'll take care of your face there, no problem."

"Okay. Let's go."

"What about the detective?" Carey asked. "We don't tell anyone?"

"No one. For all we know, he's one of them. We just go. Agreed?"

"Let's go," Wendy said, running for the stairs.

They went quietly, in single file, up the stairs. The library now lay silent, in dim amber light, sealed by the FBI after they'd wrapped up their processing. Colt led them around the tables, toward the large entry doors that opened with push bars that ran the width of each door.

He put his hand on the rail and looked back. "Okay, I'll look out. We go if I say it's clear. There's still police activity up at the house; we can't risk being seen, so we may need to wait."

He motioned directions with his hand, just in case there was any confusion as to where they were going. "Left, around to the back. Walk, don't run. Nicole, Carey, Wendy, take the backseat of the cruiser. Pinkus, you're up front with me."

He took a deep breath. "Ready?" He cracked the door open without waiting for their response. A thin shaft of light brightened the gap. He pushed it wider and froze. Wendy heard him gasp, faintly but clearly, which wasn't something Colt did at the drop of a hat. She imagined the cause: the killer leaning against a car waiting with a gun. Detective Clifton standing with his small FBI army, arms folded and frowning. Whatever it was, it couldn't be good.

Pinkus broke their silence. "What's the holdup?"

But then they knew, because Colt shoved the door all the way open and they saw what the holdup was for themselves.

The town was gone.

30

uke Preston sat against the desk he and Colt shared on occasion and watched Detective Clifton like a hawk. Steve had taken one of the Walton cops to get Luke's cruiser. They'd found it stashed behind the Sears building two hours after it had gone missing, no worse off for whatever wear the killer, assuming it had been the killer, had put it through.

Luke was here with the suits because of his direct involvement with the murder of Bob and Stacey Wrinkles, found dead in their bathtub by him. Eunice and Marty Ballworth had then been found dead on their back lawn. And a gardener, Pedro Gonzales, in the next yard over. Julie Gray and Mary Wolmak had been killed in their car after a trip to the grocer to stock up. That made fourteen. With no latent prints, hairs, or fibers left behind.

Luke had been nervous, even afraid, when it all started two days ago. But looking at that finger on the desk in front of Clifton, he was downright petrified.

Two other black-suited FBI agents and Paul Winters, the forensics guru they'd flown in from Vegas, paced or stood, all of them evidently as perplexed as Luke was.

"So they've gone AWOL," Clifton said. "Again."

"They can't just vanish," Winters said. "We're searching for Colt's cruiser as we speak. It'll turn up."

"The library?"

"Not there, not at the house, not anywhere in town that we know."

"Focus on the ranches. Check them all."

They all looked at him, as lost as Luke was. This business about the drugs had them flummoxed.

"So the drugs—"

"Forget the drugs," Clifton said. "That only tells us they were under the influence of narcotics when all this went down. We still have dead bodies and we still have a killer to catch. We follow the evidence."

He picked up the baggy that contained the half-mutilated appendage and looked at it under the light. "Human teeth marks, you say."

"Yes, sir."

"No other evidence?"

"Just the finger."

"Jerry Pinkus," Clifton said. "So at least that much of their story checks out. Takes a pretty strong stomach to chew on your own finger. Particularly if you're not forced."

"He was forced, though," Luke said. "Right? That's what you said."

"I said he claimed the killer forced him to chew on his finger."

"Exactly."

"Well, unless he's Red . . ." Luke stopped.

Clifton flashed him a look. "I said *if*."

"Right."

So Clifton thought Jerry Pinkus might be the killer. But he also thought the same about Colt Jackson, and Carey and Nicole and Wendy and the whole lot who'd gone missing. Again.

"The larger point is that we know this isn't just a bunch of hocus-pocus in someone's mind," Luke ventured. "It's real."

"Unless there's another explanation, it would appear so," Clifton allowed, then opened the baggy and pulled the bloodied finger out. At least the blood was dry, no longer oozing. He paced now, focusing on that finger, holding it in his right hand like a hot dog, as if he were considering taking a bite out of it himself. Instead, he set the finger back on the baggy and grabbed a tissue to wipe his hand.

They watched Clifton do his thing. He was feeling the air, smelling it, tasting it. Maybe *eccentric* was a good word, but *freaky* was better. Luke caught Winters's eyes, but the forensics guy averted his gaze. He probably agreed.

Clifton walked around the desk and glanced at one of the agents on his left. "What's the holdup on those files I asked for?"

"Jackson has a thick file with the department, but getting information on him before he attended the Academy is turning out to be a challenge. The rest are no better. Pretty strange group, if you ask me."

"That's the point. You tell them to dig deep. I have a feeling these five are more closely connected than they're telling us."

Images of Charles Manson flashed through Luke's mind. He couldn't imagine Colt as part of a cult. And no one was saying this had anything to do with a cult.

Looking around, his mind returned to thoughts of religious nuts. You never did know. Colt had always been quiet. The craziest people were always the quiet ones, withdrawn and shy until one day, boom, they snapped and walked into the post office with an M16. Or in this case, down First Street with a baseball cap.

'Course, Colt had been the one to take on Red. Unless that was some kind of setup, Colt couldn't be Red.

"We found hair that matched the suspects' in the basement of the doc's house," Clifton said, pacing.

Winters nodded. "Along the wall. It was consistent with the samples we took from the subjects this morning. I would say they slept there. The amount of hair we found suggests their heads had contact with the surrounding surfaces."

"No evidence of struggle."

"No."

"And nothing in the room with the computer," Clifton said. He was rehearsing details, not asking questions.

"No, sir. No evidence they were in the room at all."

"So the evidence supports their story."

"Yes, sir."

"Making the computer thing a red herring," he said. "Someone left the false door open, knowing we'd find the computer room and assume it had something to do with the murders."

"Evidently," Winters said.

"Okay, let's piece this together one more time. Up to one year ago, none of our five suspects lived in Summerville; then a cop with an enigmatic past transfers from Las Vegas after his mother is killed by a killer who fits the profile of our man. Colt's best known for his gun handling, not unlike our man."

"And his driving," Luke said. "He can tear the heck out of a set of wheels."

Clifton moved on. "Two of the strangers, Carey and Nicole, grew up in this region. They were on a camping trip nearby when they were conveniently introduced to a snakebite that forced them to the nearest doctor, who lives in . . . Summerville."

"So they are connected," Luke said.

Clifton ignored his comment. "The fourth of the five is a gamer who also lives in Vegas now. Drawn to Summerville by someone who supposedly doesn't show. That leaves Wendy Davidson, who was called by her mother to meet her at a time and place consistent with Davidson's passage through this town at this time. These five just happen to end up here on the same night and go missing? I don't think so."

"Too coincidental," Luke agreed, looking at Winters for support. The man nodded.

"All five go missing at the same time and reappear drugged with similar stories that do two things." He held up fingers as he counted. "One, they lead us to three more bodies. And two, they begin to lay a framework for an insanity defense."

Luke narrowed his eyes. First time he'd heard that.

"Possible," Winters said. "Nothing to prove—"

"I'm not interested in proving anything," Clifton said. "I'm just retracing the story as we see it and building plausible explanations for what we can't see. One of those plausible explanations is that all five are working together either as the killer or with the killer."

"They don't act like that," Luke said.

All three looked at him as if he had spoken out of turn, so he turned it into a question. "Right?"

"Right. They don't. That's been bothering me too." Clifton tapped his head. For the first time, Luke felt useful.

"You're saying they don't act like they're the killers because they don't even know they're the killers?" Winters asked.

It was all a bit confusing, but Luke thought he was starting to see the connection the detective was making. Five people with similar pasts, twisted somehow into becoming something they didn't even know they were.

"The drugs," one of the agents said.

"Delusion," Clifton said.

"So what we're saying here is that they're just doing without realizing they're doing it," Luke said. "That they actually created an evil man named Red, but it's really them doing the killing. And they do this subconsciously so that they have a common enemy who is the source of all their troubles."

They stared at him. Impressed, he thought. He could do this too. Maybe he should go back to school and get the education required to join the FBI.

Clifton walked to the refrigerator, pulled out an evidence bag, and held it up.

"What's that?" Luke asked.

"The rancher's missing hand," Winters said. "It was found in Colt's trunk."

Clifton eyed him. "This, green Luke, is the reason I don't trust anything they tell me."

31

N o!" Carey yelled. "I will not accept this! This is *not* happening." He stormed back and forth on the library's marble steps.

Wendy could identify, and in different company she might have reacted exactly the way Carey and Pinkus were to the utter absurdity of their predicament. As it was, they expressed her sentiments and then some. Anything she added would only be redundant.

"I am *not* crazy," he said, chanting it like a mantra.

Nicole sat on the steps and stared at her brother without emotion. Colt squatted on the sand and stared out at the desert. Even Pinkus wasn't reacting at the moment. They were all still swimming in disbelief.

"Is anyone listening to me?" Carey cried. "I don't have a clue what's going on, but I will not accept this any longer!"

"Oh, that will really make Red run and hide," Pinkus said.

"And you, shut up! I'm sick of your whiny, cynical yapping."

"In contrast to your words of brilliance."

Wendy looked at Colt. "Are you going to tell them?"

"What? Tell us what?" Pinkus demanded.

Colt sighed slowly. "They found traces of a hallucinogenic drug in all of our blood."

Carey looked up. "What?"

Colt told them what they knew, which wasn't much.

"So what we're seeing isn't real?" Carey said, staring in the direction of the town.

Pinkus retorted in his usual condescending tone. "Well, that much is obvious."

"Shut up, Pinkus. You can't tell me that everything I'm looking at right now, at this very minute, is just a hallucination. That's nuts!"

Nicole stared out at the desert landscape. "He's right. It doesn't make sense."

Wendy strode toward the depression made by the fallen power line. "Even if this is a hallucination, how can we see the same thing we saw last time?"

"Or the same thing everyone else is seeing," Colt added, hurrying up behind her. "Be careful."

She felt the static raise hair on her skin ten feet from the cable line. She stopped. One more step and he pushed against her.

"It's like a wall," she said.

Colt stepped past her with one arm extended, then backed up. "Exactly like before. This is more than just drugs. There has to be another explanation."

Pinkus stood beside them, gazing south. The town lay beyond the barrier, and if what they saw were the result of some hallucination, then the buildings were still there.

"It's almost as if someone doesn't want us to walk past this line and bump into the buildings," Pinkus said thoughtfully.

For the moment they were all on equal terms, united by the impossible.

Nicole and Carey stepped up to the line. "Can they see us?" Carey asked. "We can't see them, but if a cop car drove by it would see us, right?"

"They'd have to," Wendy said. "But for all we know, this isn't even the front lawn of the library. We're in a state of disassociation. What we do might be real but the environment could be totally different than we see it."

"Immaterialism," Pinkus said.

Carey frowned at him. "That's helpful."

"A philosophy that claims we can know for sure that what we see is real. You look at a spoon in the water and it appears bent, but is it? Or is something just making it appear bent? No way to know what's distorting our view of life."

Something about his words swept fear through Wendy.

Carey spun back and marched toward the library. "Your philosophy doesn't mean squat. Red's no hallucination."

"I didn't say he was."

"Then it doesn't help us, does it?"

"Shut up!"

"Knock it off," Colt said, following them. "None of us volunteered for this. The more complaining you two do, the less time we spend trying to figure our way out of this."

"And your solution is to hold hands in a circle and meditate until we wake up?" Pinkus said. "Good morning. Hey, lookie here, my finger's not missing. My face isn't cut to ribbons; my life isn't hanging in some madman's balance."

He looked at Nicole, who frowned. "Okay, not ribbons, but you get my point."

Huummmmmm . . .

They looked up as one. The black streaks in the sky again, of which there were now several dozen. Part of their hallucination?

Wendy suppressed a chill. The streaks didn't seem to be threatening, but nothing that made that sound could be good. And something that bothered her almost as much was the darkening gray along the red horizon. Like a distant dust storm, slowly encroaching.

Smog, Colt suggested, but this wasn't Los Angeles or Las Vegas.

"There, was that in our minds?" Pinkus asked.

"What if the town was destroyed by the tornado and we just hallucinated it reappearing?" Wendy said.

"Please," Colt said. "Don't encourage him." He bent to one knee, scooped up some sand, and shoved it in his pocket.

"What's that for?" Pinkus said. "Proof you were here? In case we ever get *out* of here?" But then he proceeded to shove sand into his own pocket.

Colt marched back up the steps. "As far as I'm concerned this is real." He reached the landing and spread his hands, turning. "All of this is real. That's the way we deal with it. Real sand, real sky, real flesh and blood, real killer. We don't understand it, but we respect it. Anything less and we're bound to die."

Nicole stood and walked over to him. The cut made her look like a monster. A beautiful monster, but a monster. And underneath it all Nicole was surely nothing less.

Easy, Wendy, you're judging. Judging a wounded woman who many be as innocent as the day she was born.

"For all we know," Colt said, "the town could be gone, devastated by the tornadoes, and we just imagined it all coming back. That makes more sense at the moment than this not being real. Either way, Red's here, so we have to be here." He pushed his forefinger at his temple. "Focus."

Nicole slid her hand into the crook of his elbow and looked out at the empty landscape. They looked like two adventurers gazing out at their new land. It was surreal. "Why hasn't he come?" she asked.

The question they were undoubtedly all asking. The police cruiser was gone. So was Pinkus's finger.

And so, it appeared, was Red.

"Because he isn't good and ready," Pinkus said. "Believe me."

Nicole shook her head. "But nothing's changed. He made that clear to me. If we don't do what he asked in a reasonable amount of time, he's going to kill another seven people. Then fourteen. He'll kill the whole town unless he's stopped."

Colt looked like a chastised puppy beside her. They all knew what Red was asking for. The ugliest. Colt.

"As long as he doesn't hack off the rest of my fingers, man."

Wendy glared at Pinkus. "He's killed a slew of innocent people out there on our account. He's promised to make it more, maybe many more, and all you care about are your fingers?"

"I don't see you offering up yours."

"You should be careful, Pinkus," Carey said. "He never said ugliness stops below the neck."

"Oh, you're the expert on Red now?"

"I swear, you two are about as juvenile as they come," Wendy said. But even as she said it, she realized that it wasn't them as much as it was Red. He was the one who was forcing them down this path. If it kept up, she wouldn't be surprised if they all turned into raving lunatics. They were being torn apart by competing interests as much as by competing realities.

The ugliest dies. But the ugliest is the strongest. The best man. The kindest, gentlest, quickest . . . She gave Colt, and Nicole, who had reattached herself to him, a quick glance. No one deserved to die, but she found herself wishing that if Red demanded anyone's life, it would be Jerry Pinkus's.

There, she'd thought it. She did not like Jerry Pinkus.

Or Nicole, who now had her hand on Colt's shoulder.

Nicole looked into Colt's eyes. "May I talk to you in private?"

"If you've got some idea, do share it, will you?" Pinkus said.

"Please, Colt," Nicole said. "It's important."

He nodded and led her into the library.

Wendy stared after them, terrified. For Colt. For her. For them all.

Colt wasn't sure how long he could sustain this charade, pretending to be strong when he felt so unraveled. The rest dealt with it by arguing in the desert with their lives in the balance. What else could they do? They'd talked about making a run for it, but they all agreed it was futile.

Nicole's hand pulled him into the shadows behind the checkout counter. She looked back at the door.

"Colt . . ." Her hand reached for his cheek. Touched it gently. A tingle chased by warmth spread from her fingertips. Her eyes met his own. She leaned forward and touched her lips to his.

He just stood there, because he didn't yet have the capacity to return her affection like a normal man might. His mother had messed him up. He knew that.

"Colt. We have to do something."

He followed her look to the door. "You're right. We can't wait forever."

"I'm afraid." Her voice cracked. "He took me, Colt. He hit me. When I woke up he was sitting there handling his knife, talking like nothing was wrong. He'll do it. He'll kill all those people just like he said he would. And then he'll kill all of us."

"I don't think he'll kill us. If he planned on killing us, he wouldn't bother hiding his face."

"No! He'll never let us go. I think it's me he wants. I'm so afraid."

He felt compelled to put his hand on her back. "This isn't a crime of passion; it's a sick, twisted game. But even people who play sick games play them by the rules. Otherwise there's no payoff."

"Colt, can I tell you something?"

He swallowed. "Yes."

"I've never really loved anyone before. I mean I have—I love most people. But I've never loved a man. Not in the way that I would gladly give myself for him. Not in a way that makes my heart pound and my palms wet. I've never been so interested in a man that I can't get him off my mind."

She faced him. Her eyes glistened with tears. The bandage on her cheek only seemed to accentuate her beauty. Those soft curved lips that had kissed him.

"I know most people don't think that. They assume I can have any man I want, and maybe I could. But I don't want that. I want a man with a heart of gold, someone who loves me for who I am under this skin. A man who would die for me not because he would gain from it, but simply because he loved me."

"That's good. I think that's the kind of—"

"Shhh . . ." She put her finger on his lips to hush him. "Don't say anything. I think it's a cruel twist of fate that I've found that man now. I think I'm falling for you."

Colt's face flushed with heat. She said it so simply, so stripped of seductive allure, so matter-of-factly, that he believed it might even be true.

And he had no clue what to do with this new information.

"Promise me one thing," she said.

"What?" he croaked softly.

"When we get out of this situation, *if* we get out of this situation, you'll leave this town forever."

"Why?"

"Because I could never live here. Too much has happened."

Colt couldn't mistake her meaning. He was overreacting, always overreacting, but he didn't care. He didn't try to stop the shaking in his hands. She took them in hers, then kissed him again.

Colt felt the shaking spread. It had nothing to do with her kiss. His body was reacting to the conclusion that his mind was now finally, finally reaching. He'd found meaning and purpose for the first time in his life, now face-to-face with the woman he always dreamed of.

He had found love in the very cradle of death. He knew Nicole couldn't be aware of the full depth of her words. But in the end she had spoken the purest, perfect truth.

And it made his bones shake.

"Colt!" Wendy's voice shouted from the front. Outside. "Colt!"

"Something's wrong!" He ran toward the door, flung it open, and pulled up sharp. The red horizon seemed to have darkened even further.

Walking toward them from the horizon, standing tall yet somewhat slouched at once, came Timothy Healy.

†he world according to Timothy was both absurd and simple. They had stepped past the skin of that world into this world, he said. They

had left the dimension of the plain and opened their eyes to another side of reality.

"Through drugs?" Pinkus demanded.

"Maybe. But more through Red." Timothy said. "He's letting you see it."

Colt stared at the man, now completely confused about what to think. On one hand, the presence of another person standing in the sand where grass had been not an hour ago was comforting.

On the other hand, the realization that his coconut was rather ripe made Colt feel desperate. They said some savants could indeed see things that regular people couldn't, but the rest of them weren't savants. So how could they possibly trust the opinion of this one person who'd essentially told them they'd fallen through the rabbit hole and landed in Wonderland?

"How can you see us? And can others see us?" Wendy asked.

"I can see you because I'm here."

"You're drugged?"

"No."

"When was the last time we saw you?" Wendy asked, testing him.

"In the police station."

"So you're real. And you're saying all this is real?"

"Of course."

"I believe it," said Carey. "This whole thing's spiritual. I've been there. I used to mess with the occult a little. This could really be real."

Pinkus scoffed. "This is chemically induced. Get it through your head, would you?"

"But it is real," Timothy said. "Most people just can't see it."

"And is Red real?" Wendy asked.

"Sure he's real."

"In both realities?"

"Sure."

"But . . ." Wendy seemed to run out of questions.

"If it's real," Colt said, "then it doesn't matter if it's spiritual. The point is, it's real. We aren't just seeing things. That's the point, right?"

"That's the point," Timothy said. "That and the fact that I can get you out of here."

"How?" Pinkus was now all in.

"You have to beat him at the game. He's bound by the same rules you are, right? You don't think you can just throw down Lucifer without a fight, do you?"

Colt blinked. Where had that last statement come from?

"What's that supposed to mean?" Carey, the newly confessed occultist, demanded.

"I think that's how he views himself," Healy said. "There's a connection between all of you and Red. There has to be." He looked around at the vacant desert. "Do you think the town really exists?"

"Of course it exists," Wendy said. "You just said you know how to get us out. Out of this place, not out of the town. If that's true—if you can really get us out of here and stop Red from killing—then tell us."

"The game," Timothy said, pulling her in with a soft stare. "The ugliest has to die."

"Literally?"

"Literally. Think of it in Red's way of thinking. The way Lucifer might think of it. They say he was the most beautiful once. But that beauty became his own downfall and he was thrown out. Now he roams the earth trying to drag down every last soul with him."

"How does he drag them down?" Wendy asked.

"That's the beauty of it, in his mind. He doesn't need to. They do it all by themselves. They mistake themselves as more beautiful than they are, when really they're as ugly as he ever was."

"Inner-beauty crap," Pinkus said.

"I don't think he sees the difference. Somehow you all touched off a nerve in Red. Now he's back, making you do things you never thought you were capable of. Showing you who you really are. Tell me I'm wrong."

"So how?" Wendy pressed. "How do we survive this mess?"

"You either play by his rules, or you hope Clifton puts an end to his game before you have to, which is immediately."

"Unless Clifton . . ." Colt trailed off.

"Unless Clifton is Red," Timothy finished. "Or, for that matter, unless any of you is Red. Or collectively, Red." He looked around at them, searching their eyes. "It might be better to just play by the rules."

"The ugliest has to die," Nicole said.

"Me," Colt said.

The enigmatic man who was part dumb, part a heck of a lot smarter than any of them, gave Colt a sly look. "Ten minutes ago it was you."

"You, then?" Carey asked.

"Maybe," Timothy said. "I have to go to the bathroom."

The comment was so misplaced that none of them responded immediately.

"That's great," Pinkus finally said. "Our crusader has to take a leak. Brings things back down to earth, don't you think?"

They entered the library as a troop, then Pinkus and Timothy headed to the bathroom to find some peace.

"What do you think?" Wendy asked, watching them disappear past the restroom sign.

"I think he's right," Nicole said. "The ugliest has to die. That's the only way out of this. Like you said, Colt, Red will keep his word because he's driven by the fact that this is all a game to him and games have rules."

"You think he wants us to kill him?" Carey asked.

What?

"Well, what else did he just leave us all here alone for?" Carey said. "He didn't have to spell it out."

"Is that where your mind is now?" Wendy snapped. "Figuring out who the ugliest is and how we can kill them? That's what he wants!"

"You have a better idea?" Nicole asked.

Colt wasn't sure he was hearing her right.

She blinked rapidly. "I'm not talking about Timothy, for heaven's sake. But he's right, this isn't going to end until—"

A scream from the far side of the library stopped her cold. Then another.

For a moment, none of them moved.

A dark form raced toward them from the far side of the room. Pinkus was screaming bloody murder, face white, mouth wide as a saucer.

He sprinted past them as if they weren't there, slammed into the door with a loud clank and bounced back. He slammed again but the door appeared to be locked.

Colt saw what had happened then, as Pinkus turned back. He was gripping his hands. Red hands. Bloody hands.

He'd lost part of another finger.

Nicole must have seen it too, because she gasped.

"Where's Timothy?" Colt yelled. "Pinkus?"

"He's dead! In the bathroom. He's dead!"

Colt sprinted toward the bathroom, gun in hand. He was careless—he knew that with each step—but he no longer cared. Rage had replaced caution.

He crashed into the bathroom and swept the revolver back and forth. Two stalls, two urinals, one window. Blood pooled on the floor and was smeared along the tile, up the wall, out the window, which was open to the bright, blank desert day outside.

Colt dropped to one knee and checked under the doors into each stall. But the bathroom was empty.

Red had killed Timothy Healy and dragged him out the window.

Colt stepped up to the windowsill and peered out. Blood mixed with footprints and drag marks in the sand where Timothy's body had been hauled. They ended ten feet away from the building, where Red had evidently hoisted the body and disappeared.

He turned and faced the bloody floor, head spinning.

There was only one thing they could do. If Red had intended to remind them of what they faced, he'd succeeded. There was only one way out, and that one way rested in Colt's hands.

He ran back out to the main library, saw that only Nicole remained. He pulled her toward the door.

"Colt? What are you doing?"

There was only one way out of this. Pinkus was whimpering as Wendy and Carey stuffed cloth around his hand in an attempt to stop the bleeding. They'd ripped the sleeves off his T-shirt.

"He's in there!" Pinkus cried, face white. "He killed Timothy and then cut me! This is unbelievable—I'm practically fingerless."

"You saw Red?" Nicole asked.

"Yes, yes, I saw him."

"I have a plan," Colt said. He tried the door again, but Red had locked them in. Nothing else made sense. The game was on.

"Can you stop it?" None of them were listening. "Can you stop the blood?" Pinkus repeated.

"I think so," Wendy said. "We need to get you up to the house."

"The door's locked!"

"There's a medicine cabinet in the kitchen," Colt said.

Huummmmm . . .

For a brief moment his vision darkened. All he could see was black, just like Wendy had described.

And then the light was back.

Odd.

His eyes scanned the horizon. Could he do this? He would have thought it would be Nicole down there, taking charge as the resident nurse. But her eyes were wide, and they were on him. Did she know?

"I have a plan," he said again.

This time they all looked at him.

"We have to give Red what he wants."

"He got what he wanted," Wendy said.

"You know that wasn't the deal. He said one of *us*. The desert's still out there."

"You?" Pinkus said.

Colt waited a long time before he answered. "Yes. Me."

"You mean kill you?" Wendy said, unbelieving.

"No," Nicole cried. "No, that's impossible!"

He spoke to Wendy, ignoring Nicole. "Do you know any other way to keep Red from killing more people?"

"Yes, stop him. Flush him out! Lock him up, cut off his tongue, castrate him . . . whatever they do to terrible people these days. We should be going after him, not killing you. That's absurd!"

Nicole grabbed his arm. "You can't talk like this. You can't!"

"Please, Nicole. Please." He closed his eyes, unwilling to slide back into those emotions now. He couldn't allow his resolve to waver. He looked at her pleading eyes. "I need you to do something. Everything will be fine; we'll talk in a bit. But right now I need you and Carey to take Pinkus into the kitchen and get his hand bandaged before he bleeds to death. You should bandage your cut too—it's all there. Please."

She searched his eyes.

"Can you do that? Pinkus is still bleeding."

"Why aren't you coming?" Nicole asked.

"I need to talk to Wendy."

"Why?"

"I can't tell you why. Please—"

"Tell me! Why do you—"

"Because she's the only one I trust to kill me," he said.

Nicole walked into the kitchen on legs that tingled from her heels to her hips, ignoring Pinkus's whimpering. Cold flashes kept descending her sides and back. Something was wrong; she could feel it like she could feel the floor under her shoes. She couldn't place it or understand it, but she'd felt this before, during one of those asinine Satanic rituals that Carey had forced her to sit through when he was fourteen and she was ten. A palpable sense that more was happening here than they could see seemed to swim through her.

Had Colt really just offered to die for their sakes? Was she capable of letting him do that? Certainly, they all were; she'd learned that long ago. But Wendy? Kill Colt? It seemed unthinkable.

And terribly hopeful.

If she were brutally honest, she didn't know who she really was. She knew what she'd done, and she knew the thoughts she'd dwelt on, and both were wicked enough to make the other four's blood boil.

But she still didn't know who she was. Was she redeemable from this mess called life? Could she ever pull herself from this terrible house of cards that had collapsed around her?

"If I get out of this one . . . ," she whispered to herself, entering the kitchen.

"What?"

She gave her brother a quick look, only now realizing she'd said it aloud. "Nothing. Find the bandages—hurry." She looked back through the front door as they entered the hall. No sign of Colt or Wendy.

"Is she going to do it?" Pinkus asked. "You gotta get me some pain pills, man. I'm dying here."

"Of course she's not going to do it," Carey snapped. But he offered no further explanation for his conclusion. He headed for the bathroom.

"Carey." Her brother turned back at the corner. "You should know . . ." A sharp blend of anguish and panic flooded her chest. For a moment she thought she would burst into tears. She held her tears back, but she couldn't still the tremor in her voice.

Carey stepped toward her. "What?"

"I think that if we don't do what he wants, he's going to take it out on me."

Carey's face flushed red. "I won't let that happen!"

He stood by the cabinet he'd opened, hands gripped into fists. "Never," he said, catching himself. "I couldn't live with that." But he didn't rush past her and into the library to make sure of things. He turned and reached for some bandages.

"He's losing it," Pinkus said weakly. His eyes jerked around the house. "We're all losing it. This is bad, man. Why aren't the cops here?"

"Give me your hand," she said.

"It hurts," he said.

"Enough!" She worked on his hand mechanically but quickly, torn by thoughts that were now so fragmented they left her with no thread to follow.

"Ouch, careful!" Pinkus said. "You're supposed to be helping me, not ripping my hand apart."

It took only a few minutes to bandage both Pinkus's hand and her cheek.

Nicole slapped the roll of white tape on the counter. "What happened to Timothy? You saw Red kill him?"

"You want the details? I was in the stall, I heard Timothy scream, and when I came out, he was gone and Red was standing in a pool of blood. It looked like he'd shoved the body through the window and come back for me. He grabbed my hand and cut me, then told me to get out. I got out. What did you expect me to do, box him?"

A shriek pierced the sudden silence.

They turned to the kitchen door.

"*Noooooooo . . .*"

"Wendy," Nicole said. She was the first to move.

Nicole could now hear her weeping in the main library. "I can't, I can't."

"Just do it!" Colt shouted.

Nicole brushed past her brother, ran past the checkout counter, slid to a stop beside the first cherrywood study table, and gasped. Wendy stood on the center table holding Colt's gun extended with shaking hands. Angled up.

Colt stood on the second-level railing, leaning out over the tables below. He'd cinched a hangman's noose around his neck. The other end of the rope was stretched to a large beam that ran high over their heads.

Nicole's heart hammered. "Colt?"

He refused to look at her. "Please, Wendy. You know what will happen if you don't."

Wendy was crying, face twisted in desperation. "I can't."

"Then I'll die slowly," Colt shouted. "Just do it!"

He was actually doing it.

"Colt, don't," she said, taking one step forward and stopping. "We'll find another way." She looked at Wendy. "You can't do this! You can't just shoot him in cold blood!"

Do it, Wendy. Pull the trigger.

"She can," Carey said. "She has to."

"She has to," Pinkus whispered. "He's going to kill half the town if we don't. She has to."

"He'll hurt you if she doesn't," Carey said.

"Do it," Nicole whispered in a voice no one could have heard. But Wendy looked at her, eyes flashing.

"Do it," Colt said. "Do it now!"

Wendy screamed. A loud thunderclap crashed in on Nicole's ears, and she flinched. Colt grabbed his chest with both hands, eyes wide with shock.

For a moment he teetered. Pulled his hands away bloody. His torso tilted forward, then swung off the balcony like a sack of grain. The hemp rope creaked under the weight.

Wendy let the gun clatter to the floor. She dropped to her knees, covered her face with both hands, and wept beneath the swinging body.

He's dead, Nicole thought. *Oh no, what have we done? He's really dead. He forced Wendy to shoot him by threatening to die a more painful death at the end of the rope if she didn't.*

Nicole walked over to her, eyes fixed on the dead body above them, torn by mixed emotions. She put her hand on Wendy's shoulder.

Then she began to cry with her. "I'm . . . I'm sorry for—"

"Get away from me," Wendy snarled.

She slid off the table and walked away.

Nathan Blair paced his sterile office, phone to his ear, scrambling for the right words. The moment he'd learned that Mark Clifton had taken charge in Summerville he knew there would be some explaining to do, but he'd never expected it so soon. Then again, they were up against an uncanny killer and it only made sense that an uncanny sleuth like Clifton would close in quickly.

Or there was that other possibility. That Clifton was so swift because he already knew.

"I'm telling you what I know. You'll have to ignore that fact that I waited this long to offer this information. I have my reasons."

Clifton's steady breathing filled his earpiece. "You knew we'd find traces of the drug at the gas station, in their blood. You can't expect me not to ask why you hid the facts. This isn't a game of cat and mouse."

"Frankly I'm surprised you put it together so fast. And it strikes me that you're about as cat and mouse as they come, Clifton."

That earned him a pause.

The number of people who feared the development of exotic designer drugs that could target specific areas of the brain's limbic system were too many to count. Any who had been through enough schooling to understand the extremely high probability that it was only a matter of time feared the day it would arrive.

The number of those who knew that day had in fact arrived could hardly fill his office. And now Mark Clifton was among those few.

"How does this . . . drug work?" Clifton asked.

"Lycergitide. Better known as LT by the drug jocks. Drugs are dumb. They only go where the body allows them to go. On the most basic level many can't pass the blood brain barrier that protects the mind from unwanted chemicals. On a much more advanced level some can not only easily pass but bind to specific molecules in the brain and affect them in specific ways. LT is based on a new synthetic protein that finds very specific molecules in the hippocampus, binds to those molecules to produce a very specific effect. Follow?"

"Not really, no. You're not telling me anything useful to my investigation. Tell me what starts it, what it does to the mind, and how it's stopped. Can you handle that?"

For a moment Blair imagined that Red had just spoken to him. Trying not to sound like Red, of course. It was more in the breathing than in Clifton's choice of words. Or it was more in Blair's imagination.

"Most of the mind's sensory perception—sight, smell, hearing, emotion etcetera—is contained in the rear part of the brain. Controlled by the limbic system. The hippocampus is like a relay center that directly affects the mind's sensory perception. Mind-altering drugs essentially trigger relays that result in specific perceptions. What the mind sees, for example."

"Too much detail." The scolding was measured but even tso it took Blair aback. "What they're seeing is controlled by this hippocampus; that's the point if I wade through your jargon. What the eyes see in the front of the head is interpreted by a wad of synapses at the back of the brain. This so-called limbic system."

"That's correct, yes."

"And someone has developed a powerful drug that creates very specific perceptions when introduced into this wad of synapses."

"Correct. It mimics certain psychotic experiences."

Clifton breathed.

"You know that there's more to it, doctor. You're not telling me everything."

"I'm not a doctor. I'm telling you what I know."

The phone hissed.

"So they're killing without realizing they're killing?"

"Possibly," Blair said. "Or they're being forced to play a game and Red is using LT to mess with their minds as they claim."

"Tell me how, Doctor," Clifton said softly. "How did a twisted, mustard-loving butcher like Red get his hands on this drug of yours?"

Blair sat in this chair and tried to sound as natural as he could. "That's the question we're facing, detective. Not you. Your job is to find the killer before it's too late. Before the world finds out what happened in Summerville. Leave the drug to us."

Two long breaths and then the line clicked.

Clifton had hung up.

Something about Clifton had changed, Luke thought. He'd told them that the drug had been identified but that it changed nothing. Business as usual. They had to focus on the killer. Where, what, when, why, how.

Still no sign of Colt, his cruiser or the other four. Clifton had ordered a house-to house-inquiry. They'd shifted the rest of their resources to lookouts on all roads leading to and from Summerville as well as on all main streets within the town. Red, whoever he was, had killed seven more people. That made fourteen. When this got out, the world was going to go ballistic.

Clifton didn't want anything getting out. Particularly not about Red or the five suspects who he seemed to think might collectively be Red.

"On the other hand, the severed hand does belong to the rancher. And we've confirmed the fingerprints at both ranch houses match the ones taken from the suspects earlier today. Wendy Davidson and Carey Swartz were in both the shed and the house at the ranch out west. We have Colt Jackson's prints at the other ranch. No prints for Nicole Swartz, but that matches their story."

Luke and Steve watched them, learning. It wasn't going to be every day that the FBI hung out in Summerville, Luke told Steve. They'd be fools not to soak it all up like sponges. It was clear by Steve's sigh that he didn't seem to understand the significance, but he was here just the same, watching brilliant minds at work.

"If they were the killers, why would they tell us they were at the scenes?" Fred Olrude, the agent presenting, asked.

"For two reasons, Fred," Clifton said, turning back. "One, only an idiot wouldn't realize the bodies would be discovered in short order anyway. By revealing them, they divert suspicion. And two, they're not entirely aware of what they're doing."

Clifton ran his fingers over a stack of folders that contained the five missing suspects' histories, newly delivered by the Las Vegas office. "There's more here."

Luke nodded. He'd already been through this with Clifton.

"I don't see how they could all be insane."

"Who said insanity?" Clifton asked.

"Um . . . You did. Well, I did. Drugs."

Clifton offered him nothing but a stare. "Like I was saying, there's something else. It turns out that at least four of them have met before. We're still digging out the details, but I think we'll find that there's nothing remotely random about these supposed victims. There's much more to your buddy Colt than you know."

Luke exchanged another look with Steve, then blinked at the detective. "What?"

"That's the question, isn't it?"

"But you know. So what do they have in common?"

"For one, people in much higher places than I are tracking all of this as if their lives depended on it. In their minds, none of us are safe. I'm as much a suspect as Colt. Or you, Luke. You like mustard, Luke?"

"Heck, no."

"We have a beauty queen, a jealous brother with questionable religious ties, a cult survivor, a world-class computer gamer, a whore's son made good, a redneck, and an idiot to choose from. You add up all the pieces, and my money's on the whorehouse boy."

"Who's the redneck?" Luke asked.

"You."

Oh. Better than the idiot, he supposed. Considering the detective was engaging him, Luke asked something else that had been digging at him. "Why didn't we see them?"

"You did," Clifton said.

"I saw Red shoot it out with Colt."

"Which only tells us that Colt wasn't being Red when you saw them together. There's five of them, after all."

"I guess . . ."

"Do I look like I'm blowing smoke, Luke?"

"Um . . ."

"Really. Back to why you didn't see them around town, estimated times of death on each victim match periods during which there was no active surveillance. At night in the storm, for example."

"It would be harder for them to go unseen now with the perimeter."

Clifton stared at him, and Luke wasn't sure if the detective was trying to get over how stupid his comment was, or chasing a thought he'd brought to the surface.

"The only thing that would be harder for them now is leaving town or walking down Main Street. It's dark. Considering the skill this killer or killers have demonstrated, they could kill a dozen people tonight and none of us would see a thing."

"That good, huh?"

"Better than good."

Clifton walked to the coatrack and pulled off a rain jacket—chance of rain in the forecast. He strode for the door. "I'm going out to clear my head."

Luke watched him go. People in much higher places than Clifton suspected Clifton. Now *that* was something to think about.

33

he thin and distant humming coaxed fresh sweat from Wendy's pores. She'd shut herself in one of the study rooms for the first fifteen minutes because she couldn't afford to interact with the others in the wake of the hanging.

A half hour had passed, she guessed, and she had begun to worry at the fifteen-minute mark when she'd snuck out and seen that beyond a darkness that had settled surprisingly quickly outside, the desert was still there.

No town.

No Red.

No Timothy.

She'd remained outside on the steps then, fighting off a tremor. Twice, Nicole had looked out and then retreated inside.

What was there to say? They'd done what Red had demanded and were still trapped. The only thing that had changed was the humming. It came more often, reaching into her small room through the vents. Each moan seemed to set her bones off, like tuning forks resonating with demons from hell.

This and the absence of any other change made her forehead wet. She stood and paced, knowing that she had to go in and confront the others. Red had lied to them.

Or had he? Surely he couldn't know.

A long, pure note floated on the night air from behind her. She turned around. The note flowed into a rich melancholic tune. Or was it a chant? No, it was definitely singing. If she wasn't mistaken, Carey was singing.

Wendy pulled the door open and stepped into the library, which was now filled with the haunting tune. She moved quickly to the counter and pulled up, stunned by what lay before her.

Colt's body hung by the neck, no longer moving. Directly below it, the tables had been moved back to make room for white candles that Carey had pulled from a dozen unused decorative candelabras around the library. Using books for lines, he'd laid out a large pentagram on the floor. Carey stood at the center, arms spread and low, gazing up at Colt's body, singing a dirge.

The absurdity of the scene kept Wendy in silence for a full thirty seconds as Carey sang. Pinkus was nowhere to be seen. Nicole sat at a table thirty feet from her brother, one leg draped over the other, hands folded in her lap.

He was singing in a foreign tongue, Latin maybe, but the sound of the crooning, together with the candles and the pentagram, had her at a loss. She'd never imagined this from Carey, even after his Satanic background comment.

The man had clearly cracked.

And then something else cracked. Some seam between heaven

and hell that released a distinct hum similar to the hum they'd heard all evening, only now *inside* the library.

Carey's song caught in his throat. He stepped over a candle and looked around. Silence.

He sang another note, walking slowly to his right, stepping over the books that made the pentagram. The hum came again, as if coaxed by his own song.

He stopped. The bone-chilling hum stopped.

Wendy trembled.

Sterling Red was bothered by the fact that the library's pathetic little lunchroom contained all that was required to satisfy the urges of a librarian when her belly grew empty, yet didn't offer what he most wanted. Yes, there was mayonnaise, and a healthy spoonful had eased his disappointment some. There was ketchup, plenty of ketchup, and he wasn't the only one in the building interested in ketchup tonight. He also found relish, hot dog buns, lettuce, even some sliced tomatoes in a little clear baggy.

But no nasty yellow mustard.

Instead, he kept his tremors to a minimum and held the knife with its sharp point digging into his forefinger, allowing the pain to keep his mind sharp. There would come a point when his friends—yes, he did think of them as friends, because friends were those who made your world happier, and Red had never been so happy—would start to figure out who he was, what he was, why he was, when he was. No, not *when* he was, because that much they'd already figured out.

He was now.

It had taken all of his skills to trap these five who had once plotted against him. Now he was successfully showing them that they were as black as he was Red. *Isn't that right, Timothy Healy?*

They were breaking. And still not a clue as to what he was asking them to do. The bodies would be stinking up the streets of Summerville before they even understood how much danger they were really in.

His friends should know better; they really should be considering what they'd done. But like most people blinded to the realities that governed the daily grind, they still hadn't connected the dots.

People who don't connect the dots are like fish that refuse to jump out of the water barrel and into a barrel of mustard, where they could hide from the gun waiting to shoot them. Stupid.

The analogy itself was also stupid, he realized, but his hunger for mustard had brought it on.

Ah, well. Time to get down to business.

Something whooshed through the air above them, like a bat's wings. A huge butcher knife flew at the rope holding Colt, severing it, and Colt dropped like a sack of rocks.

Wendy caught her breath.

He was halfway to the library floor when another object flew in and hit the carpet with a loud thump.

With that thump Colt came alive. He flexed his legs and spread his arms for balance, landed at the center of the pentagram, deftly reducing the shock of his fall, and stood up, seemingly no worse off for the wear of hanging from his neck for half an hour.

Nicole was on her feet with a gasp. Carey could only stare.

Colt ripped the rope from his neck and two additional loops that he'd snaked under each arm to support his body weight. He flung the rope at the ground and scanned the balcony for whoever had thrown the knife.

"What?" Pinkus exclaimed. "He's not dead?"

"But we saw you die," Nicole said, rushing over to him.

He'd promised Wendy that he could withstand the pressure on his neck as long as he swung rather than dropped. The ropes under his arms had taken 90 percent of the weight and had been well hidden by his shirt.

Wendy's gunshot came from a blank that he'd hastily fashioned from a live round. This, along with the help of some ketchup from the library's small lunchroom, completed the illusion. The important thing had been that the others couldn't check his pulse or breathing. Hanging fifteen feet in the air had accomplished that.

But Red hadn't fallen for his faked death. He'd known. How?

Wendy rushed up to him and stopped short of reaching for his neck, which had been scraped pretty raw. "You're okay?"

"I'll live," he said. "He's here."

"You *cheated*?" Carey demanded. "He's going to kill us for sure now."

"Thank goodness you're alive," Nicole said, reaching him. He let her touch his face. Wendy grunted with disgust.

"I heard you," Wendy said in a hushed tone.

Nicole looked at her. "What?"

"I heard you tell me to kill him."

Colt's eyes flashed. "Please." His tone dismissed her so convincingly that she felt powerless to continue.

Colt searched the book cases. "He's listening. We're locked in here with him."

Nicole stepped back and scanned the library. They all did. Colt was right, Red was undoubtedly watching them at this very moment. But they would be fools to look for him. He was the master here.

Carey walked over to the other object that had fallen. A book, Wendy now saw.

"He's going to kill us," Carey said, staring down. "He's not going to fool around." The thinner Carey's nerves grew, the more his behavior resembled Pinkus's.

Nicole began to pace nervously. "What's he want? Pick it up, Carey."

"What if it's booby-trapped?"

Nicole was suddenly on the verge of panic. "What do you think he wants?" She was sounding a bit like Pinkus herself. "Open it, Carey. Open it!"

Where was Red? He was watching them, wasn't he?

Colt reached out and put his hand on Nicole's shoulder, hushing her gently. If she had anything but his best interest in mind, Colt was clearly blind to it, Wendy thought.

Carey bent down and picked up the book. He examined its spine, then the cover.

"What is it?" Pinkus asked.

"A book."

"I know that. But he threw it, didn't he?" the gamer asked, searching the rafters. "What's it say?"

Carey walked to a table and put it down gingerly. They gathered around him. "Open it, Pinkus."

"Me? I have two bandaged hands, man. What's your problem? Just open it."

"You have two bandaged fingers. Your other fingers are fine. Open it."

"I don't know why you can't—"

"Stop it!" Nicole cried. "Just stop it! Open the book, Carey. He wants us to read something, so just read it!"

Carey took a deep breath, then glared at Colt. "This is your fault. You know that, don't you?"

Wendy stepped past Carey, infuriated by his cruelty. She pulled the cover open. *Moby Dick*. An old copy of *Moby Dick*.

She picked the book up and fanned through the pages. It opened to a crease made by a card. She set the book down so that the card stuck up from the binding. The killer had placed it there; they all knew that.

Nicole grabbed a candle from the floor, placed it beside the book, then withdrew the card with a trembling hand and leaned forward to read by the light.

"What's it say?" Pinkus asked. "Read it."

She did so in a breaking voice.

When I say kill, I mean make dead.

Do I need to spell it out? Then I will.

Colt will pick the black door with the white 6, or the white door with the black 7. You go in one, your pathetic lover goes in the other. One gets hurt, one gets some mayonnaise to celebrate.

Six hours just became six minutes.

34

ho's his pathetic lover?" Pinkus asked.

They all looked at Nicole, who was staring at the note.

"What's he mean Colt will pick?" she asked. "How do we know which door's the bad one?"

Pinkus looked around. "What doors?"

No door in sight had either a six or a seven painted on it. That left the study rooms behind the magazine section. Wendy ran around several tall bookcases, followed by the others. As soon as she rounded the long magazine racks, she knew she was right.

What had been plain doors the last time they'd been trapped were now gleaming with a black seven on white, and a white six on black.

Pinkus spoke for them all. "Man, that's really messed up."

"Shut up, Pinkus," Colt snapped. "We've got six minutes. Wendy?"

She stepped up beside him and spoke in a hushed tone. "Save yourself, Colt. I don't trust her. You hear me? She's not who you think."

He didn't respond.

"Please, Colt. The drug isn't the only thing messing with us here."

Colt glanced into her eyes.

"Love is blind. You're not seeing things the way they are. For heaven's sake, listen to me!"

"Not now, Wendy," he said. She knew then that Colt's greatest enemy was not some hallucinogenic drug. He was blinded by his own heart.

Maybe they all were.

Nicole walked up to the doors, stared at them as if trying to discern what secrets they guarded. "Can we open them?"

Colt crossed to the black door and pulled it open. Stuck his head inside. "Nothing but a table and chairs. And a door at the back. Maybe a closet."

He quickly checked the other room. "Same."

"So what do we do?" Nicole asked in a thin voice.

Carey faced the doors. His red face glistened with sweat. "It's a rigged game."

"He's behind the black door," Nicole said in a cracking voice. "I know he is. That's his color." She turned to Colt with pleading eyes. "Right?"

"She's right," Wendy said. "That's how I would see it. The white door is for the mayonnaise; the black door is for Red."

"You're running out of time," Pinkus said.

"Shut up, Pinkus," Carey and Wendy said in unison. Colt and Nicole were staring at the doors.

"Colt?" Nicole slid over to him and took his hand. Tears ran down her cheeks. "I think he knows. I think he's going to hurt me."

"Knows what?" Wendy asked.

"What I did."

"What did you do?"

Nicole didn't answer the question. "He's going to do something to me."

"Are we all agreed that the black door is the bad door?" Colt asked quietly.

Carey paced. "What if it's not?"

"I don't want any more what-ifs! Just pick a door. Which one do you think is worse?"

"The black one," Carey said after some hesitation.

Colt was going to take the bad door, Wendy realized. She couldn't persuade him any differently now. She'd said what she thought, and even that much could be wrong. Saving Nicole was the noblest choice. But Wendy could hardly bear the thought of this innocent man giving himself for a woman who had manipulated his wounded heart into such a sacrifice.

She was having a hard time not hating Nicole, who clung to Colt's hand, begging him with her eyes. She stepped up to him and whispered softly, wanting more than anything to reach out and touch him.

"You're a good man, Colt." She was aware of tears running from her eyes, and she made no attempt to stop them. "You're a very good man."

He looked at her with sad eyes, unsuccessfully tried to force a smile, then turned away and spoke to Nicole.

"We could be wrong," he said. "You know that, don't you?"

"Yes."

"Which door do you want me to take?"

Her face is now wet, and her nose is beginning to leak, and still she is stunningly beautiful, Wendy thought. Even with the two bandages on her face. She took one last look at the doors, sniffed, and faced him. "I'm sorry. I'm so sorry."

"Don't be. Just tell me."

She waited one second longer, tortured by her choice. "He's going to kill whoever goes into the black door," she said. "Will you take the black one?"

He nodded. "You go through the white door first. I'll go into the black room when you're safe."

She nodded. Like two sheep headed for the slaughter, they lined up in front of each door. "Go on," Colt said.

She held her breath, opened the white door, and, apparently seeing no danger, stepped in. The door swung shut behind her.

Colt walked to her door, put his ear against it, and listened for a moment. "You okay?"

"Yes," her muffled answer came back.

He walked to the black door, opened it, and stepped inside.

"This is messed up," Pinkus said. Then, "I didn't know they were lovers."

"They're not." Carey paced, clenching his fists. "I don't think I could take it if he messes her up."

Wendy heard the bitterness in his voice and might have pressed him if her own heart wasn't lodged in her throat. So far they'd heard nothing. *Colt, dear Colt, please tell me . . .*

The black door suddenly burst open, and Colt barged out, eyes wide. He ran for the white door, gripped the handle, and pushed.

"What's wrong?" Carey asked.

It was locked.

Colt slammed his palm on the door. "Nicole!"

No response.

"Nicole!"

"What's wrong? Tell me!" Carey screamed.

Colt spun around, back to the white door. "I found a jar of mayonnaise."

A high, piercing scream reached past the wall, then another. Both came from beyond Nicole's door.

35

"He's cutting her fingers off," Pinkus said. He stood with two hands bandaged in white, staring at Colt.

"Stop him!" Carey charged at the door.

"It's bolted," Colt said, but he slammed into the door with him anyway. They bounced off. Futile. Inside, Nicole's screaming continued.

Carey's eyes and lips were peeled back. He began to beat on the door with both fists, yelling incoherently at the top of his lungs.

Colt stumbled back, drained. He'd faced hundreds of high-stress situations as a cop, but he'd never been put through a meat grinder that cut as deeply as this suicidal game.

The fall from the balcony hadn't gone as planned. First of all, he hadn't expected to hang from his neck for thirty minutes. Colt had been on the verge of freeing himself when Red cut him down.

The thirty minutes had given him a unique perspective above it all. Below him, Carey was building his pentagram. Wendy had gone outside, Pinkus had pulled another one of his disappearing acts, and Nicole had sat quietly, watching her brother. Watching it all through half-closed eyes, Colt couldn't shake the feeling that they'd all been there before.

Not here, in this library, and not them as in these five people. But something about this wasn't new.

Something about the numbers six and seven.

Something about that hum they kept hearing.

Something about the blackening sky.

Something about Red's vengeance.

Nicole's screams intensified, burning him like acid in his bones.

Wendy stood beside him, looking away from him at the white door, tears in her eyes. Then her eyes met his, searched them.

"It's not your fault," she said softly.

But Nicole was still screaming, and that added up to fault in his mind.

The thing of it was, he wasn't even sure he *wanted* to be alive anymore. He was the ugliest. The ugliest didn't deserve to live. Was this the first time he'd heard that? No. What made his pain so great now was the pain of his lover. That's what Red had written, and those few words had been the sweetest Colt had ever read, despite being trapped between lines of death.

Colt has a lover.

He swallowed in horror. What a strange, unwieldy thought. His mother had had many lovers, but not one of them was a true lover. Not like Colt's. Not like Nicole. No, that was reserved for the son whom she had tossed out with her dirty linens.

Colt has a lover. And he was now powerless to stop her pain.

Dread rolled up inside his chest like a locomotive. His legs gave out and he sank to his knees, pushed down by Nicole's now-subsiding screams. He let his hands fall by his side and began to shake.

He'd always been so strong. They wouldn't be caught dead kissing the ugly one whose breath was undoubtedly as nasty as his face, but given a burglar on the loose, he would be the first one on their minds. He'd always been the strongest, but now he was . . .

His condition had nothing to do with epilepsy. He didn't know who he was, so he shook. Those torn between conflicting realities sometimes took to shaking. He knew this. He didn't know how he knew it, but he did; and the simple truth of it wasn't pushed aside by his overpowering emotion. Odd how such clear thinking could sometimes present itself during the most inopportune times.

Hummmmmm . . .

Wendy knelt with him, coming close again but not touching him. "It's not your fault, Colt. You hear me? It's Red's fault. There is no way to win. You know that."

But he didn't know that.

"Me," he managed, hating the gravelly emotion in his voice. He could say no more.

It took her a moment to respond. "I don't think that would stop him."

Nicole's cries stopped. Carey had settled to a hard pacing, hands at his face, wiping the sweat from his brow.

"Are you okay?" Wendy whispered.

"No," he said after a moment.

"Of course he's not okay," Carey said. "He just sent his *lover* to her death."

"But you cut her!" Wendy snapped. "Why would he hurt her?"

"Because we didn't follow his rule," Pinkus said. "We haven't killed the ugliest."

Wendy looked at the door. "Colt was trying to save her," she said.

"Of course he was," Carey snapped. "The good cop with everyone's best interest in mind."

"He went into the door you picked, you heartless pig! He went in like a lamb to the slaughter."

"I picked the black door first. But no, you all said white." Carey's face twisted. "She's my sister. And do you have any idea what he's—"

The white door swung open, and Carey spun around. Colt wanted to rush through the dark doorway, but his feet remained fixed.

The door's shadow came from one of the plug lights down low, a wedge that widened as it rose. They saw her tennis shoes first, limping forward.

Colt nearly rushed her then, but he still couldn't move.

Her jeans. Her hips. Then Nicole was out and looking at them in shock.

Colt's first thought was that she was wearing a mask. One of those realistic rubber ones that looks like flesh. But the mark that covered the right side of her face was real. It started on her forehead and caught the side of her nose, the edge of her lips, then circled back up to her ear.

His next thought was of a brand. A burned scar. Half of her face had been disfigured somehow. Colt hardly recognized her profile.

She began to weave, then cry. Any movement of her facial muscles had to hurt. Colt ran forward and held her up by her waist and her elbow.

"It's going to be okay," he said. "I promise, it's all going to be okay."

Nicole's face was swollen, not bloody. Whoever had done this had used a method that included ink, maximizing the mark while minimizing the actual tissue damage. A cross between a tattoo and a burn.

Permanent. No amount of surgery would ever return Nicole to her former self. Red had made her ugly.

"Is it bad?" Nicole asked. "How bad is it?" Her eyes glistened in fear, and they were looking over Colt's shoulder, at Carey. She was asking Carey.

"Is it?" Her mouth opened in a silent cry; her eyes closed. She was getting her answer.

Colt glanced back. Carey was slowly backing away, horrified. How could he? Colt felt a rush of fury. How could this loving brother retreat from his own flesh and blood? This sister whom he had been only recently ready to defend to the death?

"Carey," he snapped. "Give me a hand."

Carey hesitated, then came forward. He was in shock, Colt thought. Not responsible for his actions.

"She needs to sit down," Wendy said, running for a folding chair. "Is it just your face, or did he hurt you anywhere else?"

But Nicole wasn't listening to Wendy. She was fixed on her brother. And she was hearing his unspoken words as if they were being screamed.

Colt looked back at Carey. "Stop it!" he yelled.

Carey blinked. Looked at him with questioning eyes.

"Help us."

Finally, the brother stepped up and tentatively put a trembling hand on his sister's shoulder. But it was too late. Nicole's eyes were closed, and her shoulders were shaking with silent sobs that quickly grew to a guttural groan so terrible that Colt felt alarmed.

Then, abruptly, she stopped.

Nicole shrugged them off and walked away, looking for her reflection in one of the glass windows. She seemed strong enough, an encouraging sign. But her mind would have to adjust to this new reality. Colt had always been ugly. He didn't know what it was like to lose such a treasure as she had.

Then Nicole found her reflection in a section of window properly lit. She stood motionless for a few long seconds, then grew totally silent. At least she didn't seem to be in terrible physical pain. But still . . .

He neared her and spoke softly. "It's okay, Nicole."

Without warning she whirled around, grabbed a chair behind her, and slammed it against the window with all her strength. The thick bulletproof glass bounced it off harmlessly, out of her hands and across the carpet.

"It's not okay!" she cried, turning on Colt. "Stay away from me."

"No . . ." Colt took a step forward. "You don't mean that. You're hurt, but—"

"Stay away!" She backed up, then sat hard in another chair.

"We should get some salve on—"

"He said if I do anything to heal it, he'll burn the other side," she said in a low voice.

She'd changed, Colt realized then. Shock, yes, but maybe more. Clearly the seeds planted by her mother when Nicole was very young hadn't been entirely uprooted as Carey claimed. They were flourishing under her skin, hidden by a beautiful face.

But now that face was gone.

Until she realized that he would love her as much without such a beautiful face, she would stay in retreat. Colt had no intention of letting her do that. But neither did he have a clue how to change her perceptions.

He glanced at Wendy and saw that she was staring at him as if it was he, not Nicole, who'd just been wounded so deeply. Given how Nicole had made him respond earlier, Wendy must think he was a fool.

"Wait here," he said and ducked into the room with the white door.

To all appearances it was identical to the other study rooms in the library, but Colt was more interested in the closet door. If that's what it was.

It wasn't. The door led to an unfinished hallway, sided by open walls with pink insulation stuffed between the two-by-fours on one side and the concrete foundation on the other. The ceiling was lined with plumbing works.

A gurney rested at an angle on his right. Beside it stood an adjustable bedside table.

Colt walked to the table and picked up a heating torch. The syringe Red had used to prepare her face lay on its side, but any branding iron or tattooist's inks were missing.

He considered following the access way but decided doing so in the dark would be pointless. Some light spilled in from the door behind him, then quickly faded to darkness in both directions.

He replaced the plastic protection cap back over the syringe's needle, wrapped it in a cloth that lay on the tray, and shoved it into his pocket. He took the torch with him. They represented the best physical evidence he'd found so far.

"That's what he used?" Wendy asked when he stepped out of the study room.

He nodded and looked at Nicole. "Did you see him?"

She turned her eyes from the torch in his hands. "No."

What was he thinking, showing her the instruments of her torture? He set the torch on the shelf.

"We have another problem," Pinkus said.

Colt looked at the gamer, who'd been unusually quiet for the last few minutes. Carey was still staring at his sister like a deer caught in headlights.

Pinkus spoke what they were surely all thinking. "We still haven't killed anyone."

"Thanks for the reminder, Pinkus," Wendy said. "You're so thoughtful when you put your mind to it."

"I'm not saying we *should* kill anyone. He's not killing us, after all. He's taking it out on the town."

"You're saying you're okay with the wholesale slaughter of a town? And you know sooner or later he'll get to us."

Pinkus eyed her. "You're right. There's only one way to win. He's a gamer. Gamers play by rules."

Timothy Healy said something similar, Colt thought.

"We have another issue," Pinkus said.

They looked at him.

"Colt's no longer the ugliest."

Nicole didn't even flinch.

Colt hadn't made the connection, but it screamed through his mind now. Red hadn't just taken Nicole's beauty; he'd made her the ugliest. Which clearly meant that Red wasn't after Colt alone.

"How can you discuss all of this so casually?" Wendy demanded of Pinkus.

"Because those are the cards we've been dealt. Someone has to be practical here."

"And if you were the ugliest, would you be as practical?" she shot back.

"I'm not, though."

"Inside, maybe you are, Jerry."

"Look," Pinkus said, undeterred. "We know he's obsessed with physical beauty, and we know that Nicole is now the ugliest person here. That's just the way it is."

A buzz lit through Colt's mind. The punk was right. Man, he was absolutely right.

"He wants us to admit what all of us are really thinking," Pinkus continued. "What everyone in the world really thinks. Well, I'll say it! Ten minutes ago I thought Nicole was hot. But Red changed that." He looked at Colt and quickly added, "Not me, man. *Red.*"

Colt walked over to Pinkus, grabbed him by the collar, and shook him hard. "If I hear one more word about this, I swear I'm going to make *you* the ugliest. And if you think anyone here would have a problem killing you, you're not connecting with reality. Do we understand each other?"

"I'm just saying it like it is," Pinkus said.

"And I'm not interested in hearing it," Colt snapped. He gave Pinkus a parting shove and turned back.

"He's gonna kill us all because you refuse to face the truth," Pinkus said. "That's the whole point. You said it yourself: he doesn't want to kill us; he wants us to admit who is the ugliest and kill that one person."

"Shut up!"

Carey's voice crooned through the library. Only then did Colt realize the brother had slipped away. His song wasn't haunting or melancholic as it had been before. It was now the sound of raw anguish and bitterness, swelling from the center of the library.

For a moment they all stared at each other, letting Carey express what they were all feeling. Oddly comforted by it. But then Carey abruptly dropped the tune and began to scream obscenities. At Red. At this whole inhuman farce.

"Wait here." Colt moved, alarmed by the possibility that Red had shown himself to Carey.

They found Carey standing at the center of his pentagram. Half the candles had burned out, but the rest gave off enough light to cast an amber hue on his face, which was tilted to the ceiling, eyes clenched.

Shouting, screaming, spit flying. Cursing black, perhaps in reference to the black door or evil. The black arts. Spewing words of hatred toward a long string of things, but the only one Colt locked onto was Nicole.

He was cursing Nicole.

"Stop him!" Nicole cried. "You have to stop him!"

"Carey!" Colt shouted.

But Carey wasn't listening.

"Carey!"

"Colt?" Wendy had walked away from them toward the front. But his attention remained on Carey, who had become so erratic and filled with rage that they all had reason to be concerned. Maybe fearful.

"Carey!"

"Colt!"

"Not now, Wendy. He's going to—"

"The door's open!" she said.

Carey stopped. His last few cries echoed through the library. They turned as one toward Wendy, who was staring through the front door. Daylight streamed in.

"Is it . . . ?" Pinkus began.

Then they were all running for the front door.

They piled up behind Wendy. Stumbled out. And stood on the library's marble steps, gawking.

The town was back.

36

Wendy traced her hand over the chair's hard plastic arm rest. It felt perfectly real.

She stared at the light-board next to Clifton as they waited for the doctor to present his findings. The Summerville clinic was a small building with three examining rooms, a waiting area that contained six green chairs that could stand reupholstering, a lab hardly large enough to house the X-ray machine with chipped black paint that filled one whole corner, and the conference room in which they now sat.

Real, all real. None of this could possibly be figments of her imagination.

They'd been out of the library for three hours but it felt more like three minutes. Colt's cruiser had found its way out to a shack a mile east of town—how, no one knew. What they did know was that it contained traces of the drug everyone kept referring to.

Wendy was slowly coming to terms with the idea of the drug coursing through her veins, never mind that she didn't feel it in the least.

SKIN

The minute they'd flagged down a cruiser and made contact with Clifton, Colt had demanded with as much urgency as Wendy had seen from him yet demand that they have their bodies X-rayed. Drugs could not account for the experience they had just endured, he insisted. Not a chance.

Clifton had taken their sudden reappearance with his usual ease, almost as if he'd expected it.

The medical work-ups had taken two hours between all five. In addition to a light rash on her left calf and lower back, Wendy learned that she had blisters on both heels, from her trek into the desert, she assumed. Otherwise she was in good health. This is what she knew so far.

She glanced at Colt who'd returned Clifton's eerie silence with his own for the last hour. He was watching her, she realized. His eyes lingered on hers. Wendy wasn't sure what constituted imagination any longer, but if her intuition were still functioning properly, there was more guilt in those soft eyes than she would wish on any man.

She wanted to reach out to him, tell him that it was okay. None of this was his fault. But she felt like a specimen under a microscope in the small room. All eyes seemed to be on her.

She continued to focus on Colt, tried to encourage him with a gentle smile, but feared it looked more like a grimace. His eyes shifted into space.

She swallowed the lump in her throat and looked at the agent who stood like a tree at the door. They were being treated like prisoners. Someone should say something. They should be defending themselves.

But there was no defense that could possibly satisfy Clifton. They'd told him everything, naturally, and he didn't doubt that they believed every word. But they alone had been witnesses to the events they ascribed to Red.

The door suddenly opened and agent Winters escorted Dr. Hurtz, who'd been flown in during their absence.

"Sir?"

Clifton nodded. "Go ahead."

The doctor crossed to the light-board, hit a switch that lit a sea of fluorescent bulbs behind the smoked glass, and began shoving eighteen-inch square negatives into the clips that lined the case. The plastic flapped with each expert thrust as they went up.

Five negatives. Five heads. Four angles of each. A white tab at the bottom labeled the X-rays: Jackson, Davidson, Pinkus, N. Swartz, C. Swartz.

Wendy sat up and studied the pictures of her skull. Bones and brain. Surreal.

Dr. Hurtz cast them an accusing glance, pulled out a telescoping pointer, and tapped the first negative labeled Jackson. Colt's head.

"You'll notice the cerebral cortex—"

"No jargon, Doctor," Clifton interrupted, eyes fixed on Colt. "Tell us what you found. We don't have all day."

"Yes, sir." He tapped a BB sized sphere of white at the base of Colt's brain. Wendy had seen the spot and assumed it was a marker on the film. It didn't look anatomical.

"All five subjects have some kind of implant in the same proximity of the hippocampus." He walked down the line of X-rays and tapped each. "Without removing them we can't be sure of their purpose, but they appear to contain an electrical charge consistent with a transmitter." He paused, studying his own handiwork. "Or a receiver."

Colt stood abruptly. "That's it!"

"Sit down, Mr. Jackson," Clifton said.

He sat, eyes pinned on the light-board. "That's it, right?"

The detective ignored his question. "Can you tell how long have they been implanted?"

"That's just it. There's no sign of any wound to the tissue surrounding the implant that I can find. No scarring on the skin, no bruising or trauma. I would say a long time."

"How long?"

"Very long."

"Please, be more specific."

The doctor hesitated, tapped his palm with the pointer. "It doesn't follow any logic, but what I see suggests they've always been there."

"You mean since birth."

"Something like that. Yes."

A very long, heavy pause. Wendy felt suffocated. There was a mistake here, that much she knew beyond the slightest doubt.

She reached behind her head and felt the skin at the base of her skull. No bump, no scar, no pain. Nothing.

Pinkus jumped to his feet. "Then cut it out," he said.

"Sit down—"

"You have to cut it out! Don't you see what's happening? That's how he's triggering it all! You take it out and he can't touch us! Cut it out!"

"Impossible," the doctor said. "Not without a complicated surgery. Even then it could be risky."

Wendy stood and walked to the light board. Clifton made no attempt to stop her. The small white dot on the film wasn't solid, she saw. The faint outline of thin lines curled through the center.

"I thought you said this was all drug-induced," she said, searching for a way to dismiss the implications of the black and white image in front of her.

She'd directed the statement at Clifton but Hurtz answered. "I've never seen anything like this, clearly, but it's plausible that a device could control sensory perception if a . . . if the right drug . . . one with a receptor spectrum that mimics particular psychotic experiences . . ." He stopped. The links to his logic were all there, he was just having difficulty actually making the connection between the theoretical and the actual, Wendy thought.

She blinked and searched his blue eyes. "But this is all possible, that's what you're saying."

"Theoretically." He looked at the implant in the X-ray of Pinkus's brain. "Maybe ten years from now. Not now, not so soon. Everyone knows it's only a matter of time before ordinary sensory perceptions can be precisely mimicked to duplicate ordinary experience. You think you see a red Mustang when you're actually looking at a white wall. They've done it with owls . . ." He was speaking quickly, almost to himself.

"Drugs do it now all the time on a less specific plane. Synthetic proteins that bind to specific molecules in the brain to create a desired effect. Even seeing particular images or colors. Perception is controlled by electrical impulses and chemical reactions. Our response to those impulses is conditioned through experience . . . it's all possible, of course it is. But . . ."

"Why do we all have this?" Carey asked. He was still in a sort of stupor. "I mean . . . This means we're messed up." His hands were trembling.

"This means were royally freaked," Pinkus said.

Nicole shoved her chair back into the wall, eyes piercing, unflinching as the metal chair crashed against the wall. "Get us to a hospital!" she bit off. "Fix this." She jabbed a finger at her cut cheek. "Fix *this*!" Then slammed her palm on the table. "Fix all of this, you filthy pig! Now!"

Clifton looked as cool as an unfired six-gun barrel. "Thank you, Doctor. You can leave us."

"I should take this film to—"

"Leave!" Eyes still on Nicole who faced him, red-faced and unblinking.

The doctor made a quick escape, closing the door on the small conference room. Clifton stood next to Wendy. One agent at the door.

Wendy walked to the back of the room, turned around. Crossed her arms.

"You have two choices, Miss Swartz." The words rolled off Clifton's tongue with what could only be pleasure. His eyes sparkled bright. "You can do exactly what I say without the slightest hesitation. Or you can buck me. I suggest the first option. Buck me and the chances of you surviving the day will fall dramatically."

"You're threatening me?"

"No. I'm stating the obvious. This fancy doctor-talk might have you feeling all victim like, but the fact is, Red is still out there. Or in here. He's made good on his threats. I doubt he intends to stop because we've found a little round BB in each of your skulls."

"Go easy," Colt rumbled. "She's been through more than any human being—"

"You're just going to sit there and let him bully me?" Nicole snapped at Colt. "Stop this!"

It was the last straw. Wendy stepped forward. "Back off! What's your problem? This man offered his life for you!"

"And look where it landed me!" Nicole pointed a shaking finger at her burned face. "This wasn't supposed to happen!"

"Sit down, all of you!"

Wendy turned to Clifton who had palmed his gun. It hung from his hand, aimed at the floor.

Wendy sat. Nicole cursed and righted her toppled chair. The blackness, as Wendy had come to think of her spells, smothered her world for a few seconds, then faded. They were increasing in frequency. And growing worse.

"Thank you. I realize that you think I'm just a smidgen insensitive, but being cuddly isn't part of what I do. I flush out the truth. Stop injustice in its ugliest form. Isn't what this is all about? The ugliest?"

For a second Wendy thought Red, not Clifton, was speaking to them. She let the thought fade.

"You aren't being entirely straight with me," he said. "That much I know. Truth is being hidden."

Colt seemed to have recovered from Nicole's attack enough to bring his mind back to the room. "What makes you say that?"

Clifton walked around the table. "The evidence we're gathering is starting to tell a story that doesn't match yours."

"What evidence?" Wendy asked, as eager to make sense of this as he. "We just found evidence that clears us."

"Your pasts. The fact that each murder thus far was committed at a time when one or more of you were unaccounted for or near the victim. The fact that you all conveniently go missing at night. Our time, that is. You then emerge the following day with the kind of stuff normally reserved for true-blue psychos. Like Red."

"Those X-rays explain our behavior," she said.

"They explain *why* you might be disturbed, but not *what* you do. The way I see it, the drugs have nothing to do with your so called manipulation. They just change your perception. The skin of what you see, so to speak. Not the choices you make. Interesting, I admit—we'll let a psychologist issue a paper on this when it's all done. But none of this helps me stop Red."

Clifton lifted his gun in line with Wendy's head. "I could make the same threat here and now. I could say, 'Kill the ugliest or I'll put a bullet in your head.' It doesn't matter if you're in this room or in the desert. Doesn't matter what you think you see around you; the real question is who's the bad guy and how do you beat him?"

Wendy stared at the black hole at the end of his barrel, wondering what it looked like to see a gun fired head on.

"We get the point," Colt said. "Put the weapon down."

A bead of sweat ran past Clifton's left eye.

"Clifton . . ." Colt warned.

The detective spun his gun once and dropped it home in the holster at his side. "Will the real Red please stand up."

"The minute he gets around to chewing your ear off or something," Pinkus said, "you'll get around to believing us. For all we know, you're as nuts as you think we are."

Clifton drilled Pinkus with a blank stare. "Comments like that don't inspire confidence. Just a heads-up."

"Have you checked the blood on the bathroom floor in the library yet?" Colt asked.

"It's Timothy Healy's. So is the blood on your shoes. Blood but no body. Where's the body, Colt?"

"Red took it. If we knew, so would you. Tell me you didn't find the other bodies exactly as we said you would. Tell me you've found any evidence to suggest we've done anything other than what we've said."

"Well now, you haven't told me about all the bodies, have you?"

"Of course we have," Wendy said.

"All. Even the latest?"

"The five you found this morning?" Colt asked.

"Very good, Mr. Jackson. So you did know we found five more in addition to the two before you went missing. That's fourteen total.

What I need is for one of you to tell me how you could have that information. None of us gave it to you."

"I was guessing," Colt snapped. "He said he'd kill seven more. Clearly, he did."

"Quite a guess. No physical evidence leads to any Red character outside of this room."

"What about the syringe I took from the library?"

"We'll know soon enough."

"Where did you find the bodies?" Colt asked.

"You know, don't you? Someone in this room knows." Clifton watched them carefully. "Two older couples on the east side. A gardener in another backyard. All five were killed about two hours ago, while you were supposedly playing games in the library. Why didn't you tell me about the hand we found in your trunk? It belonged to one of the victims, a Mr. Stratford."

That was new. "You really believe I would be so stupid?"

"Depends. Why were you digging holes behind the doctor's storage shed, for example."

"We told you about that. We were checking to see if the town was under the sand."

"Really. People who bury bodies do that kind of thing. That's not the half of it, Colt. We've got more. Much more."

No one reacted.

"You need to know that more law enforcement than any town this size has ever seen is about to descend on Summerville. The word is out. We have a killer who's managed to make every serial killer in United States history look like amateurs by comparison. The governor has called up a special unit of the FBI to move in; they'll be here within twenty-four hours. The FBI has five agents here now, and that will soon double. We're stalling the media, but a reporter managed to snake past our perimeter last night, and he got enough of the scoop to bring on the big blowout. Any of you ever been through a blowout?"

Evidently not.

"That's what I call the point when the media hounds get ahold of something, doesn't much matter what, and they blow it out of proportion. A thousand people die in Las Vegas every year, but it's the one that they decide to cover day and night that gets the world screaming. This has the makings of the biggest blowout we've yet seen. And this time, it would be hard for them to blow it out of proportion."

He frowned. "I don't care who this Red fellow is; he's not going to be able to move come morning. A confession now, before your hands are forced by all that coverage, will go much further with the judge."

"I think Pinkus is Red," Carey said.

"And why's that, Mr. Swartz?"

"For starters, he told us not to trust you."

"Really? Why would you tell them that, Mr. Pinkus?"

"Because he says you aren't real," Carey said.

"Is that so?" Clifton walked over to Pinkus and slapped him on the cheek, hard enough to make his face flush red. "Does that feel real, Jerry?"

A knock sounded.

"Come."

A technician entered, pulled Clifton to one side, spoke under his breath, gave him a small box, and then left.

"Did I happen to tell you how the victims we found this morning were killed?"

"No," Wendy said.

"They were poisoned. Not the typical poison, like cyanide, but a very rare poison, as of yet unidentified by our people. A helicopter delivered a sample to our lab in Vegas an hour ago. We do know that the poison paralyzes the victim's muscles, the heart muscle being the last to go. The killer evidently burned the victims' hair off with a torch after administering the poison. We found the torch that did the burning on a shelf in the library, where Colt said he put the one he found."

What was Clifton saying?

"Did I tell you how the poison was administered? It was injected using a syringe." He pulled the syringe Colt had found from the box. "This syringe, actually. It matches the victims' puncture wounds. Unfortunately, there are no fingerprints belonging to anyone we know named Sterling Red. The only prints on this syringe belong to Colt Jackson. A rather condemning bit of evidence, don't you think?"

"That's ridiculous—"

"So's your effort to cloud the issue by acting this way."

Clifton rapped on the door. Two uniformed officers came in.

"Lock them in a holding cell. No one releases them unless I say so."

"Yes sir."

37

"Now we're finished," Pinkus said, running his hands through his hair, oblivious to the bandages. "Totally. That fool hit me, you see that?"

"You're safer in here than out there, Pinkus," Colt said. "Take it easy."

"Are you nuts? Since when do a few bars stop Red?"

Nicole sat on the concrete floor in the corner, bunched up. She started to cry softly, head bent and rocking. Carey glanced her way, then turned his back. His jaw muscles flexed.

Wendy watched them all, perplexed by the vast change in the people she'd been thrown together with less than forty-eight hours earlier because of a storm. They'd all changed, although Pinkus the least, perhaps because he'd come to them already changed after his finger had been cut off.

Yes, of course they'd all changed. Or had they? What did she really know about the pasts of these four people locked in this cell with her? Something about their pasts interested Clifton. Something besides the fact that they all had unexplained spheres in their heads.

Colt kept glancing at Nicole and then at Wendy. She didn't think she'd ever met such a loyal, sincere man as Colt. More than that, she couldn't help thinking that she was falling for him.

Facing the brink of extinction had a way of stripping away all but the truth.

And what about you, Wendy? Have you bared the truth about your own heart? Your fears, your desires, the demons you face every day?

Wendy walked over to Colt and followed his gaze to the door. "You okay?"

He seemed to shake off whatever cobwebs were weaving their net about him and nodded. "Yeah."

"Yeah?" Pinkus said. "What do you mean you're okay? None of us are okay. It isn't going to end until he gets what he wants. You all know that. We have to do what he wants."

"You lay one finger on her and you'll spend the rest of your days in prison," Colt said. "If you're lucky enough to survive me."

"So then you're okay with him killing again? Not a problem for Ugly-as-Sin as long as he gets to fantasize about Uglier-than-Sin."

Wendy had to focus to keep from slapping him.

Colt ignored him. "We're missing something."

"We have to do what he's demanding," Nicole said softly. "We still haven't done that."

True enough.

"Maybe Timothy was right," Wendy said. "Maybe he's bound by the same rules we are."

"You're right," Colt said. "We have to get out of here. We have to play the game. And we have to find a way to beat him at his own game."

"So you think that under that stocking Red's really the ugliest?" Pinkus asked. "He wants us to kill *him*? Fat chance."

Colt shook his head. "I don't think so. No, it's more complicated than that."

"Then what?"

"I don't think Red will stop until he gets his revenge."

Yet for the life of her, Wendy couldn't understand what was driving this need for revenge. Surely nothing she'd done. And it wasn't just Colt, because Nicole was now in Red's sights.

The darkness—an opaque wall that shut off the world—came with a stunning hum, and she froze. But this time the episode was worse. Much worse. And not simply black.

Wendy had the distinct impression that she was lying under a heavy weight, or wrapped in a hot blanket. Her chest was pulling hard for air, and her extremities seemed to be tied up. All of this was consistent with the previous episodes.

The blurred light in her peripheral vision, however, was new. A ring of gray iridescence that seemed alive to her. And motion. Something in the circle seemed to be moving.

And then it was gone.

Colt put his hand on her shoulder. Then dropped it. Part of her wished he hadn't.

Sterling Red. He loved the name. Normally you would think a word like *sterling* would go with *silver*. Sterling Silver. And you would be right. But Red wasn't interested in normally. He was abnormal to the marrow, heck yeah.

And it wasn't just the fact that he'd contracted a case of the shakes so long ago now that he couldn't remember when. Like an epileptic.

It wasn't just his casual brilliance or his on-the-go reasoning power, both of which would put most normal folk in the hospital with a paralyzing headache.

It wasn't even his self-confidence or his baseball cap worn backward or his occasional donning of a freaky stocking or his love/hate of mustard. All interesting, yes, he had to admit.

But none of that made Sterling Red terribly unusual. Rather, what made him different was his passion for the kill. Silver like a weapon. Red like blood. Like a gut-wrenching novel, only real, real, real, right down to the slipping and sliding of blood through his veins.

Sterling Red. Silver the killer.

He glanced at the plain masquerade mask he'd decided to wear when he faced them the next time. Really this was all about masks, he knew. They were all wearing masks, not just him. They, unfortunately, weren't catching on fast enough. Maybe this would clue them in.

Unfortunately, the many new law enforcement personnel in town made moving around both more difficult and easier than before. More difficult for a mad killer on the loose. But easier for a mad killer dressed and riding like a cop. Red drove the cruiser fast so that they couldn't see that the man behind the wheel was shaking like a blender. Cop hat too, of course. Soon they'd catch on, but by then he'd be gone.

He brought the cruiser to a sudden halt on Harbor Drive, which was crap because they weren't within a thousand miles of a real harbor, and slipped the shifter into park. He stood from behind the wheel, rounded to the trunk, popped it, and pulled out two five-gallon gas cans.

He'd come to Harbor Drive on the west side of town because at the moment the wind was blowing in an easterly direction. One thing about most normal people, they were so maddeningly predictable as to drive exceptional people like Red to suicide. Which was one reason he liked to kill normal folk—it was a kind of payback for an offense first instigated by normal people.

Among the most predictable habits of normal people was their tendency to run from danger. Boring and infuriating, yes, but today Red would use that tendency. The fools had even written their fleeing into law!

The moment he spilled these two canisters full of chemicals, they would spew into the air a noxious gas that would quickly blow east, into the town. By law, all those in the path of such noxious fumes had to be evacuated. The law had first been written by the Department of Transportation to regulate the transportation of hazardous chemicals in large trucks, but its application was as appropriate here.

Red faced the wind and drew a deep breath of clean air. See, that was another thing about normal people, even normal serial killers—in the end they usually died because of their habits. Take Ted Bundy. Though Red hadn't been around when the good-looking fella had killed his forty-some-odd women, he held him up as a fallen hero of sorts. But even Ted Bundy had been caught because he'd used the same old Volkswagen, crutches, "Can you please help me?" shtick too often.

Red, on the other hand, had started this little spree with a rifle on the highway, then switched to a pistol to gun down the chief, then taken up a chicken to club his next victims, then his fists, then a knife, then a syringe, and now he was using gas. This time his intention wasn't to kill; but still, the variety of his techniques demonstrated versatility.

Thinking about it made Red hungry for mustard.

He faced the wind and stilled his shaking muscles. It was all coming to a head, and he could feel his triumph already. He stilled a final violent shake, took a deep breath, and dumped both containers on their side. Liquid splashed out with twin *gluck, gluck* sounds.

Red ran to the car, jumped in, and was halfway down the street before he called it in.

A flurry of radio activity followed, all of which he smiled through. And then the call he'd been waiting for came—the call that he knew made them all so pathetically normal.

"All units, all units to the west side."

"All? What is this thing? You don't mean—"

"I mean you, Steve. All Walton police, anyone with wheels. We have to get the place evacuated and keep that crap from killing the whole town."

"What about the police station?" Frank wanted to know. "Will it be safe?"

"Depends on the wind. Just go, Frank. We need to get those people out! This is coming from Clifton."

"What's Clifton got to do with this?"

"Just get it in gear. You hearing me?"

A long pause. "I'm on my way."

"Of course you are," Red said softly. "You'll all be on your way."

38

Never before in Colt's memory had he been so emotionally drained as he was now, juggling impossibilities that all felt certain to destroy him if dropped. The fact that he hadn't slept for over twenty-four hours didn't help, but he'd take the physical challenges over the mind games any day.

He'd always been a man who prided himself in finding the most elusive solution, no matter how unlikely. His childhood negotiation with the owner of the strip club, for example. In the end he'd shown them all that he could survive, however difficult the circumstances.

They hadn't seen the detective since he'd interrogated them. Colt would have thought the man would want to talk to each of them at length. Unless, of course, Clifton himself was associated with the killer, or worse, *was* the killer.

Wendy had comforted him in his loss, and he relished that comfort.

Loss? Yes, that was how they both seemed to be understanding Nicole's transformation. The Nicole he's embraced seemed to be gone, at least for the time being.

Wendy spoke quietly beside him. "I've been thinking."

"What have you been thinking?" he asked.

"That this has more to do with the past than the future."

"How so?"

The door suddenly crashed open. *Bang.* They all spun as one. But no one stepped in.

Pinkus was the first to speak. "Hello?"

The lights went out, and for a moment Colt thought he was going through another blackout, of which he'd now experienced three. But Wendy was beside him—he could just see the whites of her eyes.

"Becky?" Colt said.

She responded with a muffled cry. A slap sounded, silencing her.

"Becky! What's wrong?" But he knew what was wrong. Red was wrong.

A shape slowly filled the dark doorway, backlit by soft indirect lighting from several emergency exit lights in the adjoining room. The man stopped just inside the door, arms by his legs, staring at them through that a bland masquerade mask. He wore jeans and a black T-shirt and a blue baseball cap backward above the mask.

A pistol hung in a holster on each hip.

"Hello again," Red said. And he shivered. "Have you figured out why I'm here yet?"

Nicole was cowering, face turned away. Wendy's fingers dug into Colt's wrist, but she was driven more by anger than fear, he thought. Carey and Pinkus stood behind Colt—he could hear their steady breathing but nothing more.

"No," Colt said.

"That's too bad. I'm running out of patience. I would have expected more of a fight from such formidable foes after the first sound beating. Instead, I'm having a hard time remembering why I thought I had to be so careful."

"Sorry to disappoint," Colt said.

Red shook violently again. "No need. The cops are closing in and we're getting to the end of the sixth day, so we need to draw this contest to an end."

Six days? What is it about six?

"You're sick," Wendy said.

"I think that's the point. Question is, are you? Since our time is short and none of you seem terribly motivated, I'm upping the kill load from seven to seventy."

"What do you want?" Nicole screamed, startling Colt.

"I want you dead," Red said in a cold voice. "But let's start by getting you all back in the game in a way that improves the mood. Since Colt fancies himself with a gun, I think he'd be best."

"Best for what?"

"Best to fight Becky in a fast draw, of course."

Red stepped back, reached behind the door, and yanked a woman from where she'd remained hidden. Colt couldn't see her features clearly in the dim light, but there was no mistaking Becky's familiar figure. Her hands were restrained behind her back, but with a flip of his wrist, Red freed her. Gave her a nudge forward.

Becky shuffled forward, passing through a shaft of light from the adjacent room. Now Colt could see her teary face, hair matted to her forehead, eyes searching the cell for assurance that this was all a mistake. Gray duct tape was strapped over her mouth. She held the cell keys in her hand.

"It's okay, Becky," Colt said softly. "Everything's going to be okay."

"Don't listen to him, Becky," Red said. "Everything's going to be quite horrible, I promise."

Colt moved over to the gate that Becky struggled to unlock. He was thinking clearly now, thoughts of Nicole's predicament, his own dilemmas, the fate of being up against a faceless threat, all stripped away by a very real and tangible adversary who stood fifteen feet from them.

He whispered to Becky, "Let your body go when I shoot you. Don't fight it."

She stopped struggling with the lock. The sound of her breathing through her nostrils filled the cell.

"It'll be easier, trust me." He knew Red could hear him, so he'd chosen his words carefully. "Open the lock."

She did, then stepped back, numbly.

"Just Colt. The rest of you will have to wait your turn to die. Come back to me, honey pie."

Becky whimpered, refusing to move.

"You have no choice, Becky," Colt said, easing out of the cell.

Fifteen feet separated him and the killer. Any other opponent and he might have taken his chances, but he'd seen the man move. Becky shuffled back to Red, who snatched a gun from his left hip, twirled it once, and handled it in his palm.

"Don't worry, Becky. I think you can beat him. You have me on your side." He unbuckled one of the hip holsters, dropped it on the floor, and kicked it over to Colt. "I'm the snake. Nicole knows about the snake, don't you, sweets? Don't think about Nicole, she's nasty-ugly now. Think about Becky. Red will crawl inside Becky and make her quick as a snake."

He motioned to the holster on the floor and spoke to Colt. "It's loaded and cocked. Pick it up."

Colt picked up the leather hip-hugger and buckled it around his waist. The man was going to force a quick draw. Why would he take the time for such antics now, in the police station? Unless he'd found a way to instigate a response. The faint crackle of radio chatter reached them from the front. Everyone sounded like they were dealing with some new emergency. Colt couldn't imagine what it might be. But sooner or later they would stop assuming Becky had gone off the air for a bathroom break and send someone back.

"Hands on your head," Red said when Colt had adjusted his gun so that it hung by his front pocket.

He put his right hand on his head, leaving his left to dangle free.

Red lifted his own weapon, stared at Colt for a moment, then stepped behind Becky, who stood trembling. He dropped his gun into the remaining holster on his hip.

"Okay, honey pie, reach back and put your hand on my gun. Go on."

Becky whimpered behind the tape on her mouth.

"Go on," Colt said softly.

"Go on, honey, reach for my gun." Red wrapped a hand around her gut and pulled her tight to him.

She groped behind her, felt his hip, then his gun. He put his hand on hers and pressed it on the butt of his gun. Her body covered most of his, shoulders down, but his head was above hers, providing an easy shot at this range.

Colt doubted Red had any intention of giving him that shot so easily. He would duck as Colt pulled the trigger, pulling his shot down, into Becky's head.

The man was no idiot. He probably knew what Colt was planning already. He was dangling a carrot, his own head in this case, near Becky's.

Red slowly lifted his right hand to his head. "Keep your hand on my gun, honey pie. When we go, you jerk that gun out and shoot old Colt dead. You hear me? If you don't shoot him dead, he'll shoot me. But he won't be shooting me, because you're me. And if he doesn't shoot you or me, I'm going to shoot you in the back before I shoot his eyes out."

Colt felt the sweat gathering on his palms. His muscles had coiled tight. He'd been here before, facing targets on a range, but never a dispatcher and a snake.

"Anyone have any mustard?" Red asked.

Mustard?

"On three, Colt."

Becky began to make annoying squeaking sounds behind her tape. Red reached up and slapped her lightly on her cheek. "Focus!"

Colt went then, on the *c* of *focus*. But not his right hand, which remained on the crown of his head, unmoving.

His left hand flashed right, snatched the butt of the gun from his holster, and had it halfway out before Red moved.

But when Red moved, he moved with a speed Colt had never seen. Dropping his hand over Becky's.

One of her fingers cracked loudly as the gun cleared leather.

Colt already had his weapon angled for Red's head when the man shifted down, precisely as Colt had predicted. A head shot was out of the question, and he was out of time.

He dropped the barrel a fraction of an inch and pulled the trigger.

Twin gunshots boomed with two flashes, one from Colt's gun, one from the weapon in Red's hand.

Colt's bullet drilling into Becky, high in her center body mass.

Red's bullet slammed into Colt's gun, ripping it free from his hand. It flew across the room and clattered to the concrete.

Colt grabbed his hand and dropped to one knee. For a moment no one moved. And then Red released Becky and let her slump to the ground.

"You killed her!" Pinkus cried.

"Not true," Red said. "But not bad. There's only one way for any of you to survive the day and save a bunch of old folks from wicked things. I'm giving you exactly six minutes to get back into the library to finish the game you started."

Red moved back, stepped to his left behind the door, and was gone.

Wendy was the first out of the cell, rushing past Colt to Becky's fallen body. She hit the light switch. Light stuttered, then flooded the room. Becky's white blouse was turning slowly red. It was almost as if Red really had crawled inside her and was now leaking out.

A single glance at the weapon on the ground told Colt that it was destroyed. "Stop the bleeding," he said, running for the first aid closet in the adjoining room. He came back with some gauze.

The other three had come out of the cell now and were staring at the body. Wendy had ripped Becky's shirt open to expose a puncture below her right shoulder.

"Unless I'm wrong, it's a flesh wound," Colt said. He tossed her the gauze. "She's out with the pain, but she'll be fine. Shove some of this in the wound, but be quick."

"What do we do?" Pinkus asked.

"What he's forcing us to do."

"Are you nuts? I'm not going back there."

"Suit yourself," Colt said. "But I can guarantee you he'll put a slug in your head, haul your dead body back to the library, and then continue with the rest of us."

They all looked at him, knowing he had spoken nothing but truth.

Colt turned and strode into the station.

Wendy started to protest. "Wait . . ."

"I'll be right back," he said.

"Where you going?"

"To get some firepower."

39

They ran from the station, five in a row, led by Colt, who'd grabbed five pistols from the armory. They would be nearly useless in unskilled hands against Red, he pointed out, more harmful than good. But it was clear he had an idea.

The thought of a weapon in Wendy's hands wasn't unappealing. There were risks—Pinkus could up and shoot Nicole, for example. But if Colt could live with that risk, so could she.

Carey and Nicole took their guns without bothering to look at them. Pinkus kept looking at the triggering mechanism, but he didn't do much more. Only Wendy seemed to know what to do with the gun after Colt's quick lesson in the library.

Red had destroyed the radio in the station. And the one in Colt's cruiser. No other cars were in the lot.

"Where is everyone?" Wendy asked. "I've never seen it so empty."

"Something's happening," Colt said, firing the car. A man ran past on the street, and he swung the cruiser around, giving chase. He caught the man, rolled his window down.

"Hold up. Where you running in such a hurry?"

The man slowed to a walk beside the cruiser, panting. "They're evacuating the town. You don't know?"

"Why?"

"A chemical spill over on Harbor Drive." His eyes darted over Pinkus, Nicole, and Carey packed into the backseat. "You don't know?" he asked again.

"What?" Pinkus said in a high-pitched voice.

"My radio's out," Colt said to the runner, who kept looking west. "I want you to get to the first police officer you can find and tell them that Becky's stuck in the station. She's been shot."

"Shot? What are *you* doing?"

Colt hesitated. "Going to save the town," he said, then pulled ahead and whipped the car through a U-turn.

They sat in silence as Colt raced through empty streets. There was nothing more to say. They'd been here before, rushing into the jaws of death; only this time they all knew it was the end.

"This has to do with our pasts," Wendy finally said.

"I don't understand why we have to go back to the library," Pinkus said. "Every time I go into the library, I lose a finger. Why can't we just do it out here?"

"Because he wants us in the library," Colt said. Carey and Nicole maintained the same silence that had gripped them since coming back into the town. "His arena, where he can control most of what happens."

"And we want to be controlled? Why not go to the cops?"

"*I'm* a cop!" Colt snapped. "For all we know, *he's* a cop!"

They flew around the corner behind the library, and Colt brought the car to a screeching halt. A Walton cruiser sat near the building like a black-and-white lump of candy with a cherry on top. They could see the officer behind the wheel, staring ahead. Colt pulled up, parked behind the officer, and climbed out with Wendy.

The cop hadn't moved—a fact that made Wendy consider returning to their car. But she'd changed in the last few days—the thought of a dead policeman horrified her less than it once had.

She shielded the window glare with one hand and peered inside. The cop had been shot through his forehead. The bullet had come in through the front windshield and pinned him to the headrest.

Wendy felt suddenly nauseated. Maybe she'd overestimated the change in herself. "He's dead," she said.

"The radio's destroyed," Colt said. He motioned the others to get out, retrieved the guns from the trunk, and passed them out.

He led them toward the library's back door. Open.

"Okay, we know the drill," Colt said, one hand on the knob. "But this time we hunt him. Take your—"

"How?" Pinkus interrupted.

"I'm telling you how. Take your safeties off." He showed them. "Keep your guns pointed at the floor. I'm the only one here who stands a chance of actually engaging him, so my gun is the only one with live rounds, but you shoot near someone's face and you could put out an eye."

"What?" Pinkus cried. "These things have blanks in them?"

"That's right. We call them *training rounds*. You think I'd give you live ammunition?"

Wendy couldn't suppress a wry smile. He'd brought them here where there was no opportunity to reverse his decision before telling them their guns were useless. That meant he had a plan besides simply gunning for Red.

"I think that's smart," Wendy said. "What do we do with them?"

"We're going to kill each other with them," Colt said. "All of us. I want all of us dead on the floor."

"You mean pretending to be dead," she corrected.

"Yes. Within a ten-foot radius."

"Why?" Carey asked. It was his first word since leaving the station. "You did that once and it failed miserably."

"If we're all on the floor, presumably dead after a convincing fight, he'll have no choice but to check to see if we're actually dead. Think about it."

"Isn't that something we should agree on?" Pinkus said. "You can't just spring this crazy plan out here and tell us to go shoot each other. Why didn't you say anything in the car?"

"I don't trust the car. I don't trust the cops. I don't know *what* to trust."

"It makes sense," Wendy reiterated. "It could work. If we put on a strong enough show, he would at least have to check us. And that's when your real gun comes in?"

He nodded. "That's the idea."

"Can you beat him straight up?"

A shadow crossed his face. "He's fast."

Pinkus put it more clearly. "Faster than you. Right?"

"Not if I take him by surprise."

"Red doesn't get surprised."

"There's always a first."

But even to himself, Colt sounded less than convinced. They stood in a group around the door and stared at each other.

"Anyone have a better idea?" he asked.

They placed themselves around Carey's pentagram at the center of the library, waiting to begin, although how they were supposed to do so was still a mystery to Wendy. Did they just start yelling?

Colt's makeshift plan was ingenious precisely *because* they'd done something similar at his faked hanging. Who would try the same thing twice? Red would wonder. Regardless, he would have to check to see if they were alive or dead.

There were some rather large holes, of course. Red might decide to check by shooting a bullet into one of their legs from his hiding place, Colt had said. They would have to resist moving if he did so.

And there was the simple fact that Red was fast, very fast, blazingly fast, too fast for Colt.

But they had to play the game or risk far greater consequences. At least Colt's plan offered some hope, however thin.

So here they stood, five lost souls leaning against the tables Carey had pulled back, staring at each other, ready to start an argument, but unsure what that meant.

"Okay." Colt spoke naturally, with enough volume to be heard without sounding like it was staged. His eyes skirted the balcony. "Our hands are tied. The inescapable fact is that if we don't do what Red's demanding, more people will die."

"Just like that?" Wendy demanded. They had to work up some emotion. In fact, the more the better. "Just throw principle out the window? Will you pull the trigger?"

"On who? Nicole?" Pinkus said. "And who's going to kill Colt?"

They looked at him.

"We can't risk not killing the ugliest, right? There are only two ugly people here, and yes, I would have to agree that Nicole looks pretty sick with her face half burned off, but Colt's no star. The fact is, Nicole's got more to her than her face. She's a woman and Red's a man, we know that much."

Wendy had never considered that perspective. "We don't even know that by *ugly*, Red's referring to physical beauty," she said. "If you want to—"

"Sure we do," Pinkus said. "He told us beauty isn't in the eye of the beholder. You see it, I see it, we all see a beautiful person and know they're beautiful. Cut all the crap about it being skin deep."

"That's still an assumption," Colt said. "I agree, it would be impossible to figure out which of us is the ugliest inside, and I don't think that's what's driving him; but technically speaking, Wendy's right."

"The point is," Pinkus pushed, "I think Red may still consider you the ugliest here. Naked, that is."

"That's the most ridiculous thing I've heard!" Wendy cried. "You're playing with lives here. Stop talking about him that way."

Her own anger surprised her. Maybe because it went deeper than moral outrage.

You like him, Wendy. You like him way too much.

He deserves my love, she answered herself.

"I keep telling you," Pinkus said, "this is about what's on the surface not inside. What we see with our eyes. The desert, the town—it's all about the surface. The surface. Red's telling us to guess who he'd find the ugliest. And kill them. Period."

Wendy was now too angry to respond with anything but a physical blow.

"We're past pretending," Pinkus said. "Red would find Nicole more attractive than Colt any day of the week. Face it, people. Colt is plain dog-ugly."

"Stop it," Nicole shouted. And then, to Wendy's surprise, she ran to Colt's side and literally clung to him. "Don't let him kill me."

Colt didn't seem to know what to do other than put an awkward hand on her arm. "It's okay. Don't worry. We'll beat him at his game."

"My *brother*," she cut in. "Carey wants to kill me. Don't let Carey kill me."

Colt blinked. Pinkus was staring at Carey, who had his head tilted up and was staring at the ceiling. His lips were moving, but no sound came from his mouth.

"I . . . I won't," Colt said.

"He'll try," Nicole insisted. "As soon as you go after Red." She looked around the group, one face at a time. "You don't believe me, do you? He'll do it." Then back at Colt. "You don't know him, Colt. He's going to kill me!"

"No," Colt said. "Listen to me. I won't let him."

"But that's where you're wrong, piggy," Carey said. He leveled his head, lifted his gun by his ear, and walked forward. "All this love talk is enough to make even the most loyal Harlequin Romance addict heave. The fact of the matter is that Red is going to kill us all if we don't kill the ugliest person here now."

Wendy forced her way into the exchange, alarmed by the change in Carey's voice. "Stop. You don't know who—"

"Shut up!" Carey screamed, spinning with his gun at Wendy. One look in his eyes and Wendy knew he had pushed himself to the brink. "Just shut your piehole and end this stupid game."

"What's your problem, man?" Pinkus said.

Carey turned his gun on Pinkus, trembling from head to foot. "Shut up! Shut, shut, shut up!"

Had he forgotten that his gun held only blanks? He turned back to Nicole, who was clinging to Colt, and pressed the barrel of his gun against the back of her head. When he spoke, his voice was stretched to the breaking point.

"She's the ugliest here, inside *and* out. It's about her. You don't know who Red is; well, I'll tell you. He's some jilted lover who's come to end her life the way she probably ended his."

"You can't mean that," Colt said. "This is your sister, Carey."

"Look at her!" Carey shouted. "Look at her face!"

"He's going to kill me," Nicole whimpered, holding Colt's face in both of her hands. "You have to kill him."

For a surreal moment, Wendy thought that Colt, Carey, and Nicole had planned this—that it was all a play being staged to fool Red. A way of making group homicide seem real.

But Carey wasn't playing, and neither was Nicole.

"Kill him?" Colt said, as confused as Wendy at this change in the siblings.

"Please, you can do it." Her voice was soft and pleading. "You have the gun."

"So do you, Nicole," Wendy said loudly, for Red's benefit. "We all have a gun. Show us all what kind of woman you are. Go ahead, shoot your brother." It was only loaded with blanks, after all.

Pinkus was frozen, and Colt looked truly scared.

Nicole spun. "Pig!" she snarled at Wendy.

"You think I'm a pig?" Wendy asked.

"Aren't we all? I'm trying to save our necks here! Go get your face torched and we'll see who's the real pig."

"I was wrong," Carey said. "She used to spit on me when I was a kid because she hated me so much. And she hasn't changed. I was blinded by my own infatuation with her beauty, with my own guilt, so I didn't see it. But here in the pentacle, I called out to the elemental power of the air, and it told me. She's the one. She's always been the ugliest, and now her face proves it."

"You didn't even know me when you were a kid," Nicole said.

"You didn't even join our happy little freak show until you were five."

"What are you talking about? Of course I was there."

"You were adopted, Carey. It was all part of Mom's brilliant plan to pay for beauty school: adopt an older kid and take the money offered by the state. But she didn't know you were the biggest freak of us all. You'd shake like a leaf, for no reason at all. Epileptic. Flawed. Needy. You started getting all the attention. Of course I hated you. I hated you all!"

"You're lying! She's lying! You think I wouldn't remember five years of my life if I lived it someplace else?"

"You aren't my brother. You're nobody. That's why they sold your soul, Brother. Gave you up for scientific research."

"She's so full of lies that she can't tell even a simple truth. She's *incapable* of telling the truth. Even now, she thinks Colt's so stinkin' ugly he makes her want to puke, but she can't even say that. You have to kill her! I swear, Red wants her dead."

Wendy could barely absorb what each sibling was claiming, but she did see how all of this could lead to a very convincing shootout, exactly as prescribed by Colt. She had another moment of doubt. Were they actually only following Colt's wishes and doing it exceptionally well? But the fact that Carey didn't just lift his gun and shoot his sister was flying in the face of their dialogue.

Colt lifted a trembling hand and aimed his gun at Carey. "Go ahead, try it. Lift your weapon. But don't stand here lying to my face."

Nicole settled. Took a step away from Colt so that she was now halfway between them. "You want me to be brutally honest, is that it, Carey? You think that will heal all your wounds? Okay. I did hate you. I still do hate you because you never forgave me for killing them. You didn't have the guts to stop me from killing them, and you never have had the guts to accept it. I think that makes you as guilty as me."

Her admission sucked the air from the room. Pinkus was the first to recover.

"You killed your father?" he asked.

Nicole ignored the question, eyes drilling Carey. A slight smile found her face. It was as if the rest of them weren't here; this was a private, forbidden conversation between brother and sister.

"And you're right, Colt does make me sick. The little girl in me molded by my sick mess of a mother wants to cheer his mother on for doing what she did to him. Poor little Colt was everything I despised as a child." Then drilling Wendy with a glare. "Does that make me worse than you, you gutless pig?"

Once again, Wendy felt gut-punched.

Colt tried to recover, but his voice was shaking. "No, you don't mean—"

"Shut up, Colt, before I throw up on you," Nicole said coldly, eyes still fixed on Carey. "And you are going to do exactly what I want again. I have no intention of dying today."

Wendy knew by Colt's vacant face that he was in a free fall. This was no planned ploy. Her mind was spinning, and it felt as if the wind had been sucked from her lungs, preempting any cry.

Carey, on the other hand, did scream, a terrifying howl of rage and fear mashed together as one. He jumped forward, wrenched the gun from Colt's limp hand, swung it up in line with Nicole's head, and pulled the trigger.

Boom!

The gun bucked in his hand. Nicole's head snapped back, eyes perfectly round with shock.

Boom, boom, boom! He emptied the gun into her chest.

She dropped back on her seat beside Carey and Colt and flopped facedown before Wendy had time to comprehend the extent of the damage.

"Nicole?" Colt dropped to his knees beside her, dumbstruck. "Nicole!"

Colt turned her over. Blood pooled under her. Real blood.

He pushed himself slowly to his feet, staring down, face white. He staggered backward; then he turned and fled the library, knocking over two chairs in his misguided haste.

Nicole was dead. Ugliest or not, she was really dead.

And by the look on Colt's face, Wendy wasn't sure that he wouldn't try to take his own life. Pinkus stood in shock with his gun pointed at the floor; Carey slowly sank to his knees beside the woman he'd killed; and Wendy ran out after Colt.

"Colt! Wait, Colt!" She raced through the foyer and crashed through the front door just as it was closing. "Please, Colt . . ."

She got halfway through the front door before pulling up. Colt was there, on the landing; the steps were there running down to the ground; but the town beyond was gone. Sand stretched to the horizon, cut by the power line that, whether in their minds or not, had the power to kill them.

And the red sky was filled with hundreds of black streaks, humming their approval.

Huummmmm . . .

40

Nathan Blair left the director's office now fully resolved to make the call. Someone with more authority had to know what was going on here, why this was happening. For that matter, those on the ground should be brought in now.

The director had refused to pull the plug on the operation. They would all die, he insisted. Red was too powerful, too smart. The director didn't even trust Clifton, and truth be told, neither did Blair. There was as much evidence implicating Clifton as there was implicating Pinkus.

But none of that mattered. Someone else had to know what Blair knew—someone outside this building. He had to cover his butt, at the very least. So he would make the call. He would tell them everything he knew and pray someone else would take the heat when it came, because when it did come, it would come hard.

41

Luke Preston climbed into his car, eased the stick into drive, and pulled the vehicle through a U-turn. Clifton wanted to see him back at the station, pronto, which was pretty interesting, because as far as he knew, the station had already been evacuated. Not a peep from Becky for over twenty minutes now.

Red tape ran the width of Harbor Street, two blocks west of where they'd found the spilled chemicals, but they'd sent everybody two miles farther east to a makeshift camp where they fed the evacuees crackers and Kool-Aid under canopies. Thankfully nearly half of the town's two thousand or so residents had used the killings as reason enough to leave town earlier, leaving only about four hundred who needed to be cleared out of the chemical vapor's path.

Summerville was like a ghost town. Luke had taken three passes through the streets in his cruiser and had seen only two people, both of whom he'd sent packing. True enough, the chances of this chemical mess actually killing anyone were pretty slim, but they had their orders. The diehards didn't want to leave their houses when ordered, but they would be the first to file a lawsuit if they woke up with a red rash, that was for sure.

What if the wind shifted? Everyone wanted to know. That was a chance they'd have to take. If the wind did shift, they could always pack up and move. Fact was, the noxious fumes were already spread so thin over such a large area that it wouldn't matter anyway.

Luke rolled down First Street, glancing at the gas mask in the passenger seat. He hated the way the thing hung off his face, but as his mother used to say, you don't cut off your nose—or in this case your mask—to spite your face.

He steered with his knees and pulled the contraption on over his head. Sounded like Darth Vader in here. Looked like the same from outside, no doubt.

An ambulance sped past him doing at least sixty, headed the same direction he was. The drivers weren't wearing masks. Someone was hurt? Maybe worse. Things had gone so crazy these last few days that nothing would surprise him anymore.

Why weren't the fools wearing masks? Maybe he should take his off. Then again, he'd just spent an hour yelling at everyone about the dangers of this chemical spill; waltzing around town now without a mask would look a bit irresponsible, assuming anyone was watching.

He parked to the right of the ambulance and walked into the station, thinking again about the call that had come from Clifton. He'd wanted Luke down here—not any of his own people, but Luke.

The first thing Luke noticed walking in was the disabled dispatcher's radio. Someone had smashed the transmitter to bits and torn the wires out of the back.

Now on edge, he walked into the workroom. Clifton was bent over the plain paper fax, scanning pages that had just come in. His eyes lifted to meet Luke's. The two paramedics who had passed him knelt beside a body on the floor by the back door. Becky.

Becky lay on her back, covered by a blanket.

"Take that thing off your face," Clifton said. "You look like *Plan 9 from Outer Space*."

Luke pulled it off, still stunned. "What happened? Holy . . . What happened?"

"She's lost a lot of blood, but she'll be okay. A pedestrian reported running into Colt and party, fleeing the scene."

"They did this?"

Clifton set the page he'd been reviewing in an open file beside him, letting his eyes linger on the sheet. "That's the question, Isn't it? It seems there's much more to our five friends than we've assumed up to this point."

"Really?"

Clifton closed the file. Picked it up, wheels behind his eyes spinning.

"What's that?" Luke asked. He knew what it was, of course: a file. The question hung in the air, so Luke tried to help it along. "That's a file on them, right?"

"Some interesting details from Quantico that fill in a few blanks, yes. I want you to find Steve and bring him in."

"Steve? He's not on the radio? I haven't seen him," Luke said.

"Find him."

"Why do you need him?"

"Find him and bring him to the library. Just do it."

Luke knew he had pushed his luck, asking stupid questions, but he'd learned that Clifton was the kind who wouldn't offer up details without being pushed. And in a strange way, the detective liked to be pushed.

"Where you going?" he asked.

"After Red," Clifton said and left the room.

42

The sky was humming outside, but the horror screaming inside their heads made the blackening sky and boiling horizon seem inconsequential by comparison, Wendy thought.

She gazed out one of the few windows at the surreal desert outside. The contrails were lower than before and now looked more like a blanket of translucent black fog. Wendy pulled back and walked to where Colt was slumped down against the wall. Pinkus was pacing outside, likely still mumbling about the fact that it wasn't over. They'd killed the ugliest and it wasn't over. She had taken Colt away before Pinkus could accuse him of being the ugliest now.

Carey was weeping beside his sister's body. He'd taken one look at the sky outside and retreated back into his own misery.

But neither of them concerned Wendy very much. Colt was all she cared about now. And Colt was falling to pieces.

She settled in front of him and drew her legs back to one side, leaning on one arm. He had his knees drawn up and his head lowered between them.

Every fiber in her body wanted to reach out and touch him with her hand.

"Colt."

He was breathing, but nothing more. Frozen from the inside out. Her heart melted for him. A tremble lit through her fingers.

She had to push aside her emotion and help him the same way Louise and Rachel had helped her when she'd emerged from the cult. Never mind that Colt and she were both facing near-certain death—she had to help Colt be strong because in so many ways her own sanity in these remaining minutes depended on him.

She took a calming breath. "Colt. I won't manipulate you by telling you that my life, all of our lives, now depend on you because you're the only one strong enough to defeat Red, but it's true."

He didn't respond, and she didn't expect him to.

"I know that you've become that child who was thrown away by your mother again and you aren't capable of thinking like the man I've come to respect over these last few days, but I want you to become a man again."

This time he responded with a single sob. Her heart felt like it was tearing free with each beat. Her choice of words struck her as absurd.

And what about you, Wendy? Can you be a woman?

Wendy reached for him and let her fingers rest on his arm.

"Colt." His warm skin felt smooth under her fingers. She could feel the muscles along his forearm.

Surprisingly, this thought didn't frighten her. She didn't panic. Before she knew it, her hand had moved up his arm to his shoulder. As Rachel Lords had once advised her, she tried to focus on the other person's thoughts and needs, not her own fears.

"You've been betrayed by every woman you've known, Colt. How can you help but believe them all? After so many years of telling yourself that your mother was wrong, you've been convinced once and for all by Nicole that your mother was right. That you are a very ugly person."

He was trying to hold back his emotions.

"Your tears are for yourself, not for Nicole. And I don't blame you for how you felt. They say love is blind. We're learning a thing or two about perceptions. I don't blame you at all."

He didn't argue. How could he?

We all know now that Nicole was bitter to the bone. Carey was right. Looks can be deceiving. Beauty is only skin-deep after all. But that doesn't help you, does it? You still want to be beautiful."

"No, that's not it," he said softly. "It's not just about—"

"Yes, it is, Colt. It's about you. You're mourning your loss. The one woman who gave you hope turned on you. And she wasn't even what she seemed to be. It's crushed you."

He lifted his tearstained face. "You're right . . ."

Encouraged, she continued, aware that she was talking to herself now as much as to Colt.

"The guilt you feel for allowing yourself to be manipulated only makes it worse. Much worse. You feel worthless, don't you?"

He dropped his head back against the wall and began to weep. Tears sprang to Wendy's eyes. In that moment she looked at Colt and saw herself. They were one. Both ravaged and discarded. Both desperate for love and acceptance. Both in need of another's touch.

Her own shoulders shook with silent sobs, but she didn't pull her hand from him. Instead, she kneaded his shoulder tenderly, willing the pain to stop and embracing it all at once.

If they were ever to break out of their prison, they would have to face the ugly truth.

Something in Wendy's mind buzzed. *The ugly truth.*

"Colt. Can I tell you something? The truth about myself. Why I'm ugly."

She said it past the fist in her throat. Saw him lift his head through her own blurred vision. For several seconds neither spoke.

"As a child I was abused by the cult leader. I was meant to be his wife at eighteen; that's why I ran away. When I was thirteen he broke my fingers for touching another boy."

Colt became still.

"I escaped, but I'm still in his prison, Colt. In my mind I'm locked up, unable to give myself to another man. I can't seem to love the way I should."

"No," he said with a thick, angry voice. "You know how to love more than any of us. How can you say that? You're—"

"Ugly. Damaged. Listen to me, Colt." She lowered her hand and looked at one of the glass panels across the library. "I'm afraid of men."

"What do you mean?" His voice trembled.

"Touching them."

Silence smothered them. She wanted to say more, but she knew he'd already filled in the blanks. When she lifted her head, she saw that he was watching her with anguish in his eyes.

"How can you be afraid of anything?" he asked. "You're so brave."

He could have said anything, but his choice of those simple words made her want to curl up in his arms and sob into his shoulder.

Instead, she deflected her emotions with a deep breath. "Yeah, well, so are you. You're the bravest man I've ever known."

She could see his mind spinning behind glassy eyes. He was looking at her differently. With a newfound understanding. Maybe even respect.

"It makes you wonder," she said, looking at the wall. "What's

real and what's not? Who's beautiful and who's not? Our perceptions can change."

He stared off, silent. What could he say? What could any of them
say?

She pressed the point, as much because she needed to keep talking as because she wanted to understand. "Who's to say that it takes
something like a drug to mess with your perception of reality? How
did Hitler deceive a nation? How can one group of people look at
the world and see one thing, and another see something completely
different? One sees a town, another sees a desert. One sees beauty,
another sees chaos."

"The skin of this world," he said quietly.

"If love can blind you, who's to say that other emotions can't?"

"What we see may deceive us—the skin may be deceptive—but
there has to be one truth, right? It can't all just be a jumble of perceptions. So what really exists out there, beyond what we can see?
We're so dependant on the surfaces of what we see. But if we could
see past the skin of this world . . ." His voice trailed off.

Wendy looked away. "I want to tell you something else," she
said. "You won't want to believe it because your mind is shot to
pieces for this kind of thing, but your life depends on what I'm about
to tell you, so I'm going to say it anyway."

The ugly truth. Something about those few words continued to
gnaw at her even as she spoke.

"You might not think I'm qualified to tell you this, but will you
listen?"

"Yes."

"I didn't think Nicole was ugly even with her disfigured face.
And I don't think you're ugly."

He didn't acknowledge her.

"In my world, you are a beautiful man. Your face is beautiful where I come from. Any woman like me would feel so fortunate to be with you."

He lowered his head, silent. He wasn't capable of believing her. She knew because she would feel the same skepticism if he said similar words.

Did feel the same way, because she'd spoken the words for both of them.

She put her hand on his arm and traced his muscle again. "The truth is, you're as beautiful on the outside as on the inside," she said.

She knew the instant she said it that her words were more profound than either of them could know in that moment.

"I'm not being pretentious or making light of the horrors you've faced. And I know I'm not qualified—"

His hand covered hers on his arm. Their eyes met. She felt no fear.

"And you are as beautiful on the inside as you are on the outside," he said softly.

She knew what he meant, and his kindness meant everything to her.

Colt brought his free hand to her face and touched her cheek. Wendy did something then she'd never done, and she did it impulsively, quickly so that her heart, not her mind, could be heard.

She kissed Colt's hand.

And felt no anxiety. No turning of the belly. None of the emotions she had always feared.

Instead, warmth and relief and happiness. She didn't know how Colt felt, but she knew she'd never let this man out of her sight. Ever. She'd have to help him get used to that.

"I like you, Colt."

He answered by tracing her lips with his thumb. She thought she would like to kiss him. Why not? They were facing death, for heaven's sake. Why not just lean forward and kiss Colt? Bowl him over and kiss his lips and neck. It would be a dangerous and wonderful and totally appropriate thing to do.

More important, Wendy knew she could do it. Would do it. Wanted terribly to do it.

"Guys?"

She started and turned to face Pinkus, who stood between two bookcases. Colt lowered his hand.

"I think we may have a problem," he said.

"No kidding," Colt said. "You really think so?"

"No, I mean . . . The detective said something about our pasts being suspicious. Connected. I think we . . . Maybe we have more in common than we think."

Pinkus too?

"Like Timothy said before he was killed. Maybe the killer is after something ugly from our past."

"We have these implants," Wendy said. "Obviously we have something in common."

"It's what Nicole said about Carey. He was an epileptic, but he couldn't seem to remember any of it."

"Who knows if that's true," Wendy said. "Not even Carey knows."

"He didn't deny it. And what are the chances that two of us were epileptics?"

"We don't know if—"

"And we were both involved in research," Pinkus said. "Nicole said his parents sold his soul. Sounds an awful lot like getting fifty thousand dollars for participating in a test to me."

Wendy's mind scrambled for meaning.

"What could that have to do with Red?" Colt asked.

"I don't know. But I do know that my test involved psychotropic drugs used to force certain memories out during regression therapy."

"You're saying our memories were repressed?"

He took a deep breath. "What if when we were kids Carey and I were part of a study that messed with our minds because we both had frontal lobe epilepsy? A test involving an earlier version of this lycergitide, or whatever Red's using on us? And what if that study went bad, but they used the same techniques they were experimenting with to repress our memories of anything negative associated with the test?"

"Colt and I weren't epileptics."

Pinkus turned away and ran his hand through his hair. "But if this is tied to our pasts, maybe it's tied to Carey and me somehow. What if . . . what if Carey's the killer and doesn't know it? Or me?"

Panic laced his voice. Wendy understood why.

Colt wasn't disagreeing.

"That's crazy," Wendy said.

"We got a maniac out there trying to get us all killed, and we're seeing demons in the sky, and the town keeps disappearing. I mean—"

"Demons?"

"Just a figure of speech. But we're seeing something that no one else can see; you can't deny that. I think you were right. I think the ugliness Red's trying to flush out is *inside* us."

"But I was sure he was speaking about physical beauty," said Colt.

"He said beauty being in the eye of the beholder is a load of crap," Pinkus said.

"Meaning beauty isn't subjective," Wendy said. "Meaning we would know easily enough who the ugliest was."

"Or meaning that beauty isn't in the eye of the beholder because it's inside, under the skin," Pinkus said.

"Then why the fixation on physical beauty?" Colt asked.

"Maybe showing us that something beautiful could be made ugly," Wendy said. *Not the face*—that's what he was saying when he burned Nicole. *She's ugly under the skin,* and she was."

"Okay, so Carey killed the ugliest," Colt said. "He killed Nicole. Does that mean this is all over?"

"If it does, whatever's humming in the sky didn't get the memo." Pinkus bit on one of his good fingernails. "I'm not saying I've got it all figured out; I'm just saying that maybe—just maybe—Red is after us because of what happened to us when we were kids. This is about good and evil, not physical beauty. And it concerns all of us, not just one or two."

"None of us are even religious," Wendy said. "I spent the last seven years running from religion."

"Not religion. That's like outside beauty, right? Inside stuff, man. The stuff that's hiding behind our minds."

A bloodcurdling scream shattered the library's silence, and Wendy's first thought was that one of Pinkus's demons had swooped out of the sky and found its way into the library.

"Help! What are you doing? Help!"

"Carey," Colt whispered.

"No! Please, no. I can't, I can't!" Carey screamed.

With that last cry a black shroud smothered Wendy. The panic attack was so strong this time that she lost complete orientation. Felt herself stagger. She tried to suck in air but couldn't.

Her hands and feet felt like they were in a vise. Tingles raced through her bones. The light that had ringed her world during the last episode brightened, and her panic eased. She focused her sight on that ring.

Movement. White ghosts moving through the smoke.

The thought that she really was looking at ghosts swimming around her nudged her closer to panic again. She clenched her eyes. The ring of hazy light vanished.

When she opened her eyes again, the attack had passed. She stared at Pinkus and Colt, who had frozen, eyes locked in the direction of Carey's cry.

Memories. What if the light was actually memories forcing their way to the surface? Memories of her terrible past, suppressed by the pain she'd lived through in the cult?

"I can't!" Carey screamed. "I can't!"

Can't what? He was begging in terror and anguish. Red was in there with him, Wendy thought, stepping back into Colt. If she wasn't mistaken, Carey was in the pentagram with Red at this very moment.

And then she knew she wasn't mistaken, because Red's voice rang out.

"Come in, come in, wherever you are. I request your immediate presence at the center of Carey's nasty devil worship thing. I'm going to count to five. One . . . Two . . ."

Colt grabbed her hand and ran. "Come on!"

"Guys?" But Pinkus wasn't about to test Red. He ran on their heels.

"Three . . . Four . . ."

They slid to a stop by the railing that ringed the cherrywood tables, now moved helter-skelter to make room for the pentagram. Carey teetered on a chair. A rope had been looped around his neck and thrown over the same beam that Colt had hung himself from earlier. No sign of Red—just his voice.

Colt bolted forward.

A bullet cracked the chair he was yanking aside to clear his way. Thunder echoed in the hollow atrium.

"Stop," Red said, stepping out from behind a bookcase. Shadows would have concealed him somewhat even if he weren't wearing the mask, but there was no mistaking the leveled gun in his hand.

Colt stopped.

"Thank you, Colt. You're definitely smarter than you look, although I've had a few doubts along the way. Now, Carey, be a good boy and jump."

43

Fact was, Steve said, he didn't like or trust Clifton for the simple fact that the detective kept disappearing on them. Like now—he was off radio. On cell, probably, but why not radio?

Luke had finally found Steve talking to Old Man Jacobs—some political nonsense, for crying out loud.

"So tell him that," Luke said. "What you think he's gonna do, bite your head off?"

"I don't think I'd want to tick him off."

Steve eyed him with a raised brow. "That so? You and Clifton just good buds these days, is that it?"

"Didn't say we were buds. I never did think he's all they crack him up to be. He walks around like he owns the place. Everybody else is dressed citylike, and he's strutting around in jeans and a T-shirt."

"That's because he does."

"Own the place?"

"Owns all these agents' respect. Heck, he's like a god to them. He could walk around in his underwear and they'd still salute him."

"All he cares about is this killer. Everything else is expendable."

"That's what makes him good," Luke said.

"For all we know, he's not who he says he is."

Luke shrugged off the suggestion. "Let's go," he said.

"Where to?"

"Library," Luke said. "After Red."

Colt's first instinct was to draw his weapon, but his gun lay on the floor where Carey had dropped it after shooting Nicole.

"Are you deaf?" Red's voice rang. "Jump. Are you denying that you are indeed butt-ugly?"

Red was saying that Carey was the ugliest? But it wasn't that simple. True, Carey was perched on the chair, strung up with a rope, but his wasn't the only rope. Three more ropes with nooses hung from the same beam.

Wendy gave a short gasp, and Colt knew she was thinking the same thing he was.

"I knew it," Pinkus said in a panicked voice. "I knew it."

"Mighty big of you, Pinkus," Red said. "But to be real straight, I don't think you did know it. I've been growing old waiting for you to know it."

"You want to kill all of us, don't you?" Pinkus said.

"Mirror, mirror, on the wall, who's the ugliest of them all?" Red said. He shook violently for a brief moment, then stilled. Colt tried but couldn't tell whether this masked man standing in the shadows was Clifton or not. Clearly not Pinkus or Carey.

"We all are," Wendy said. "Inside, we're all the ugliest."

No response from Red this time. Just his breathing over the PA.

"You want us all to commit suicide, don't you?" Wendy asked.

The simple assertion hit Colt like a sledge to the head. That was it! Wendy had just stripped Red's intentions bare.

He had played this game willing to settle for nothing less than each of them killing the ugliest. And they were all the ugliest, equal in their hearts. Red wanted each of them to commit suicide.

"That's crazy," Pinkus said. "How can we all be the ugliest?"

"Do you know anyone uglier inside than you?" Red asked.

"Nicole," Pinkus said.

"What makes you better than Nicole?"

The gamer didn't answer.

"Why do you want us to die?" Wendy asked, unable to mask the desperation in her voice.

"Because you don't think you deserve to die."

Carey had his hands hooked under the rope around his neck and was straining to pull free, but it was too tight. "Please . . ."

Red ignored him. "Have you ever seen hell, Colt?"

"No."

"Trust me, it's as nasty as they say. Enough to give a full-grown man the shakes. Like hell, this is a no-win game—has been from the start. If you *don't* kill yourselves, then you die. If you *do* kill yourselves, then you die. Either way it's time to face the music."

"Come on, you freak," Pinkus challenged. "Show yourself."

"Agreed, I am a freak. But unlike you, I finish what I start."

"What do you mean?" Wendy asked. "Finish what?"

"You all tried to kill me because you were so sure that I was evil. There's no way I'm the only one who dies with an exquisite knowledge of just how pitiful we all are. Including you, honey pie."

"Tried to kill you?" Wendy cried. "What are you talking about?"

"Look inside—it's there, all there. Embrace it, like I did. You deserve to die."

"Why not just kill us, then?" Colt asked.

"If I have to, I will. Believe me. But you should accept this gift I'm offering. The chance to choose the means of your own death. If you don't take it, then I'll slaughter you all *and* make good on my promise to do the seventy."

Colt felt the panic bumping against his mind, and he fought to keep it out. Pinkus was breathing hard. Wendy stood perfectly still, but her eyes were pooled with tears.

They were going to die. There was no way out.

"I'm going to go up to the house and make myself a glass of tea, maybe eat some mustard. Should take about six minutes, no more. Then I'm going to come back down here, and if I don't see four bodies dangling, I'm going to lose my temper. You've never seen me lose my temper. This time the game ends my way."

None of them had a comeback.

"Good."

Red scooped up Colt's gun and strode toward the door. But as he passed the chair on which Carey stood, he gave the legs a casual kick. The chair flew out and Carey dropped hard, unprepared.

They heard his neck crack when the rope caught his fall.

"That's how you do it," Red said. Then he left them standing in the library.

44

The library looked deserted enough when Luke and Steve drove by and around to the back lot. A Walton police car sat in the lot; the cop inside looked like he was asleep. Except for the hole in the windshield, which wasn't immediately visible from Luke's vantage point driving into the lot, he would have gone over there and banged on the door.

But then he saw the bullet hole. "That . . . My eyes deceiving me, or is that a bullet hole?"

Steve grabbed his radio and was about to call it in when Luke saw Clifton's car, parked on the side street behind the library. "Hold up. There he is. Clifton's here."

Luke stopped his cruiser and gave that some thought, transmitter in his hand. Why would the detective park on the street?

He swiveled his eyes to the black-and-white Walton cruiser. Clifton had parked on the street because he'd seen the car and known the killer was nearby. Or because he'd put the hole in the Walton cop himself.

Luke scanned the lot. Maybe Clifton was watching him now. Or maybe he had his radio on and would hear Luke call the dead cop in. Sweat trickled past his right temple, like ants running down one side of his face. He set his radio on the seat and gripped the wheel with both hands.

"He's inside," Steve said, motioning toward the cracked basement door.

Luke shook his head. Clifton wasn't Red—he knew that. But he didn't *really* know that, did he? Fact was, Clifton could do anything he wanted with the chief gone, like Steve said.

"Let's go."

Luke moved more on instinct than with careful forethought. He slipped out of the cruiser, checked his weapon—fully loaded, safety off—and ran on his toes toward the back door.

"You coming?"

"Right on your tail," Steve said.

Luke was sweating when he got there, pushed by adrenaline. He reached for the back door and gave it a shove. It swung slowly in, revealing a short, dark hallway. At the end of the hall stood a man, facing away from Luke.

He went rigid. Was it Red?

Luke took a long, deep breath and stepped into the doorway, gun extended. "Freeze!"

Slowly the man turned, pistol in hand by his side. He stepped out of the shadows. "Put that gun down," he said.

Clifton.

Luke lowered his weapon, feeling a little stupid. "Sorry. Sorry . . . Steve, lower it."

Steve dropped his arms and stood straight. "Sorry, sir. Sorry."

Clifton frowned as if he'd expected this. The detective studied him for a moment, twirled his gun, smoothly dropped it into the holster cowboy-style.

Clifton's eyes darted around the room. "You saw George outside?"

The dead cop. Luke nodded. Clifton must have gotten here just before Luke, seen the cop, and come through the same open door he had.

"He's here, Luke," Clifton said. "I can smell him."

"You can? Really smell him?" Steve asked, rather stupidly.

"Really. Not with my nose, but there's more than one way to smell. I'm following the scent of deductive reasoning. Something in this library's taking Colt and his company back to their teen years."

"How's that?"

"That's what I was just figuring out. Follow me."

He nodded at a side door that looked as though it might lead to storage or utility areas. "There's space behind these walls, Luke. Space that no one would guess was there unless they looked real hard. I've been through two such spaces, both empty. Follow me."

He walked toward a door to his rear that stood ajar, gaping to darkness. Maybe he'd been sizing up the door when Luke had first entered.

They stepped past the framed wall into a passage that provided access to the concrete foundation. Clifton marched right to the end of the hall, hesitated for a moment, then pushed on the brick.

The wall moved. Swung in on a hinge. A door.

A chill fell over Luke. "I'll be . . ."

Clifton stepped past the door and slapped an unseen switch on the wall. A half dozen long fluorescent bulbs strung from the ceiling stuttered to life. They gazed around at what appeared to be a rudimentary laboratory of some kind.

"What's this?" Steve asked. On a table, midfloor, two three-foot-long solid fiberglass tubes, maybe four inches in diameter, rested on top of silver boxes. Manual open beside them.

"Portable microwave transmitters," Clifton said.

An assortment of canisters, each marked with a skull and crossbones, sat on a workbench on their right. Two refrigerated medicine cabinets on the left.

"Is this what I think it is?" Luke asked.

"What do you think it is?"

"Actually, I'm not sure. Something that doesn't belong."

"He's been forcing their minds back into a game all five of them played together seven years ago," Clifton said, walking up to the white tubes.

"What game?"

emories. Wendy searched for them and drew another blank.

"This time the game ends my way," Red had said.

This time.

As if on cue, her world once again shut off. But she made no attempt to suppress the change. The darkness came; the light around the edges came; the vises tightened on her hands and feet; the blanket smothered her; the ghosts drifted through her peripheral vision.

And she was sure then that her mind was indeed recalling something that had once happened.

The shapes in the light weren't spirits, but people, faded by whatever was suppressing her memories. Her hands and feet had once been in some kind of physical device, like a suit equipped with sensors. The blackness was some kind of hood they'd once placed over her head. Or a helmet.

It was the only thing that made sense! She was remembering, however faintly, that Pinkus was right. She too had been part of the test he'd described.

The library snapped back to full view.

She gasped.

Carey's body creaked at the end of the rope. Dead.

"We're finished," Pinkus said.

Wendy faced him. "You were right."

"About what? What does it matter now? This is it, man!"

"I think you were right. And it wasn't just you or Carey. It was all of us. We were all part of that game you played years ago. Including Red. That's what we all have in common."

Colt started to protest. "How could—"

"The blackouts," Wendy said. "Our minds are going back to the game. We're *remembering*."

Pinkus stared at her without comment. The pieces of the puzzle were falling into place behind his intelligent eyes.

"They had a suit on you, right?" Wendy asked him. "Tight at the hands and feet? A helmet of some kind? You could see around the edges of the visor if you tried—a white room with technicians."

"Yeah, that's right."

"But you don't remember anything that happened in that game?"

"No," he said.

"*Something* happened in that game," she said. "Something that upset Red."

Sweat beaded Colt's forehead. "That may explain why he's after us, but it doesn't help us now. We have to take him head-on."

45

lifton faced Luke and Steve. "According to the brief, the game they played was called Skin. The drugs in conjunction with electrical stimuli from these transmitters or ones like these are forcing memories of the game to the surface."

He picked up the operations manual, flipped through it, and dropped it on the table, where it landed with a loud slap. He stepped over to the workbench and lifted a canister that read *Fentanyl*. Then his eyes settled on another set of bottles.

"Lycergitide. Best guess, the killer's drugging them using different delivery systems at different locations—the gas station, in Colt's cruiser, here. Then he transmits a signal that triggers the implants in the brain's hippocampus. He doesn't need to send specific images—Blair claims that technology doesn't exist. Yet. All Red has to do is trigger specific memories that are indistinguishable from reality. Vivid extended flashbacks controlled by precise chemical and electrical stimuli, as the good doctor put it. Memories of a computer game they played in a virtual reality desert seven years ago. Skin."

Clifton was sounding more clinical than usual, Luke thought. "Then you can turn it off. They'll come out of it."

"Maybe . . . These aren't on. They're getting the signal from another location. Or so it seems."

He walked around the tubes. "A little over seven years ago a company called CyberTech employed a researcher named Dr. Cyrus Healy to develop a technology that would immerse the subject into a perfect virtual reality. Summerville is in this mess because Dr. Cyrus Healy, Red's first victim three days ago, retired here. Colt drew the rest. Unless Red is Colt."

"That's a bit complicated, isn't it?"

Clifton continued as if he hadn't heard him. "CyberTech's research showed incredible military applications, so, not surprisingly, the Department of Defense funded expanded research."

Steve stared at the microwave transmitters. "This is unreal—we're living in the twilight zone."

"Actually, this is as real as it gets, boys. Their aim was to use the technology with highly skilled operators. Pilots. It's one thing to fly a plane or drive a tank remotely, using a joystick and a monitor like in a simulation. But imagine doing so in the safety of a room without being able to tell you *weren't* in the plane. With that kind of experience, skills would skyrocket. That's what Dr. Cyrus Healy was working toward."

"And it actually worked? You're saying this is all real. Like we could play this game?"

"Not quite. Not unless you have frontal lobe epilepsy. Dr. Healy discovered that only a mind highly susceptible to suggestion could make the transition. Like the minds found in victims of frontal lobe epilepsy. You need the drugs, you need the electrical triggers and you need a mind with unique wiring. Like in those with frontal lobe epilepsy."

Not impossible, Luke thought. Like stumbling on a cure for cancer. Do certain things to the right mind and you get this.

"CyberTech found five willing candidates with frontal lobe epilepsy in their late teens and offered them fifty thousand dollars each to participate. Their names were Pinkus, Carey, Nicole, Colt, and Wendy. All five were strapped up to a machine and played a game called Skin for six days before it all went haywire."

"Not making the connection, personally," Steve said. "What does that have to do with Gene Stratford's severed hand?"

Clifton looked at him with a raised brow.

Steve explained. "We got us a real severed hand in the morgue, not some computer simulation, right?"

Clifton looked away. "The five subjects had their minds stimulated with a specific series of microwave bursts." He touched the transmitters. "The same sequence of pulses administered today could slam their psyches back into vivid memories of the game they played seven years ago. At least of the environment they played in. The desert reality."

Steve still wasn't buying any of it. "That's really possible? You can really think you're in a desert when you're not? Just like that?"

"Not just like that. The mind's a freaky place and someone stumbled on a way to control the way it's fooled."

"You think Dr. Hansen was involved?" Luke asked.

"No, Red killed Hansen, remember? Try to think straight, Luke. When the game went crazy seven years ago, Dr. Cyrus Healy pulled the plug, but the subjects refused to come out. They had to be forced out with drug-induced hypnotic therapy. The implants were surgically inserted to keep the memories in permanent repression. That was the plan, anyway. They went home healed of epilepsy, $50K richer, missing a week from their memories. Except Pinkus, who recalled some of what happened and became a gaming master."

Clifton gingerly tapped the gray box that powered the transmitter.

"Why none of them have a scar to show the implant surgery, I don't know. There's still something wrong here. Something out of whack."

Steven exchanged a glance with Luke. "So this was all a game they're playing again now? I don't see how they could think—"

"They're not playing the game, Steve. Focus. They played the game seven years ago and it went wrong. Now they're being forced back into this desert reality from that game. Not the game itself. No one was threatening to kill the ugliest back then. People weren't being picked off in a town. The killer's just using their memories of the game to control their environment."

Luke thought he was getting this. It actually made some sense. "So that explains the desert they keep seeing. But not Red."

"According to the brief, Skin was a game that required the players to enter a desert world in which evil was part of the physical reality. Then they had to fix it. Make it beautiful. Something about the Horde, who wore evil on their skin. The game involved shifting realities that required the players to find and defeat evil at its source. They were inserted into the virtual world, fed intravenously, and given seven days. Creation 101. They lasted six days before it went wrong. Did I say there were five subjects?"

"Five," Luke said.

"I lied. There were six. And in this particular playing of the game, the sixth quickly became the greatest, the best at the game. It wasn't until the end of the sixth day that the others began to feel trampled on by the sixth player, who'd become the most powerful by far. Instead of eradicating evil, he became it. He began forcing his decisions on them—and on the computer-generated characters in the game. It got ugly when he started to hang the artificial characters, calling them dissenters. The other five real players decided that the sixth player had to be killed."

"Which would only make *them* evil," Luke said.

"Exactly. They tried to kill him in the game—hang him, the brief said—but the plan backfired and everything went crazy, thus forcing Dr. Healy to pull the plug."

"And the sixth subject?" Steve asked, eyes wide. He glanced around, nervous.

"The sixth went by the name Silver. Sterling Red. They never killed him. The other players came out of the game and went home, none the wiser. But not Red. Turns out he's been killing random victims ever since. And now he's after his fellow players, in the real world. That's who we're dealing with, boys. He'll do anything he can to kill these five players who tried to destroy him seven years ago."

"Six," Luke said. "He's used that number more than once."

Steve raised a brow. "Do you realize how ridiculous this sounds?"

"Is that hand in the morgue real?" Clifton turned his question back on him.

"Yes."

"Then this is real."

They faced off in silence.

"Seven years ago, that would make them eighteen or nineteen when this all went down," Luke said.

"So you're saying that they're not really experiencing all of this?" Steve asked.

Granted, Luke had more time to process the possibility of drugs influencing Colt and the others, but now Steve was coming across like an idiot.

Clifton obviously thought the same. "The only difference between these five and you," he said, "other than intelligence, is that when they look outside, they see a desert landscape where you see grass and buildings. Each time they've disappeared, they did so at night and only for a relatively short time, so we haven't caught them yet. I think we'll find they spent most of their time in and around the library, while our attention was on the ranches and the gas station. For all we know that was all a designed distraction." Then he added, as if to make it clear that he was only guessing, "For all we know."

"And the whole time they were reverting, like a soldier getting flashbacks of the war," Luke said. "Post-traumatic stress syndrome. Joe Goodman had that. Freaked everyone out down at Alice's once when he jumped on the table and hurled a ketchup bottle across the diner. Thought he saw choppers coming in, he said. Definitely heard them."

Clifton stared at him.

"Only these guys are trapped in a landscape from their memories—from Skin," Luke finished off.

"Yes, but only when Red wants them to." Clifton brushed away a fly and set his eyes on the transmitter. "At least that's what he wants everyone to think. This game now involves us all. He's playing against us, this cat and mouse game of his." Clifton grinned. Eyed Luke.

"If they die in the desert, will they die here?" Luke asked.

"I suppose it's time to find out." Clifton walked toward the door. "Keep your eyes peeled. And watch my back."

Luke watched the detective's back, and Steve's for that matter, but the honor was now compromised with the persisting thought that one of the two backs climbing the stairs just ahead of him might belong to a ruthless killer who'd managed to kill more than a dozen people in Summerville over a three-day span. The back on the left, to be more precise. Clifton's back.

Word had leaked to a national tabloid, the world was coming unglued over this crazy killing spree in a small town about two hundred miles south of Las Vegas, and here was Luke Preston, gun trained on someone who just might be responsible.

Clifton led, moving ghostlike up the library's outside stairs. He slipped his gun out, opened the door, and eased inside. Not a sound. He held up his hand for caution, then led them along a bookcase toward the center. Dead silent, except for the soft thump of their feet and the pumping of his heart.

The ropes were the first sign that something was off. Luke caught his first glimpse of them through the gap above the books as he crept forward. Several ropes, just dangling above the tables.

That was strange in any case, but plain freaky in light of the fact that Colt had supposedly tried to hang himself here yesterday. What was it with hanging in this place?

Luke pulled up behind Clifton, who'd stopped and was staring out at the ropes. Three ropes with empty nooses. The fourth rope, however, wasn't empty.

Carey's neck filled that fourth noose. He was hanging limp, deader than a rock.

Clifton scanned the balcony. "Colt?" His voice echoed through the library.

Luke walked out, his eyes fixed on the dead body. Carey's face was purple, and his tongue was sticking out like a lollipop. "You think Colt killed him?"

"Red did," Clifton said, moving toward the tables. He stopped, fixed on something low.

Luke saw Nicole's body then. She faced the ceiling, eyes wide, dead, maybe even deader than Carey, at least timewise. The thought of such a beautiful creature gone seemed somehow more tragic to Luke than Carey's death. Such a waste. Not because he felt anything special for her, but man . . . what a waste. The same thought had spun through his mind when he'd seen her with the awful brand on her face.

Clifton walked up to the bodies. He nudged Carey's limp form and watched it swing. "He wants them all to kill themselves," he said. "Because they're all the ugliest. That's what he's doing."

So how *did* Clifton know so much? The "brief"? Pure detective work? Or was it more?

Luke's skin began to crawl. It was a good thing Steve was here.

"He's already killed two out of five," Luke said, looking around. What if the killer wasn't Clifton, but was smiling at them from the shadows right now? He studied the shelves. "You think he's here?"

"This body's still warm," Clifton said. His gaze drifted to the front doors. "Best guess, the house. If he's not here, then he's probably there."

"I should call for more backup," Luke said.

"You can be sure any cops who go up against Red will end up dead," Clifton said. "He's too good."

"What about us, then? This is nuts! We can't just walk up there; he'll pick us off. We need a plan. You have a plan, right?"

"Not really, no. Just following my nose, Luke. Follow yours."

"Hold on. Just hold on! We can't just follow our noses to Red. He'll find us first, and it'll be with a bullet, man. We have to think this through."

"Not Red, Luke. Colt. Colt's on the inside, and we now know that he's not Red. None of them are. Red's the sixth player, come back for revenge." The detective hesitated, thinking. Always thinking. "You have a shotgun in your car?"

"Yeah."

"Okay. Get the shotgun and check the house with Steve. You hear anything, you fire your weapon."

"What about you?"

"We split up. You flush him out." He twirled his gun twice and let it slap back into his palm. "I put him out of his misery."

Split up? Why? Because Clifton wanted to be alone?

A tremor ran through his hands. He couldn't let the man know of his suspicion for the obvious reason that if he was right, Clifton, being Red, would end it. *It* being his life.

"You expect us to go up against this guy by ourselves?" he asked. "You just said any cop who faced him would end up dead."

"He'll force them back into the library."

"How do you know?" Steve asked.

Clifton looked up at the nooses. "These ropes look like they're here for a reason to you?"

Steve glanced up. "Yeah."

"Good thinking. So they'll probably be back to use them." He tapped his head with a bony white finger. "You have to think, Steve. This variety of perp is beaten up here."

"You really think Colt's in the house?" He had to play along. Not that he knew Clifton was Red. The rest would probably laugh at the suggestion. Still . . .

"Pony up, Luke," Clifton said. "Am I alone here?"

Luke glanced at Steve, who was watching him. They were cops with sworn duties.

"Okay, let's go." He turned toward the stairs that led down to the back entrance. Once he had that shotgun in his hands, he'd feel better. You didn't have to be a crack shot like Clifton with a shotgun.

46

Colt led them along the garage side of the house, picking each step as if they were walking through a minefield. He stopped and looked back at Wendy and Pinkus, who both stared back with fear-fired eyes, hoping against hope that he could pull off a miracle.

But he wasn't going to pull off a miracle. He knew that now. Miracles were in short supply.

He'd demanded that they leave the library and come up here to face Red head-on, because there was no way they were going to just hang themselves. Besides, the way he looked at it, going head-on with Red was its own kind of suicide. He would make that abundantly clear to Red and then try to kill him. If Red killed them all, the killer would be obligated to leave the town because they would have essentially committed suicide, thereby killing the ugliest. All of them.

But that's not what he'd told Wendy and Pinkus. How could he?

He hadn't actually told them he had a plan, either, but he'd implied it with his show of bravado, which was tantamount to saying he had one. It was a lie.

He met Wendy's eyes, sure that his eyes now betrayed a fear that matched hers. The profound connection between them in the library had flipped a switch somewhere deep in his psyche, but he didn't know what bearing it had on their predicament.

"What?" Wendy asked.

"What? I don't know what."

"So what's the plan?" Pinkus asked, looking around with furtive glances. "Level up and kick his butt?"

"'Level up'?"

"It's a gaming term. To beat the bad guy at any level, you have to become stronger, which means acquiring the skills necessary to kick his butt. Otherwise you die." He broke his eye contact with Colt. "We can't get stuck out here. Maybe we should go back."

"And hang ourselves?" Wendy snapped.

"We're not doing that," Colt said. "Like I said, the last thing he'll expect for us to do is come after him. We have to take him head-on; it's our only chance."

"But how?" Pinkus demanded. "You're leading us out here with our pants down. How the heck we gonna take this guy head-on?"

"I'm going to," Colt said. "But I have to talk him out of a gun to do it."

"That's crazy, man!"

"Shut up, Pinkus," Colt whispered as loudly as he dared. "He's doing all of this out of some convoluted sense of vengeance. I can play on that."

"Then why can't Wendy and I go back? We can't get past the electrical lines, but we could make a circuit around and go for help."

"That would take hours! If you survived. Last time we tried something like that he used Nicole for target practice."

"I don't *want* to go back," Wendy said. "Colt's right, he'll come down and kill us."

Colt looked from his right to his left at each house corner. "Besides, I need you up here."

"For what?" Pinkus asked.

"For bait."

"I don't want to be bait. You crazy?"

"You have a better idea? You do, I'm all ears, buddy. Until then, try to keep your whining to a minimum. I'm trying to think this through here."

"How much time do we have?" Wendy asked.

"Maybe five minutes before he heads back down." Colt took a deep breath, closed his eyes, and tried to think. But nothing significant was coming.

Huummmmm . . .

Wendy looked up at the blackening sky.

"He's isolated us," Colt said.

"Haven't we been over this?" Pinkus asked. "Man, if you don't have something better than using us as bait to pick a fight—"

"Shut up, Pinkus," Wendy snapped. She brushed past him and strode toward the back door.

"Wendy? Where you going?"

"To find Red," she said. "To get this over with."

Luke led Steve around the back of the library, up the grassy slope beside the side wall, shotgun firmly in both hands. A tall tree spread its leafy branches over the roof, shading the incline. He could see the doctor's house ahead, alone and quiet under the sun.

He had to play along; he knew that. And he had to do it without calling for backup. Or telling Steve that he suspected Clifton, for that matter.

None of them would believe him. They'd undoubtedly spill the beans to Clifton, who would then either play dumb, in which case they wouldn't be able to pin anything on him, or worse, kill Luke.

This time, Luke had to pony up, as Clifton had said, and deal with Clifton when he showed his true colors. The notion made him sick with fear.

He pulled up behind the tree and faced Steve. "See anyone?"

"No. But I think we're nuts, man."

Luke looked up at the sky, searching. "You think they see what we see?"

"I think this is just plain nuts. Why can't we call for more backup?"

"You heard him. And this killer knows how to disappear. We come out here with a ton of guys and he's gone, guaranteed. Like the man said, Steve: pony up."

Luke fixed his gaze back on the house, already considering. But first, the house.

"Ready?"

"Ready."

"We cross the ground quick, okay? Can't be out in the open long. Stay low and run to the garage. When we get there we go in the back, but go slow. No sound."

Luke looked at the western horizon. "Let's go."

Crap.

47

"D o you see him?" Wendy asked in Colt's ear.

He lifted his hand for silence. He'd rushed past her as she approached the back door that led into the kitchen. If there was any man who had the physical skill to go up against Red, it was Colt. But Colt was sweating badly—he'd lost his confidence long ago. And Wendy could hardly think straight for all the impossibilities crashing through her mind.

They should be running away from Red, not toward him! But running would certainly sentence only God knew how many to their deaths, and there was no way they could deny that in good conscience.

It was then while Wendy was pressing up close to Colt, nerves strung like guitar strings, that she saw the black horse on their right, at the top of the rise behind the doctor's house. She didn't know horses well, but she knew enough to notice that the tackle on this one looked different. Old.

"Colt?"

She glanced past his shoulder; the kitchen was empty.

"Colt, I think you should see this."

"See what?"

"It's a horse," Pinkus said. "What's a horse doing here?"

Colt followed her stare and stepped back from the window. "A horse," he said after a moment. "With a sword."

He was right. There was an old blade of some kind sticking out of a leather scabbard. The horse looked at them and snorted.

"Don't move," Colt said. "Stay put."

They let him go without protesting. He ran in a crouch up the hill, hand extended in invitation to the horse. He almost made it too, but at the last minute the horse shied away and disappeared over the crest.

Colt stopped at the top, stared over for a second, then walked out of sight.

"Where's he going?" Pinkus demanded.

"After the sword?"

A fly buzzed by her face and she swatted at it. The house creaked and she pulled back from the door. For what seem like an endless stretch nothing happened.

Pinkus was getting twitchy. "Where is he?"

The question had started to bother her as well. Surely Colt hadn't gone into the desert after the horse. He should have either caught it by now and returned with the sword, or let it go.

"Something's wrong," Pinkus said. "We should go back."

Colt stumbled over the hill, stared at them for a moment as if trying to get his bearings, then hurried toward them. His face was red and wet with sweat, and his eyes had a frantic look that suggested he'd seen a ghost.

"What happened?" Wendy whispered.

"It . . . it's gone."

"What took so long?"

"Nothing."

"You don't look like *nothing*," Pinkus said. "Something's wrong, I knew it."

"In case you hadn't noticed, everything's wrong, Pinkus," Colt snapped. "Everything! And I'm not just talking about drugs and implants. That horse just vanished." He took a deep breath, put one hand on the door knob, and steadied himself. "It doesn't matter. Red's real and he's killed enough innocent people to fill my nightmares for a lifetime. We're running out of time."

"You sure you're okay?" Wendy asked, trying to sound calm.

Colt turned the knob, pushed the door slowly open, and, seeing nothing, stepped in on his toes.

"Red!" he shouted. "I got a proposal for you."

Wendy cringed, rooted to the concrete landing outside the entry. The house sat silent inside.

"Red!"

He walked farther in with a show of purpose, and Wendy felt isolated outside. She hurried after Colt, followed by Pinkus, who was whispering under his breath. "This sucks, I don't like this . . ."

"I know what you expect us to do, and that may be the only way to end this, but I've got a proposal." Colt strode down the hall, nearly shouting the challenge now. "You want us to kill ourselves, fine, but we're not giving you that satisfaction until you come out here and face us."

But there still wasn't any response.

"What if he's not here?" Pinkus whispered.

They exchanged stares. Wendy fought a sudden urge to run out the back, into the desert, let the town fend for itself. But she couldn't.

Colt swore and began to run through the house, searching frantically now. Wendy and Pinkus stood still, frozen by the spectacle. *He must have a plan,* she thought. Either that or he was panicking. Whatever element of surprise they hoped for was long gone. The only thing left for him to do was to talk Red into some kind of alteration to his plan—what kind of plan was that?

Colt rushed into the kitchen, panting. "He's not here."

"That's good," Pinkus said.

"No, that can't be good." Colt whirled toward the front door. "Time's up. Time's up and he's gonna start killing."

He bolted down the hall and disappeared around the corner, headed for the front door. For a long moment, neither Wendy nor Pinkus moved, could move.

Wendy tore herself free and ran, and she could hear Pinkus pounding the carpet after her. Colt stood at the front door, which he'd opened, staring out at the desert. Or had Red left that door open? He was outside? She pulled up just behind him.

"What is it?"

A hot breeze blew from the black skies.

Huummmmm . . .

"What is it, Colt?" she whispered.

He stepped outside, down the steps. They followed his gaze to the horizon. Nothing had changed that she could see. Still no town, still no Red, still no sign of any cavalry stampeding in to save them.

"Colt?"

Colt walked farther into what had once been the front lawn—now desolate desert landscape. He scooped up some sand and let it run through his fingers. "What if Red isn't real?"

She hurried after him, scanning the library for any sign of movement. For Red. "We've been over this, Colt. How—"

"What if we *are* Red? Isn't that what Clifton thinks? What if he's right?"

"You're losing it, man," Pinkus said. "You're going loco."

"And you're not?" Colt snapped, whirling back. "*You* don't see this sand? You see the town instead of desert here? Maybe we're all nuts, deranged by a sick past. Isn't that what you said?"

"This isn't the time for this, man," Pinkus said. "You think Carey and Nicole aren't really dead? What, you think you or me or Wendy pushed that chair he was standing on? We branded Nicole's face? We may be a bit weak in the head, drugged, whatever, but we're not him."

Colt was red-faced with frustration, beyond himself. "It's impossible. I don't believe any of this. I *refuse* to!"

The desert rang with his words.

Luke and Steve saw that the back door was open when they were still at the corner of the house, backs flat against the wall. At least *Luke* had his back flat against the wall. Steve didn't seem to understand the word *stealth*.

He stepped past Luke, who reached out and pulled him back. "Stay behind!" he whispered.

Fact was, there was no sign of Colt, no sign of any of them. This meant they had to at least peek into the house, maybe go in the house, and Luke was even less eager now than he had been five minutes ago.

An ambulance siren drifted through the air. Maybe something to do with Becky. They were on the edge of town, no buildings on their right. Just the back lawn, then some scrub oak and rocks.

This just wasn't right. He crept closer to the open door. Could see into the house now, into the kitchen. Looked empty.

Clinging to this small morsel of encouragement, Luke eased up to the window next to the door and peeked in.

Nothing.

Looked like any deserted kitchen on a lazy summer morning. He held the shotgun out, finger on the trigger, and shifted into the doorway.

Nothing. Empty. No killer smiling in the corner with six-guns drawn.

A yell suddenly cut the silence, and Luke almost fired the shotgun. His pumping heart thumped in his ears. "What was that?"

The cry came again from the front of the house. ". . . *refuse* to!"

Luke's initial terror was pushed aside by the certainty that the voice belonged to Colt. And it had sounded like it came from the front yard, not in the house.

Another voice, the gamer's voice, was arguing with Colt, which probably meant that Red wasn't out there. They wouldn't argue with Red standing there. He ran through the kitchen and down the hall, spun into the foyer, and bounded for the front door.

"Hold up," Steve breathed.

Luke pulled up hard. Colt and company were on the front lawn, green grass underfoot, arguing with each other.

"I refuse to believe the sky is black or that we're standing on sand," Colt said. "But *I have to*, because that's what I see. Drugs can't explain this. You think a computer chip can make sand?" He threw a handful on the ground.

"Yes. It can," Pinkus said.

Colt wasn't buying. "The only thing that makes sense is that we're nuts, and you'd better believe that's what Clifton's thinking. Something crazy happened to us seven years ago or whenever and we're plumb loco. They'll pin the whole thing on us!"

"What does it matter if we're killed?" Pinkus returned. "Which is what you're going to get us—killed. And for the record, I think Clifton is Red."

"Exactly, and he'll walk away after he frames us."

Luke stepped through the door and onto the porch. "Colt?"

Wendy turned to face him. Her eyes bored past him into the doorway. "I thought I heard something," she said. "You hear that?"

The other two glanced past Luke, then turned away.

"Of course you heard something," Luke said. "You . . . you can see me, right?"

"How could they not see us?" Steve asked. "Of course they see us."

But Wendy's eyes drifted toward the horizon, and Luke knew they couldn't. They were standing thirty feet from Colt, Wendy, and Pinkus, and none of them could see Luke and Steve because Clifton had been right. Their minds had been yanked back into the world of Skin, or whatever their game had been called. They actually thought they were standing on sand rather than the grassy front lawn.

"I don't think so, Steve. I think they think they're in a desert."

"They really can't see us? Or hear us?"

"Nope."

"Holy smokes."

For a while they just stared at the trio, trying to come to grips with the prospect of being invisible.

"Hello?" Steve called out. "Hey, Colt!"

"Hush, man!" Luke motioned for him to be quiet. "The whole world'll hear you!"

"And that's bad?"

"Could be. What if they're right? You want Clifton hearing us out here, yelling?"

Pinkus strode south, then spun back. "I say we head south and put some distance between us and this place. Forget the game."

"We can't cross the electric line," Colt said. "It'll kill you. And we can't just let Red go on killing. We're finished. Totally finished, end of story."

"I'm willing to give the electric line a running start," Pinkus said. "I'd rather be electrocuted than strung up."

"What, they can't pass the electric wires?" Steve asked.

Luke studied the high-voltage lines that ran along the south edge of the lawn. He recalled Colt explaining how the wires had fallen but still held a charge, forcing them to stay north of the town.

"They can feel things," he said. "If they headed south, I bet they'd run into the buildings."

"What do you mean?" Steve asked.

Luke flung an arm out. "That's gotta be it! The reason they're buying this desert of theirs is because there's no evidence that the town is here. Red's making them stay wide of the buildings so they don't run into them and realize that it's all in their minds."

Steve considered this. "So?"

"So that means they can feel things."

"Then why don't they feel the grass when they reach down to touch the 'sand'?"

"Shoes? Maybe it's all about . . . you know, contrasts. Grass is too similar to sand to tell the difference. Who knows how the mind works?"

He picked up a pebble and threw it at the woman. The pebble hit her on the head and bounced off.

Wendy grabbed her head. "Ouch!" She faced Luke, eyes wide. "What was that?"

"What was what?" Colt asked.

"Something just hit me on the head! Hard."

"You're going nuts too," Pinkus said.

"See?" Luke said. "Holy smokes, you see that?"

Steve grabbed a big stone and cocked his arm.

"Whoa! You trying to kill them?"

"You think?"

"'Course it could. Put it down."

Steve lowered the stone.

"But that gives me an idea."

Wendy knew something had hit her on the head. No denying the lump forming. A small bump, but real enough. She looked up at the sky.

"You think whatever's up there could have dropped something?"

"Yes, of course," Pinkus cried. "The demons are crapping on our heads now. Hard turds that feel like rocks. Never mind the fact that you can't see them; if you don't dodge them, they'll beat you to death!"

Something nudged Wendy's shoulder. Squeezed it. She jumped back with a sharp cry.

"Something's here! Colt?"

Colt hurried to her side. "What is it? I don't see anything."

"Something touched me. It grabbed my shoulder."

Two hands touched her cheeks—one on each. She swung at the invisible hands out of panic. None of them could deny the loud smack of flesh against flesh as her hand came in contact with something or someone who stood directly in front of her.

"Someone is here!"

Colt stared at the empty space, incredulous but without rebuttal.

"What is it?" she cried.

Pinkus stood still, boldness gone.

"They didn't hurt you," Colt said. "If they wanted to hurt you, they would have."

"They threw something at me!"

Colt extended his right arm and felt the air. He stepped forward, groping, then pulled up sharply.

"Colt?"

His hand gripped something. Formed a handshake. "I . . . I'm holding someone's hand."

A beat passed.

"Luke?"

Wendy knew that Colt had seen something as clearly as she'd felt something, and in that moment her perception shifted. The world around her changed. Suddenly it wasn't empty air that Colt gripped, but the police officer Luke's hand. The man shook his hand, shotgun cradled in his right arm, looking on with a dumb expression.

"Hello, Colt."

Luke wasn't standing on the sand. There was grass under his feet.

Wendy glanced over to the house. The sky had brightened to blue. She turned her head slowly to the right. The town was back.

Beside her, Pinkus gasped.

"It's back!" Colt said, releasing Luke's hand. "The town's back."

They stood in stunned quiet for several long seconds. So then it *was* in their minds, totally in their minds.

"You can see me now?" Luke asked.

"We see you," Colt said, staring around. "Do you know what's happening?"

"We found a room in the back of the basement with microwave transmitters and the mind-altering drugs. Clifton says Red is someone you all knew as Silver seven years ago. You were all part of the same test that Jerry Pinkus participated in. It did something to your minds, and now Red's forcing your memories of the game back to the surface using drugs and microwave pulses. All five of you had frontal lobe epilepsy."

Colt stared at Wendy. Then back at Luke. "We did?"

"You did. This all only works with people who have that kind of . . . you know. Mind."

"Okay, that was seven years ago," Wendy said, unable to accept his claim and ignoring her doubt at once. "Why were we seeing the desert now?"

Luke told them why. He told them about the game called Skin in which six subjects were to defeat evil, which they tried to do while totally immersed in the world of Skin. But a player named Silver had become the new evil and the rest had tried to hang him. It backfired and the plug was pulled by Dr. Cyrus Healy, the architect of the game. That's why, Luke theorized, Healy and his son, Timothy, had both been killed. Revenge killings. And that's probably why Timothy had such insight into the desert reality. He'd probably at least messed around with the game his father developed. The game called Skin.

Either way, Silver now went by the name Sterling Red, like bloody silver.

Suddenly the reasoning of Red's game made perfect sense to Wendy. The most beautiful in the game had become the ugliest because of his own pride. He'd been overthrown and was out to destroy those who'd turned on him. That was Red's game!

Assuming that all of what Luke said was realistic. But she wasn't ready to assume.

"Our minds are that fragile?" Colt asked.

"Not fragile, man," Pinkus said, his eyes wide as always, but the fear had been replaced by excitement. He was buying it all, which would make sense—he'd lived with a partial memory of that week ever since. "You're all like me. They paid us all fifty thousand dollars to lend them our minds because they were *special*, not fragile. Normal people would never be able to connect like we did."

"Connect?" Colt said.

"Into the gaming environment."

"That was seven years ago," Wendy said. "If he can force us back into that environment today that easily, I'd say we're as fragile as newborn babies. Practically idiots."

"Fractured, maybe, not fragile," Pinkus said. "Ask anyone who's gone up against me in a tournament—I'm no idiot. As for easy, I wouldn't call a world-renowned physicist's discovery that you can stimulate a person who has frontal lobe epilepsy into an alternate state using a combination of drugs and microwaves a simple discovery. And he's using that microwave with implants that are tied into the limbic system. Feasible. Completely plausible."

He had a point.

"So our memories of that experiment were suppressed, and now this microwave stimulus triggers it so we think we're in this desert reality," Colt said. "Why? If he wanted revenge, why not just force our hands without all the trouble of kicking us back into the desert? He could play this same game without the desert, right?"

"Poetic justice, man," Pinkus said. "Trust me, I'm a gamer. He doesn't just want to kill us, he wants to rub our noses in our own pathetic defeat. He wants each of us to beg, grovel, and then kill ourselves. Pull the plug on our miserable lives. It's the perfect game."

"Revenge," Wendy said. "Plus he's not wholly sane."

Pinkus nodded.

"And if we're being tripped back to this waking nightmare by having our frontal lobes jogged by microwaves, how does the town come back?" Wendy asked.

"When the drugs wear off." Pinkus lifted both hands to his temples and rubbed hard. "I knew it, man! That game was nuts."

"It's not real, then," Wendy said to no one in particular. "The desert isn't real. And we saw the house and the library only because he wanted us to. Included them as part of the game. This construct or whatever. Same with the two ranches."

"And the boy," Colt said.

"Boy?"

He looked back at the house. "There was a boy with that horse we saw. Said some crazy thing about the Horde and water and then vanished. Faded right in front of me like a hologram turned off. Sounds like a construct from the game we played. Memories playing tricks."

"Horde?" Luke said. "The game, Skin, has something to do with a Horde."

Wendy recalled the horse she and Carey had seen at the ranch several days earlier. At the time she'd thought she'd seen a boy riding it.

"Way I remember it, the desert reality in Skin had all kinds of characters," Pinkus said. "You were tripping back, man."

Colt faced the library. "Either way Red is real, not some construct. And he hasn't failed to deliver on any promise yet. He's still going to force our hands. This isn't over."

Luke looked around nervously, shotgun now leveled at his hip in firing position. "I think I may know who Red is," he said.

"Clifton," Colt said.

Steve swiveled his head. "Not a chance."

Luke eyed him. "Clifton. I'll explain later, trust me."

"Where *is* Clifton?" Colt asked.

"In the library."

They all stared at the library.

"He's lost his advantage," Colt said.

354

"What if he jacks us back in?" Wendy asked.

Pinkus frowned, eyes drilling the library. "I don't think he can, now that we know. But it doesn't matter. Colt's right, the game goes on, desert or not. He's still playing. For all we know, watching us right now. We do anything but play the game, he pops us. We're finished."

"Clifton's good," Luke warned. "Very good."

"We don't have a choice," Colt said. "We have to end this."

No one disagreed.

48

You'd better get down here now." Beth Longhorn's voice held a slight tremor that spoke with more volume than had she screamed. "They know."

Blair jumped to his feet, sending his chair crashing against the wall behind him.

"They're going after him now," Longhorn said.

"Get the force in there!"

"You know we can't do that."

"I don't care what the consequences are—just get it stopped!"

"He'll kill Colt, Wendy, and Jerry."

"We have to reach him."

"Clifton?"

"Who else? Yes, Clifton!" he snapped.

A beat.

"What if he is Clifton?"

49

ustard would have been nice, and iced tea, too, but it was all coming down and he had to play the game perfectly now. His excitement was at a fevered pitch, and the shakes were screaming to come out, to rattle his body to a blur. He couldn't allow any such indiscretion in the face of victory. Jerking muscles could spoil his aim.

Sterling Red hated them all, not only because none of them had the shakes, but because all of them knew or understood how terrible the shakes really were. They lied to themselves, like most fools, convincing themselves that there really was no conflict within themselves and thus blissfully traipsing through the tulips. It only made him realize how terribly he hated them all.

Red chided himself for getting so worked up at this crucial moment. It wasn't over yet. This was his finest hour.

He knew he'd embraced the very evil he'd set out to destroy with the other five in the game, which made him nothing less than a conflicted version of evil, thus causing his constant shakes. He'd often told himself that once this mission was done, he would lie down and die; but he knew he couldn't do that because he was already dead in so many ways.

Instead, he would go after another group of deeply deceived black souls. Maybe politicians. Or those preachers who pretended. Maybe just anybody, because he'd never met anyone who wasn't as evil as he.

But first, the game.

Come to me, children. It's game time.

And pass the mustard.

Colt approached the library cautiously, fully aware that they were caught in a terrible guessing game that had in no way resolved itself. They knew a few things now, but they didn't have anything that could end Red.

Other than a gun.

He'd taken Luke's sidearm, never so thankful for the feel of steel in his palm. Nine rounds. Luke followed with a shotgun. Then Steve, with another sidearm.

"When we go in, stay behind cover until we know what's in there."

"I don't like this," Steve whispered. "This ain't right. None of this is right."

Colt pushed through the door, gun cocked. He'd thought about asking the others to remain outside but rejected the idea, unwilling to leave them unguarded.

"Just be ready."

The library was eerily silent and dim. He moved forward on soft soles, nerves stretched tight, arms relaxed and hands loose on the gun. His exit avenues printed themselves on his mind with each footfall: a roll to his right behind the counter, then up and firing from cover; around the bookcase on his left, down the aisle between it and the next one to bring fire on a target across the way.

But all of these could be easily negated with a single bullet from the shadows. If Red had a bead on him now, no amount of gun handling could save them.

But if everything they'd guessed was right, Red wasn't in this for a bullet to their heads. He could have done that two days ago.

No, Red was on a vendetta that had taken him years to prepare. He wouldn't end it with a few simple shots. He really did intend on forcing them to hang themselves, even if he had to break all of their bones in the process.

The ring of cherrywood study tables came into view. The three empty nooses. Another noose ending with Carey's limp body. Colt quickly searched the balcony, saw nothing but bookcases and shadows.

"Where is he?" Luke whispered. Good question. He answered himself. "Maybe he's downstairs, in the room."

Colt glanced back, saw that Wendy and the other two were tucked behind bookcases, and stepped past the counter toward the center. The pentagram was still undisturbed. The body was still dead. This was as real as it got.

"Luke, I want you to stay here with Pinkus and Steve. Keep them behind you and keep that shotgun ready. Wendy and I will check the basement. We force him to split his focus. Can you do that?"

"He's good, Colt; he's fast and he's good."

"I think we've established—"

A loud thump behind Colt stopped him short. Another louder crash. He spun to the sound and saw nothing but empty space at the end of the bookcase that Steve had been standing behind.

"What?" Luke had his gun around and trained on the floor.

The counter cut Colt's view off waist high. He bounded back, weapon up in both hands. Steve lay on the floor, facedown, either dead or unconscious.

Luke was breathing hard. "Oh, man . . ."

"Get back! Cover!" They all scrambled past Colt to cover themselves from any fire that might originate behind Steve's fallen body.

The library went silent.

"Detective Clifton?"

Nothing.

Colt scooted back to where Wendy and Pinkus knelt behind the counter. Luke crouched behind the bookcase about ten feet off, shotgun ready, eyes on Colt.

Wendy grabbed Colt's shirt and pulled him close to her. He could smell her, feel her breath on his cheek. The sound of feet running rose just above their breathing, then faded.

Red.

Colt's hands were shaking. He knew he had to move now, before Red managed to cover them from a new angle. They were sitting ducks.

Boom! A gunshot cracked from the far side of the library. Luke's shotgun clattered to the ground, trigger gone.

"Crap! Crap!" Luke held his bleeding hand as he rolled for cover next to Colt. All three of them now huddled behind the counter; Pinkus was on both knees at the other end.

"Stay here," Colt whispered. "Don't move!"

Wendy grabbed his shirt. "Colt?"

"Just stay put." He ran around the counter in a crouch, rolled across the gap to the bookcase where Steve lay, and came to his knees behind the books. He pressed two fingers against the cop's neck, found a pulse. Blood seeped from a wound on his head. He would keep.

Premeditation was the key to survival in any firefight, but calcu-
lated thought had to happen in fractions of seconds. He'd already
wasted four or five.

Colt stood and sprinted forward, around the bookcase, straight
toward the back, where the last shot had been discharged.

Still no target.

Boom!

Thump!

Colt spun back. Carey's body had fallen. The rope had been cut
in half by a bullet, and this time Colt couldn't place the origination
point. The bullet ricocheted around the room like a ping-pong ball.

"Colt . . ." Red's whisper chased the dying echo. And then loudly
in a matter-of-fact voice, "Mustard, anyone?"

He still couldn't tell where the sound came from. But hearing it,
he thought he could make out Clifton's voice in it. Similar enough,
anyway. They were caught flat-footed, he saw. Red could probably
pick any one of them off at will, and the fact that he hadn't done so
confirmed Colt's guess that this was all about Red's vendetta.

Colt pressed his back against the vertical beam he'd stopped behind
and considered his options. If he could just find a target, he could
attempt a shot. But Red clearly had no intention of that. Could he
have managed to climb the stairs to the balcony? Possible, but the
man would have had to move like the wind.

He could try to distract Red—run out of the library. But even in
that short time, he would have his way with the others. If Red was
on the balcony, he could try to get the others out with him under
some covering fire.

"Colt," Wendy cried.

"Sorry, honey, Colt was too slow," Red said.

Colt whipped around to face the counter, now far to his left.

"Look out," Pinkus whispered, as if he knew it was too late.

Colt saw the man in the mask then, beyond Wendy and Pinkus, between two bookcases, half hidden by shadow. He had a gun in one hand and a bowie knife in the other, and he was staring directly at Colt.

The shot was dangerous, far too close to Pinkus's head, but Colt took it anyway. He fired at the form.

The gamer screamed and ducked.

Red had pulled back.

"Run, Wendy! Get outside before—"

"No, Wendy, no, not outside," Red's voice said. "To the ropes, or I put a hole in the mutt's face."

Mutt, meaning him.

"Colt?"

"Move!" Red screamed.

Wendy and Pinkus stumbled forward, over the pentagram.

"Heads in the noose and one of you will live, I swear it on my black soul."

"Colt?" Wendy whimpered.

They were cornered. Colt tried to think, but his mind was slugging through a sea of fear. This time it was going to end. Luke was still in a position to try something, but they all knew he lacked the resources to present a true threat to Red.

"Colt?"

"It's okay, Wendy."

"You expect us to put our heads in those ropes?" Pinkus cried. "We can't—"

Boom!

"Aaaahhhhh! Aaaahhh, aaaahhhhh!"

Colt poked his head out for a shot. Pinkus clung to a newly bloodied right hand.

Boom! A second slug splintered the post beside him. He jerked back.

"You keep testing me and I'll blow all ten of them off," Red said.

Colt could hear a table scrape, a chair topple, a curse from Pinkus. His vision blurred. He had to do something, anything, maybe put a bullet in his own head, but something.

"Now you, Colt. Walk out with the gun above your head. Lower the gun and I put one in your arm. Don't walk out and I put one in her leg."

He took a deep breath, lifted the gun over his head, and walked out. No sign of the man, but he was there, lurking in the shadows. Wendy and Pinkus stood on one of the tables, heads level with two of the ropes.

Colt pushed his way past two tables that had been squeezed together to make room for Carey's pentagram and walked to the middle, moving as fast as he dared without raising suspicion.

"Eager to die, Colt? Set the gun on the floor."

He didn't set but rather dropped the gun so that it slid a few feet, closer to Luke.

"Up on the table with the others."

Luke sat against the wall, searching him with frantic eyes. Scared stupid. "That's not him," he whispered shakily. "He's dressed different."

Not Clifton? But Clifton could have changed easily enough.

Colt walked to the tables, hoisted himself up, and stood next to Wendy, who immediately latched onto the back of his shirt.

"Stay calm," he whispered.

"We're *all* the ugliest," she said.

Sterling Red stepped out, clad in a black T-shirt and jeans, mask snug against the backward baseball cap. He strode to the center of the floor and stared up at them. Behind him, Luke pushed himself up a bit, then jerked back down. Like he'd seen something.

"Seven years is a long time to wait to bring this whole thing to a joyful end," Red said. "But I'm now quite confident that we're all gamed out."

"Timothy Healy said something about you," Wendy said.

"I don't care what anyone said. And if you talk out of turn like that again, I might lose my temper."

"You're going to kill us anyway," Pinkus said. "What difference does it make?"

Red shifted his weight and twirled the gun. "You're right. We're running low on time, and I've pushed this thing to the bitter end, taken all kinds of silly chances, all in the hope of helping you see just how ugly you all really are. Vanity, vanity, all is vanity. But there's still one last trick I want to show you before I go ahead and bring this game to a close."

"Don't move!"

The words hadn't come from Red, who'd frozen, gun by his ear. They'd come from a man who now followed his gun out from behind the same bookcase Red had come from.

Detective Clifton.

"Not a muscle," the man said.

Clifton crossed quickly and pressed the gun to the base of Red's skull from behind. "Put it down."

Colt's blood pounded. Luke had known that Red wasn't Clifton when the killer had stepped out earlier.

"Really?" Red asked. "Why don't you just pull the trigger, Detective? You of all people should know how dangerous I am."

"Shut up and lower the weapon."

Red lowered his gun. "You want to know, don't you? All of you. Who is Red? Who is the blazingly fast killer who seems to know your innards as if they're his?"

He dropped the bowie knife and lifted his left hand to his face. He pulled off the mask.

They stared into the face of Timothy Healy, now grinning wickedly.

"Hello, Colt. Hello, Wendy. Hello, Pinkus. Now who's the ugliest shape-shifter in the land?"

No sign of any deformity in his right hand—he'd played the role to perfection.

"Silver," Wendy said.

"The one and the same," Sterling Red said. "The one you all tried to kill seven years ago because I was an ugly blight on your precious little world."

"That was a game," Pinkus cried.

"Really? Someone forgot to tell my father. He *gave* me frontal lobe epilepsy so that I could participate. The game only worked on freaks, so he made me a freak, just like you all. I became the best of the freaks, so the other freaks tried to kill me. Oops."

So what Luke had learned from Clifton was right. Silver's mind had fractured, probably before he'd even entered the game, which he'd never quit playing. He was taking his revenge here in the real world, out to destroy those who had cast him out.

Timothy had entered the desert reality and faked his own death to provide cover. They'd never found Timothy Healy's body, only his blood on the bathroom floor.

He had murdered his own father, who'd made him Silver, the sixth player. The most beautiful had become the ugliest in the game called Skin.

They all stared at Red for several long seconds, connecting the dots.

"Drop the gun and place your hands behind your back slowly," Clifton said.

"You can't really shoot me, Detective," Red said. "Not in cold blood. A slug would tear my face off, and a bullet from the back would be hard to explain."

"After what you've done? I don't think it would be a problem."

"And even less so after this," Red said.

He jerked to his right, ever so slightly but with blurring speed that made the movement almost intangible. For a flash, Colt saw the hole at the end of Clifton's barrel facing nothing but air.

Fire flashed from the muzzle as Clifton shot into thin air.

Red's gun was already up and around. He shot into the detective's chest, point-blank. Their close proximity muffled the gunshot.

Clifton's face went white.

Red spun around, lifted his foot, and shoved him hard.

The detective staggered, discharged a round into the floor, then stopped and fell straight back, like a toppled pillar.

Red faced them. "I hear he was quick. Get your heads in those nooses before I start shooting more fingers off."

Watching the man's speed again, Colt knew there was no way to beat Red straight up. Red was lightning fast. And the element of surprise had obviously gone by the boards.

"Because we're ugly," Wendy said. "We have to die because we're ugly, you said."

"Too late, honey—the game is over."

"But that's what this is all about, you said. Evil is ugly and we're all evil. That's your point?"

Red didn't respond. Which in his world meant *yes*.

"The ugliest have to die," Wendy pressed, voice tight. "That's the rule of the game, and if you're still playing, you're bound by it. We're all the ugliest because we're all evil, to the bone. But that includes you."

50

Sterling Red heard her words, and they worked their way into his brain like any other words might. But these particular words didn't stop at his mind. They sank deeper, beyond his quick reasoning to the place where the shakes originated. For a brief moment, he lost focus, but he quickly recovered.

"Right," he said.

That's all he had to say? "Right"?

"We are like you," the woman said.

"Yes," Red returned. But this wasn't what he'd planned.

"And you're like us."

He wondered if he should just put a bullet in her mouth to change the subject; but he was a man of considerable truth and she seemed to be headed that direction, so he kept his finger off the trigger.

His mind seemed to have slowed.

"We may be ugly, but you're as ugly as we are," she said.

The shakes started in his toes and ran up to his knees, and he suddenly wasn't sure he could stop them. But they hadn't reached his upper body, his arms, his head. His gun.

"Skin was a game," she said, growing bolder. "You're trapped in your own pathetic past, isn't that right?"

"You're annoying me," he said.

"Why did you destroy Nicole's face?"

"She got what she deserved. So will you."

"Because ugliness deserves to be hated," the woman said. "Ugliness deserves to be killed. You made her ugly. But it's not really physical ugliness but the ugliness inside. And we're all ugly to the bone, so we all deserve to be hated and killed. We're no better than this Horde from Skin that we tried to defeat. We essentially became them. Ugly inside and out. Isn't that what Skin proved?"

She'd said it so succinctly that for a moment Red thought he should spare her. But the sentiment was gone before he could entertain it.

"And now that I understand, I agree with you," she said. "We are all ugly to the bone and deserve to die. But can't you make something this ugly beautiful?"

"No," he said.

"Simply destroying ugly evil doesn't solve a thing. There has to be a way to make what was once ugly beautiful."

The shakes were so bad now that he had to take his mind off the woman and bear down on his own body. He got the trembling under control. He'd always known there was a possibility that he was fooled by his assumption that he'd risen above them all, but for first time he wondered if his shaking was linked to that fact rather than the fact that he was forced to live among worms half his worth.

Perhaps he should change the rules. Again.

"You have a problem," she said. "Because you're one of the ugliest too. You have to kill yourself with us."

He knew this was where she'd been leading. But Red's innards didn't seem to like hearing it. Even as he reasoned calmly and with complete confidence as he always did, his muscles began to quiver. A seizure like the one he'd often imagined must afflict Lucifer 24-7 swept through his body. Red shook like a skyscraper under the full assault of an earthquake.

The conflict between his abject hatred of these last three and the terrible suspicion that he was bound by the same fate as they were wasn't something he could just tell to shut up.

More than ever he craved mustard.

Wendy took a step back when Red started to shake. Epilepsy, or something else? The rest of them had apparently shed their symptoms following the game, but not Silver. His eyes bulged, face red. Sterling Red. Silver gone bloody angry.

Colt had stepped up beside her and was mouthing something, but she refused to look at him, afraid of breaking the spell her words seemed to have cast over Red.

"You all have to die," Red said.

Luke was up on all fours behind Red, like a cat, creeping, eyes peeled round.

"She's right," Colt said, grabbing his rope and swinging it to the side. He stepped forward atop the table. "She's right; you're one sick, ugly son of a whore. And I know what that feels like. So I'll tell you what, you get your neck in one of these and we'll do it together, how's that? We'll all go together."

Red was shaking so badly now that Wendy thought he really might be having an epileptic seizure. But he managed to lift his gun.

Luke moved with more deliberation. Quicker. Eyes rounder.

"You can't shoot us unless we refuse to kill ourselves," Colt said. "We'll kill ourselves with you."

Luke reached the gun, grabbed it. Colt shoved his finger at the killer and yelled to cover the sound. "You hear? *With* you!"

But Red was already moving. He dropped, spun, and fired back at Luke. The bullet slammed into the deputy's shoulder, sending Luke's own shot high and wide.

Colt hit Red in the back, then rolled over him toward the reeling Luke.

Wendy's foot was suddenly off the edge of the table, falling, but none of this stopped the thought screaming through her mind.

Kill him, Colt! Boom!

She landed on her right arm. Pain shot up her side, whether from a bullet or from contact with the floor she didn't know, but she began to scream.

Pinkus wailed in a high-pitched voice behind her. Someone was screaming in Red's direction, either Red or Colt.

Boom!

Pinkus went abruptly silent.

Wendy rolled once, twice, like a toppled mummy, half-expecting a bullet to smack into her at any instant. The cries from Red's direction were so vile, so guttural, that she was sure they'd tear a throat apart.

Boom! Boom! Boom! Boom!

Wendy rolled to a stop and instinctively flung her arms over her head.

The library quieted. No one spoke. No one shot. No one kicked her to see if she was still breathing.

Red had killed them all? Before she could ever really come to know Colt? It didn't seem fair. It—

Wendy flung her head back. The library spun as oxygen flooded her blood. She saw it all in one glance.

Red and Colt faced each other like two gunslingers, fifteen feet apart. Both were bleeding: Red from his left leg, Colt from his left forearm.

Both leveled guns at the other: Red, his own; Colt, Luke's weapon. Neither was shooting.

"Kill him!" Pinkus cried. "Shoot him!"

Sweat trickled down Colt's cheek. Wendy wondered why he didn't just pull the trigger. Was he suddenly confused about killing someone who was a product of the same childhood as he? Or afraid?

The answer dawned on her quickly. Both guns were leveled to the other man's torso. A bullet from either wouldn't necessarily kill immediately, thereby allowing the other to shoot in return. Neither was interested in killing only to die.

Colt could jerk his gun up and shoot Red in the face, but he surely knew that the killer would fire at his slightest movement.

A smile slowly spread Red's lips. "Well, well, well. Aren't we all in a bind."

"I will if you will," Colt said.

Will what?

"Then you'll die," Red said.

"I'm willing to take that chance."

"No!" Wendy cried before she could stop herself. Because Red would kill him. He was faster. Colt knew that! What was he thinking?

"Lower together," Colt said.

"Colt, please!" Wendy said.

For a full ten seconds Red just stared at Colt, who had evidently just challenged him to a draw or something similar. The whole scene was surreal, two gunslingers facing off in the library like in a spaghetti

Western. The floor was strewn with bodies. A bullet had punched through Luke's shoulder and he was out but alive. Steve was also still alive. But Nicole, Carey, and Clifton were all dead.

Pinkus breathed heavily on Wendy's left. Her own breath came shallow.

But Red and Colt stared each other down unblinkingly, as tense and as calm as any two men Wendy had ever seen.

Then Colt's gun hand edged downward.

"You're a fool," Red said, but his gun followed. Both eased their weapons down and into their belts.

They now stood with hands loose at their hips, legs spread and flexed, eyes pinned on each other.

"This is crazy," Wendy said. "Can't we work this out? It was seven years ago! Seven years. We all have new lives. You can't hold what happened in a stupid game seven years ago against us."

"I can," Red said. "I will. I am. And it's really, really tripping me out."

"You're going to kill him? He's a cop!"

"Yes, I am," Red said.

Twenty minutes had passed since Wendy had last blacked out. Her world crashed about her hard in that moment. The smothering darkness, the vises on her chest, hands, and feet. The memories raged to the surface, and she felt herself stiffen, then drop back to the floor.

Her head hit with a bang that filled her mind with a flash of light.

Once again she stared at darkness. And the ring of light. Wandering ghosts. But this time there was something more.

She could hear herself breathing. A steady hissing and rushing of air. Sweat tickled her temples.

Wendy spread her eyes wide, desperate for the episode to pass so

372

that she could stop Colt from committing suicide by sacrificing himself in a gun battle he was sure to lose.

That was his plan. He really was going to get himself killed this time.

A streak presented itself to her from the darkness directly above her eyes. Strangely enough, it looked very much like the streaks in the sky that had turned dark outside.

A faint hum whispered through her ears. Like the hum in the desert world.

She closed her eyes, opened them again. It was as if she was staring up at a translucent glass, streaked with shadows or something.

She moved her fingers. Felt a cool metallic glove.

Wendy was already frozen in the grip of her panic attack when the simple thought first walked uninvited through her mind and made her go stiff like a beam.

You're in a suit, the thought said.

She blinked rapidly several times. What if the episodes of darkness weren't memories washing to her mind's surface at all? What if she was simply waking?

Now.

With a helmet on.

Her heart began to hammer.

51

Nathan Blair burst into the white room, as the employees of CyberTech called it, letting the door slam against the wall behind it. He'd seen it a hundred times, and every time his skin had crawled. Except for the yelling, nothing seemed to have changed.

Beth Longhorn gave him a knowing stare. She clearly knew that something had changed, and it had turned her face paler than usual.

Seven technicians in white lab coats stood at the control counter, looking past a thick pane of glass into the inner sanctum, hands gripped into fists. Three of them paced. The gray-haired doctor stood on their right, stiff like an ancient tree.

"We have to stop it!" exclaimed Nancy Rengald, the project coordinator. "Now, before the rest die."

"What is it?" Nathan demanded. He glanced up at the six monitors filled with green and white lines. Two of the monitors showed flat lines.

No life.

According to the screens, Carey and Nicole were dead.

He spun to the bank of monitors that showed the technicians what each of the primary players saw inside the game. The wall contained twenty-two screens to depict the points of view of a number of the primary computer-generated characters as well as five of the six human players, not unlike any multiplayer computer game.

Clifton's monitor showed nothing but black. Dead. But he was a computer-generated character who didn't concern Nathan. It was the six humans playing the game who . . .

He locked onto the monitor showing what Carey saw. Black.

Below it, Nicole's. Black.

"Stop it," Nathan cried.

"You know we can't," Director Healy said. His voice sounded like a fingernail on a bass guitar string. Definite but deeply troubled. His own son, Timothy Healy, was one of the six. "Extraction takes at least an hour. We programmed the game for seven days. You could kill them all if you rush it; you know that."

"Dr. Healy, you have to reconsider," Nancy said. "He's already killed two. They're all going to die!"

"They'll all die if you bring them out too quickly."

Nathan ran forward. It was happening. His worst fears were coming to life. This was what he'd warned them about. The military had agreed to fund the project with CyberTech only on the condition that an internal auditor retained full authority to shut the project down. He'd come within a breath of doing so a dozen times as the updates rolled in.

They were messing with the lives of human beings. Teenagers, really. All of age, but young enough not to grasp the danger of their gamble. Fifty thousand dollars was hard to resist for an eighteen-year-old.

Blair was halfway to the glass when the pulse monitor on one of the six screens began to chirp loudly. The sound sent a chill to his heels.

He slammed into the glass and peered into the sanctum.

"Wendy's coming out!" Rengald whispered. "On her own?"

Wendy lay on her back, unmoving except for the rise and fall of her chest, face covered by the visor through which she saw the gaming world. No sign of change other than the monitor that indicated she was pulling herself from the game.

The game Skin was hosted by a huge white circular disc, roughly seven feet in diameter, around which the six modified dental chairs were symmetrically positioned.

The six subjects reclined on the chairs, dressed in white suits. Their feet were inserted into sensory pods, as were their hands. Each wore a helmet, not dissimilar to those worn by fighter pilots. Each was connected to the central computer with a dozen electrodes and two tubes through which both nourishment and psychotropic drugs had been delivered intravenously. The microwave transmitters that stimulated the frontal lobes of the six epileptics were situated above each chair, not unlike dental lights.

Dr. Healy had created this game, the first of its kind, to replicate a desert world filled with evil. It was a collaborative rather than competitive game; the players were given the goal of eradicating the various evil entities within seven days.

They'd entered Skin six days earlier and had masterfully defeated evil at first. And then Silver had begun subjugating the others by forcing them to follow new rules he created, going so far as to hang a few computer-generated characters when they got in his way.

The other five players recognized Silver as the new evil that, by the game's very own rules, had to be defeated. In real time, that had been six hours earlier. In game time, three days ago, just before Red had strutted into the gaming construct called Summerville.

After the failed attempt on his life, Silver had managed to reset the game from the inside, giving each of the other five players new skins in which Colt, Wendy, Carey, Nicole, and Pinkus were seven years older than they were in real life, complete with memories of those seven fictional years.

He presented the players with a new setting—an imaginary town named Summerville filled with artificially intelligent citizens, including a very intuitive detective AI called Clifton.

Then he'd restarted the game, which really constituted a continuation of the old game. Six human players, with fresh identities, and hundreds of computer-generated players in Summerville who each played their part as the game unfolded.

The technicians had watched in wonder as the screens reset themselves to show Summerville instead of the original desert world. It was like watching the fantasy world in World of Warcraft blink off and then blink back on as Grand Theft Auto set in a small town. Then blink back and forth between both Warcraft and Grand Theft as Colt and company went in and out of the two constructs.

They had a window into all of their world . . . except for Timothy Healy's. He'd managed to block their link to all but his vitals. Until he'd actually unveiled himself in the library they had been forced to assume he could have switched skins with one of the other players in the game. Or one of the computer generated characters like Clifton, for that matter.

Either way, all of them, including Silver, were bound by the rules of Red's new version of the game. The ugliest must die. It was a twisted restatement of the game rules before they had turned against Silver, which had been to destroy all evil.

To start the game rolling, Silver had killed a character modeled after his own father, Dr. Cyrus Healy, who now stood on Nathan's left, face white.

The only aberration Blair was aware of were the implants. There were no implants and no scars. They'd used noninvasive forms of stimulation, external electrodes, masks, body suits, devices that could be duplicated with military pilots.

But in the game the players believed they had implants. They were part of the construct. The computer's clue to them that not all was right in their minds. If they could X-ray Red they would find he too showed an implant, because he too was hooked up to the computer.

"What's happening?" One of the younger technicians was having difficulty coming to grips with what they were all witnessing.

Blair searched the bodies of Nicole and Carey, both reclined. Their monitors indicated that they were dead, *here in real life*. But how . . .

Then he saw it. Thin trails of blood trickled down their necks from ruptures beneath the helmets. Eyes, nostrils, ears—maybe all three.

Beside them, Timothy Healy's body began to tremble as it had sporadically ever since he'd changed the game. The frontal lobe epilepsy his father had given him was making its presence known.

Nathan glanced to his right and saw that the doctor's tightly drawn face had turned red. Remorse or anger? He'd found a way to simulate epilepsy in his son's brain, and for that Timothy had killed him within the game. Plus two other non-AI players and counting.

"She's waking!" someone yelled. "She's pulled herself out!"

Nathan spun back to the sanctum. Wendy was hyperventilating, sending her monitors off the chart. Her head wagged back and forth as if she were trying to fling the helmet off her face without unlatching it.

Then Wendy Davidson sat up in her chair.

Wendy felt light-headed as the blood drained from her head. So it was real, then. She was sitting up. With a helmet on. In a suit.

She was at this very moment in the very game that they had all assumed they'd played seven years ago.

Wendy lifted her right hand to free her mask. Something tugged at her arm, a restraint or worse.

Fighting back a fresh wash of panic, she grabbed at her mask, fumbled with a dark translucent visor through which she could see her gloved hand groping.

Light seeped in from the edges of the visor, and now she could just see the white room that she'd seen a dozen times in her black-outs—which were clearly awakenings, not blackouts.

And the streaks in the sky . . . hundreds of thin wires or tubes that evidently created the three-dimensional world in her visor.

Her fingers snagged a latch, and the visor flipped up. Bright light blinded her.

Slowly her eyes adjusted. She was in a white suit like one an astronaut might wear, only not as thick. A heavy cord snaked from her right boot into the circular machine at her feet. It was humming.

Huummmmm . . .

Wendy was so amazed at finding herself in such a clinical environment after so long in the gritty reality of Red's game that she could do little but stare at the suit and slowly catch her breath.

She knew then, with certainty, that this was the real world. The library, the desert, the town of Summerville—all of it was less than real.

Or was it the other way around?

It took her nearly a full minute to remember that she hadn't been playing the game alone.

Colt.

She turned her head to the left and saw two supine forms in dental chairs like hers. Their names were on their helmets. Carey. Nicole. They didn't appear to be breathing.

And blood was leaking down their necks.

Wendy's heart crashed into her throat. She spun to her right and saw the others: Pinkus, Colt, Timothy. Chests rising and falling through deep breaths, lost in the library.

Red was going to kill Colt.

Panic smothered her. She reached up and pawed at her helmet, managed to pull it free. But there were wires connected to her head. She had to get out and stop Red.

"Don't!"

Wendy swiveled to the voice behind her. A gray-haired man in a white smock stood at an open door. Technicians peered into the room from their places behind a glass wall.

"The electrodes are inserted beneath your scalp. Don't pull them out."

"What's going on?" she cried. Her voice cracked hoarsely, raw with fire. "Red's going to kill Colt! You have to stop them!"

She tried to swing her feet off the chair, but the cable that led to the computer caught. An IV tube tugged at the crux of her elbow.

Directly in front of her, Nicole and Carey lay dead.

Wendy's mind snapped. Her thoughts refused to connect with logical constructs. She went berserk, knowing full well that she was, but unable to stop herself.

She screamed past her dry throat and tugged at the cords that bound her to the contraptions. The boot with the cord yanked free, and she threw her legs to the floor.

Needles beneath her suit pulled from her skin with a bite. A small real pain that she wanted more of.

She grabbed the wires from her helmet and ripped them out of the lining.

Then she was free, staggering across the floor.

She was still crying out when her gloved hands struck Timothy Healy's helmet.

He jerked.

"Die! Die, you—"

She turned and dived for Colt's suited form instead, thinking through the fog of panic that it might be easier to wake Colt than kill Red. She had to stop them, save Colt, end this madness in the library, because if she didn't, Colt would die, and she wasn't sure she could live with Colt dying.

"No, stop! You can't. You'll kill all of them."

She made it halfway to Colt's body before strong arms wrapped around her waist and pulled her back. They belonged to two technicians, and both were yelling at her.

"Easy! Easy . . ."

"You can't force them out without killing them. Just calm down!"

Wendy swallowed her cry and grasped for the meaning of these words. She yanked free and spun to the men. The gray-haired man who'd first come in stared at her in amazement. A man with a name tag that identified him as Nathan Blair pushed into the room.

They were fixed on her, every one of them.

She stared back, panting. "You have to stop him," she said, but it came out scratchy and weak. The room tilted dizzily, then corrected.

None of them were telling her they would stop it. Or could.

The one named Nathan Blair was the first to speak. "Wendy. Please . . . You have to calm down."

"Can you stop him?"

They didn't answer.

No, they couldn't. At this very moment in another reality that was as real as this one, she was passed out on the library floor. Colt and Red were facing off fifteen feet from each other.

Red was going to kill Colt.

She tore for Timothy, shrieking again. This time they knocked her sideways before she could lay a hand on him. Her foot caught on the chair's pedestal, and she sprawled facedown on the floor.

She lay there, shaking with sobs, unable to plot any kind of course that might offer hope. With each minute awake the profundity of what she'd just been through became more and more real.

Her name was Wendy.

She had escaped a cult that had left her ravaged. That much was true.

And she had frontal lobe epilepsy.

But her memories of college, life in Southern California, abortive relationships with men—all that she'd apparently created, imagined, while asleep in this room. In the game. That was part of her character in the game. Part of her skin.

A month ago, at age nineteen, roughly a year after running away from the cult, she'd volunteered for this very test, eager for the $50,000 it would earn her.

Six days ago she'd entered the world of Skin.

Six hours ago, Timothy Healy must have changed that game without their having any recollection of the previous game. He'd introduced new stakes.

In that game, Wendy had faced her greatest fear and fallen in love with a man named Colt.

And now Red was going to kill Colt.

Wendy pushed herself up and faced them. All four sets of eyes inside this room were locked on her. Beyond the glass several technicians were bent over monitors.

Beside her, Colt, Pinkus, and Timothy Healy all breathed deeply. They might not even be aware that she'd passed out on the library floor.

She faced Nathan Blair. "Okay. Okay, tell me there's a way to stop this."

The gray-haired man with dark eyes and deeply creased forehead stepped up. Only now did she see that this man was Dr. Cyrus Healy. The man behind the game.

"We can't pull them out without killing them," Healy said.

"Are you *sure*?"

"Nothing is a certainty."

"Except that Red will kill them if you don't wake them!" she snapped.

"Colt can be quite inventive."

"You know your son will kill him. You know he's faster."

No answer.

"He's already killed two others. Please, Doctor, don't let him do this."

"We have to let the game play itself out."

"He's right, Wendy," Blair said, moving to the doctor's right. "Pulling them out will almost certainly kill one or all of them."

She faced the three heaving bodies and clenched her teeth. Fresh tears wet her cheeks. Then what? Her head spun, more from exhaustion than from confusion. In fact, she had no confusion. For the first time in days, she knew exactly what was happening.

Wendy stilled her breathing. Except for the soft hum of the computer, the beeping of monitors indicating pulse, the rush of hot breath under helmets, the room was quiet.

"How do I know this isn't just an imagined reality, like the desert?" she asked no one in particular.

"You don't," the older man said. "But we do. Trust me, you've been lying on that chair for six days. No desert, no tornado, no library, no Clifton—not in this life. That's all part of the game. The only real people in Skin are you, Colt, Pinkus, Carey, Nicole, and Timothy."

"And the implant?"

"No implants. That's how it looks in the game, but in this room we use more traditional means."

"Drugs?"

"Yes. And the suits. Helmets. Electrodes. Microwave technology that stimulates the hippocampus."

A faint glimmer of hope sliced through Wendy's mind. It was something Pinkus had said in the game.

She slowly turned to the gray-haired man whose son was going to kill the man she'd fallen in love with.

"You have to let the game end on its own terms."

He hesitated. "Yes."

"I am one of those terms."

"I—"

"I'm one of the players."

The short silence was followed by someone's soft mumble. "Wow."

"Put me back in," Wendy said. "Let me finish the game with them."

"That's . . . We don't have time. That would take ten . . . fifteen minutes!"

"Put me back in!" Wendy cried. "You know you can. An hour here can be a minute there. Let me back in; it's my choice."

"He'll kill you. If you die in the game, you die here."

He too knew that Red would win.

"I'll take that chance. Put me in. Now!"

52

Wendy lay on her side, cheek pressed to the library's floorboards, when she opened her eyes in the game.

Her mind raced through a dark fog. Fragments of her time in the white room crowded her thoughts, and it took a few seconds to place them in an order that made any sense to her.

They'd hooked her back up to the computer, fed her veins with more of the drugs, administered a number of pulses from the microwave transmitter above. Her transition had been gradual at first; then her senses had shut down in the white room and been awakened here, in the library.

How much time had passed?

She pushed her head up. Red and Colt were still staring at each other like hawks. She'd made it back in time. Maybe less than a minute had passed. Maybe only seconds.

"Colt?"

She got her knees under her and slowly rose.

"Colt, you have to listen to me."

He didn't acknowledge her. His entire focus was fixed on Red, the man who would kill him.

"The blackouts weren't blackouts," she said. "We were seeing the real world. In that world we have black visors covering our faces. We're still in the game, Colt. Right now, at this very moment, all of us are hooked up to a computer in a white room, playing this game as if it's for real."

"What?" Pinkus cried.

"Nicole and Carey are dead," she said. "In both worlds."

Pinkus came again. "That was seven years ago."

"No, it wasn't. Red gave us all new skins in which we were all older, but we're not. We're all still younger and still in the game."

Colt blinked. His hands were spread, coiled to draw.

"You can't beat him, Colt."

"You're going to get us killed, Wendy," he said softly.

"Yes, you are, Wendy," Red said. "You're going to get all of you killed."

"You have to believe me. We're in a game!"

"Stop it," Colt said. "Stay back."

"Yes, back off, Wendy," Red said with a shrewd grin. "What you think is real there could be as unreal as what you think is unreal."

He was right. But she refused to accept it.

"*This* is the game. And in this game, Red's faster than you, Colt."

Colt breathed steadily, mind racing behind his eyes.

"How would Colt beat Red in the game, Pinkus?" She spoke without looking at the gamer.

"I'm not sure . . ."

"No, what did you say earlier? About leveling up?"

A beat passed.

"He would become more skilled in the game and level up."

"You have to level up, Colt. How does he level up, Pinkus?"

"He . . ." Pinkus stepped forward and spoke with a little more confidence. "You work within the game construct to achieve a higher level of excellence than your opponent."

"And what is the game construct? What is the point of this game? And what if Red changed it? How does someone become more powerful than the creator?"

"This game is about understanding who is ugly," Pinkus said. "Who is evil. In this game you outwit your opponent."

The moment Colt flinched, Red's hand would move, faster and deadlier, Wendy thought.

"Okay, Pinkus," she said, keeping her voice calm. "Tell us *how*. How can Colt outwit Red and become more powerful? Tell us how he levels up."

"It could be knowledge. Understanding." He hesitated, perhaps just now realizing the implications of his own conclusion.

"Not likely," Red said.

But Wendy followed a thread of logic that she'd begun earlier, with Red. "By accepting what Red can't? That we're all born ugly. That we all have evil in our bones. That you can never judge a book by its cover or a person by their skin. And what's born ugly can't make itself beautiful. That's why none of us could beat the game, Skin. Not even the best of us, Timothy Healy."

"Hocus-pocus," Red said.

"That hocus-pocus will take you down," Wendy said, voice trembling.

Pinkus took another short step forward. "She's right, Colt. In the construct of this game, you have to draw power from the *truth* to level up. Realizing your own weakness makes you stronger."

"Shut up, please, please shut your filthy mouths." Red sounded self-assured, but a line of sweat snaked down his cheek.

"The truth?"

"That you're no better than he is. He, on the other hand, believes a lie, which is that he's better than you."

"Please, Colt," Wendy said. "You have to embrace the truth. He is faster than you, but you can be faster. The truth is stronger than his lies."

Silence engulfed the room. Wendy could barely hear the humming outside, just beyond the skin of this world. Her heart thumped like a drum.

"Well, Colt, what's it going to be?" Red asked, still confident. "You want to test this nonsense against my hand? The truth versus lies and all that crap?"

No answer.

"She is right about one thing. I am faster than you. What she doesn't know is how much faster."

Still no answer.

"Wanna trip, baby?"

Wendy felt her face wrinkle in desperation. Her words came out in a whisper. "Colt. Please."

But Colt didn't answer. Didn't flinch. Didn't seem even to be breathing. He drilled Red with a stare.

"Mirror, mirror, on the wall," Red said, "who's the most beautiful of them all?"

"I don't know," Colt replied softly, "but you're one ugly son of a whore."

And then they went. Two blurs at their waist; heads and feet and knees and chests unflinching.

Just their right arms. Just the guns. Like the wings of a hornet, fanning, barely visible.

Wendy blinked, and the crash of gunfire filled the room while her eyes were momentarily closed.

Boom!

She couldn't stop the cry on her lips. "Colt!"

Both stood still as if nothing had happened. Both were fixed to the floor. Neither was dead; neither was wounded; neither appeared even bothered.

The only difference between Red and Colt was that Red's gun was pointed at an angle. Down.

Down?

Wendy's heart seized like an overheated piston.

Red's gun was pointed slightly down because he'd never gotten it up any higher; that had to be it. But there was no evidence that Colt's gun had put a bullet in him.

The killer's body suddenly began to tip backward. Only then did Wendy see the hole in his left eye, hidden till now by the bridge of his nose. She knew Colt had put that hole there, right through the man's brain.

His body stayed tall and rigid as it tipped backward and slammed onto the floor like a slab of meat and lay still.

Colt shifted his aim back to the killer; otherwise, nothing moved.

"Is he dead?" Pinkus asked.

Beyond Colt, Luke stirred.

"He's dead," Wendy said. "Is he dead, Colt?"

"He's dead." But he still didn't take his gun off the body.

Wendy swayed and tried to clear the fog from her mind. A hundred voices whispered together, but above them all rose one truth that had saved their lives.

Ugly, it said. We're all ugly to the bone.

Colt lowered his gun. "Tell us how to get out of this game, Wendy."

Epilogue

Wendy sat next to Colt and Pinkus in the debriefing room, head still reeling from the bits and pieces they'd been told over the five hours since they'd come out of the game. The most disconcerting bits and pieces naturally being those concerning Timothy, Nicole, and Carey, who were all dead.

Dr. Healy had adopted Timothy from a monastery when the boy was fourteen. It didn't take much to guess that Healy may have had all of this in mind when he'd first taken Timothy into his house. There would be an investigation.

Nicole really had killed their parents several years earlier.

Timothy, Carey, and Nicole were all human and all very much dead.

Until a week ago Wendy hadn't known any of the other five players, who had all been recruited because they, like she, suffered from some form of frontal lobe epilepsy. Having escaped from the cult two years earlier, and having no real concrete direction for her life, an advertisement in the Arizona *Daily Star* for paid volunteers with FLE had been a prospect she couldn't pass up.

She'd arrived a week ago, on August first, and after a day of testing she'd entered the world of Skin with the others. How Dr. Healy had done it she had no clue, but she could swear she'd lived seven years in the last six days.

The game itself could have gone a thousand directions. Indeed it had started in the deserts of a world far away fighting the Horde, and ended in a place (or a map as they called it) Timothy Healy had created called Summerville, but the next time it could look quite different. Players, not programmers, determined the direction of the game.

Wendy lifted her hand and stared at it. "I still can't get over it," she said. "I'm nineteen, not in my twenties."

"And I'm not a cop," Colt said. "I'm headed that way, but not yet."

"Clifton . . . the town. It was all this . . . what did they call it?"

"A construct," Pinkus said. "In the game." He lifted his hand and flexed his mouse finger, still intact. "Thank the stars in heaven."

Wendy looked into Colt's eyes. Although none of what had happened in the game had actually happened, their histories were real—everything up to a week ago. Not the intervening five to seven years that each of them had been led to imagine. Colt had been raised in a whorehouse. She in a cult. Nicole and Carey were brother and sister.

They'd poured out their hearts and bared their souls. In a terribly unnerving way it all mirrored the fall of Lucifer, Lucifer being the best at the game, the most beautiful, like Timothy Healy. Thing of it was, however demented he was in his obsession to bring them all down with him, he had proven one thing: They really were as ugly as those in the game called Skin—this Horde whose disease was visible. In the game they had proven themselves incapable of achieving the objective to make what was ugly, beautiful. Timothy had failed miserably and proven them no better.

All of this because beauty wasn't about the skin, either the skin of their flesh or the skin of this world. For that matter, what they *could* see with their eyes—the desert, the town, the library, Nicole, even Timothy Healy—had turned out to be very different than the way they'd seen it. The mind was easily deceived by seemingly obvious perceptions.

Instead, beauty was found beyond the surface. *It was there, beyond the skin of this world, that a cure of ugliness could be found,* she thought.

She looked at Colt. When she'd first met him a week earlier, he'd been extremely shy. Now he returned her stare with soft eyes. It was good to see him younger, wearing faded jeans and a well-worn rust T-shirt with the words *Forest Guard* stenciled on the front. He didn't know what they meant—just a shirt he'd picked up at the Salvation Army, he said.

Somehow he didn't look nearly as homely here, in real life. Not so rough around the edges, not nearly so plain. Or had her perception of him changed?

She could smell the musk of his cologne. Well muscled with a long scar on his forearm. He couldn't remember where the scar came from.

The Horde, he said. They'd chuckled.

"Now what?" she asked.

"Now they wipe all of this from our memories," Pinkus said.

"They can do that?"

He shrugged. "They got us into the game. Our minds are a bit fractured. I'm sure they'll find a way."

Wendy looked up at a calendar on the wall. August seventh. They really had been in the game for six days.

The door behind them opened, and Nathan Blair, an inspector from some government watchdog group, walked in.

"Sorry to keep you all waiting," he said, crossing to the desk in front of them.

Something about that calendar bothered Wendy. August seventh. Six days.

Blair sat in the desk chair, scooted in, and looked at them, blue eyes piercing. "Well. Here we are."

"When can we leave?" Pinkus asked.

"As soon as we get things back to normal," Blair said.

"You're going to hook us back up, aren't you?"

The man stared at Pinkus, then slowly nodded once. "You want to live the rest of your life with these memories?"

Wendy didn't, and silence from the others indicated agreement.

"Three people died here today," Colt said. "Including Dr. Healy's son. You gonna just sweep that under the rug?"

"I'm here to make sure that doesn't happen, Mr. Jackson. You'll have to trust me on that."

Wendy had her doubts. But they had little choice.

Blair drilled her with a hard stare. "You three, on the other hand, present more of a problem."

Something was wrong with the way this man spoke to them, Wendy thought. The concern he'd shown toward them when they'd first come out of the game was gone. He appeared cold.

She glanced once again at the calendar just beyond and above the man. "How long was the game programmed for?"

He hesitated. "Seven days. But that doesn't—"

"We only played six days . . ." Her heart began to beat heavily.

Nathan Blair blinked.

She saw it then, just for a second. The man's left eye had lost its blue hue and flashed gray. The gray static of a television that had lost its signal.

Then it was gone. Both of his irises were blue again.

"You've got to be kidding," Pinkus whispered.

Wendy slowly turned to Colt. "Did you see that?"

When he spoke, his voice came soft and hoarse.

"You have *got* to be kidding," Pinkus said again. "It's not over?"

Blair looked at him with a raised brow. "What do you mean, son? Of course it's over."

It occurred to Wendy that Blair didn't know. He honestly didn't know.

"Figure of speech," she said. "Maybe it is over. Or maybe it's never really over. We have to play the game to the end. We have to figure out what's real and what only wants to be real. Isn't that right, Mr. Blair?"

He shrugged. "Fair enough." Once again his left eye flashed gray for split second.

Pinkus grunted.

Wendy took a deep breath. "But Pinkus asks a good hypothetical question," she said. "What if we are still in the game?"

Colt looked at Wendy, eyes wide. Back at Blair. "Then we play it to the hilt. I'd say we know how now."

"Do we?"

He hesitated. "We know where the truth hides."

Her heart swelled. She took his hand in hers without looking and held it tightly. In that moment she wasn't sure she could ever let it go.

"Beyond the skin of this world," she said.

Colt spoke softly, in a steady voice. "This time we play the game together."

Wendy nodded without removing her stare from Blair's blue, then gray, then blue, real, not-real eyes.

"Together."

THE HOARD'S
BEEN MISSING YOU

DIVE DEEP FEBRUARY 2008

Journey back to the alternate reality of the circle trilogy where
the only hope for the Forest Guard rests in the hands of four
untested young fighters who must lead the charge for Elyon as
they set out to rescue the seven missing books of History.

Simultaneous release of Book 1 (*Chosen*) and
Book 2 (*Infidel*) in the epic 6-novel circle series.

HAVE YOU JOINED THE CIRCLE?

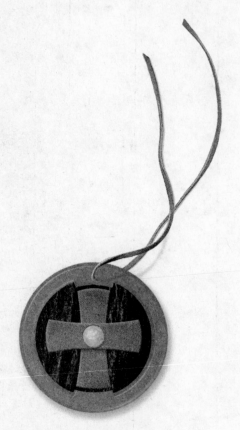

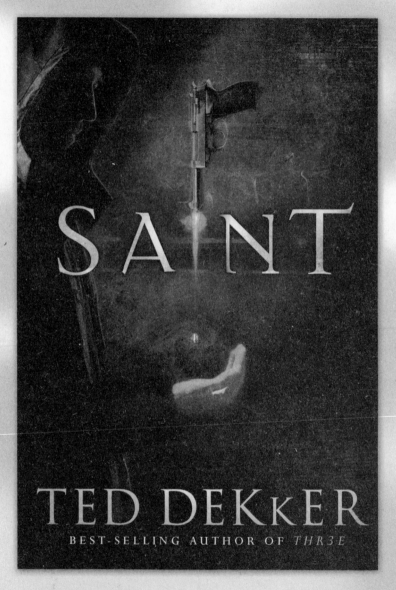

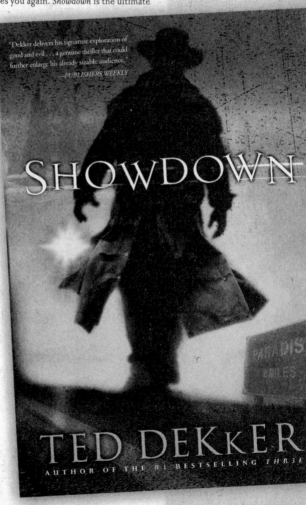

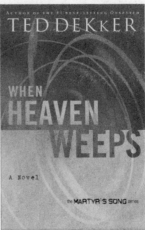

THE WORLD IS HARDLY READY FOR A BOY LIKE CALEB.

THOMAS NELSON, INC.
Since 1798